SHEA
GOOD-BYE

THE UNTOLD INSIDE STORY
OF THE HISTORIC 2008 SEASON

Keith Hernandez
with Matthew Silverman

TRIUMPH
BOOKS

To Kai

Triumph Books and colophon are registered trademarks of Random House, Inc.

Library of Congress Cataloging-in-Publication Data

Hernandez, Keith.
  Shea good-bye : the untold inside story of the historic 2008 season / Keith Hernandez and Matthew Silverman.
     p. cm.
  ISBN 978-1-60078-170-4
  1. New York Mets (Baseball team) 2. Shea Stadium (New York, N.Y.) I. Silverman, Matthew, 1965—II. Title.
  GV875.N45.H48 2009
  796.357'64097471—dc22

                                                            2008055275

This book is available in quantity at special discounts for your group or organization. For further information, contact:
  Triumph Books
  542 South Dearborn Street
  Suite 750
  Chicago, Illinois 60605
  (312) 939-3330
  Fax (312) 663-3557

Printed in U.S.A.
ISBN: 978-1-60078-170-4
Design by Patricia Frey
All photographs from AP Images unless otherwise noted

CONTENTS

ACKNOWLEDGMENTS

No book is completed without the help of many hands. The authors would like to acknowledge the following sources: baseball-reference.com, retrosheet.org, newyork.mets.mlb.com, sports.yahoo.com, and *The 2008 ESPN Baseball Encyclopedia*. Thank you to the New York Mets, SportsNet New York, Brian Jacobs, garykeithandron.com, Connie and Gary "Country" Cline, Brion Wollum, Katy Sprinkel, Adam Motin, Dan Carubia, Jon Springer, Greg Prince, Greg Spira, the Hernandez and Silverman families, and the Triborough (now Robert F. Kennedy) Bridge Authority.

This book was culled from dozens of interviews and discussions during the 2008 season. Predictions—right or, more often, wrong—are included as they were made during the highs and lows of the season. No one who was there will forget the final year of Shea Stadium.

Chapter 1

THE OFF-SEASON

JANUARY 29, 2008

Winter is barely a month old on the calendar, but it feels as if it has been going on since time began. Or at least since September. September 30 was the day winter began for the New York Mets.

After taking over the division lead in mid-May, the 2007 Mets had built up a seven-game cushion by September 12. That's when the roof collapsed. The Mets were swept in a weekend series at Shea Stadium by the Phillies, who beat the Mets eight straight times (including six in a row at Shea) on the season. But what truly doomed the club was going 1–5 against the fourth-place Nationals during the final two weeks and dropping two of three in a must-win series at home against the last-place Marlins to end the season. The division went to the Phillies, who also erased their name from the top of the list of largest blown leads in history. The Mets squandered seven-game lead with just 17 remaining, which caused them to miss out on both the division and wild-card, trumped the

6½-game lead with 12 games remaining coughed up by the Phillies in 1964, back when a team had to have the best record in the league to reach the post-season. The 2007 Mets endured the most frustrating finish ever for a franchise whose history is filled with agonizing endings.

The off-season did not start any better for the Mets. A trade with Milwaukee to rid the club of flammable reliever Guillermo Mota brought back pedestrian catcher Johnny Estrada, to whom the Mets subsequently did not tender a contract. New York did not negotiate with Paul Lo Duca, the club's catcher for the previous two seasons, and broke off negotiations with Rockies free agent backstop Yorvit Torrealba. When they finally landed a catcher in Brian Schneider from the Nationals, it drew howls of protest. Lastings Milledge, whose attitude seemed to rub the veterans and front office people in Flushing the wrong way, was sent to Washington for Schneider and outfielder Ryan Church. Many considered Church a platoon outfielder and an afterthought. Outspoken scribes, fans, and voices in the ever-increasing Mets blogosphere blasted the club for giving up too soon on a highly touted prospect, even though the Mets received in exchange a good defensive catcher and a right fielder who had shown promise in his first season, starting more than 100 games.

Part of that anger may have been frustration because the Mets were at the time deemed a distant third in the Johan Santana sweepstakes. The Yankees and Red Sox mulled over prospects to send to Minnesota for the prized left-hander, while the Mets were dismissed as having nothing comparable to offer. While the two American League behemoths sloughed off the Twins' demands and decided to keep their cherished prospects, Mets general manager Omar Minaya remained in contact with Minnesota GM Bill Smith. The Twins kept busy, signing two of their top everyday players—Michael Cuddyer and Justin Morneau—to extensions worth a combined $104 million. And they still had Santana.

Then, on a damp Tuesday afternoon in January, Santana was dealt to New York—not to the Bronx but Flushing. And the Mets managed to keep their best prospect, outfielder Fernando Martinez. They said goodbye to minor leaguers Philip Humber, Carlos Gomez, Kevin Mulvey, and Deolis Guerra...and hello to Johan.

Keith Hernandez, inducted into the Mets Hall of Fame as a dynamic first baseman with bat and glove and now a broadcaster for the club, first arrived in New York with a similar thunderbolt in June 1983. Coming off a world championship with the St. Louis Cardinals, Hernandez became the foundation for a Mets renaissance built around young, skilled, and passionate athletes. In 1984, Hernandez had as superb a season as any Mets hitter to that point. He then led the team to a world championship in 1986. A year later, he became the first team captain in club history. His defense at first base remains unmatched; he collected 11 consecutive Gold Gloves. His six-plus seasons with the Mets represents the greatest period of prosperity in franchise history. The deal that brought him to New York—for pitchers Neil Allen and Rick Ownbey—is still considered one of the best trades ever by the franchise. The Johan deal looks to be right up there, too.

Santana: Art of the Steal

You have to have a true ace to be successful in this game, and the Mets have one now. Johan Santana might be as good as any pitcher in baseball.

I have no reservations about any of the players sent to Minnesota in the deal. I thought it was the steal of the winter to get Santana. You have to give Omar Minaya credit for holding on to Fernando Martinez, a player the Mets one day hope will bat in the middle of a lineup card that also has Santana's name written on it. Trading Jose Reyes to get Santana was never in the cards—that was speculation by the press. You don't fill one glaring hole by creating another.

Reyes is the franchise's shortstop, leadoff hitter, and catalyst. There's no question in my mind that Omar never really entertained the thought of trading Jose.

I do, however, question the Minnesota general manager for having a two-time Cy Young winner and not getting more in return. Mets fans have lamented for more than 30 years about Tom Seaver being traded to Cincinnati for four prospects—well, this is what it's like on the other end.

I'd rank this deal right there with the David Cone trade the Mets made with Kansas City just before the 1987 season. GM Frank Cashen got Coney, who'd just turned 24 and had never started a game in the majors, in exchange for Ed Hearn, Rick Anderson, and Mauro Gozzo. The Royals even threw in a minor leaguer named Chris Jelic. It turned out to be one of the great trades in Mets history.

Anytime you can get a pitcher of that quality with years left in his arm, that's the name of the game. Today's pitching is watered down by the extra four teams added since 1993. There's just not enough major league–caliber pitching to go around. Take those four extra teams—Colorado, Florida, Arizona, and Tampa Bay—figure in a 25-man roster for each club, and that's 100 players scattered throughout the majors who would have been in the minors if not for the expansion. With many teams now keeping 12 pitchers on the roster, you multiply that times four, and that makes almost 50 pitchers in the big leagues who shouldn't be here. You see the results of that every day. Pitchers who are constantly falling behind in the count, giving up more walks, and hitters taking advantage in predictable counts when the pitcher has to throw a strike.

A 1–0, 2–1, 3–2 game is as fun—to me, it's actually more fun—than a 15–12 game. The pace of baseball has slowed to a crawl. It's like the American League was when I played: one base at a time and wait for the three-run home run. The National League was always about speed, the hit-and-run, bunting, and doing the little things that make the game so beautiful. Well, that's all gone now. It's like the 350-pound lineman in the NFL or the 7-foot-3 center in basketball. Subtlety and skill have given way to brute force and size. Bigger players, bigger scoring. Forget the lure of the game with its layers of strategy and the constant decisions demanded of both the players and the manager.

But the rules still say you have to get 27 outs in order to win a baseball game. It all boils down to one thing. What it's all about is what it's always been about: pitching. So whenever you can get a pitcher—a bona fide ace, a two-time Cy Young winner like Johan Santana—you have to go for it. I'm glad the Mets did it. I can't wait to watch him go about his business 30-plus times a year.

FEBRUARY 1, 2008

The Mets have a 72-hour window that expires at 5:00 PM in which to sign Santana. If they can't work out a contract, the trade is off because of Santana's no-trade clause in his existing Minnesota contract. The Mets ask for and receive a two-hour extension from Major League Baseball to finish the deal. In the early evening hours, Santana agrees to the richest contract in club history and the largest to this point for a pitcher: $137.5 million for six years (plus a vesting or club option for 2014). The deal is finalized with a physical examination the next day.

Suddenly the once-creaky Mets rotation is considered among the best in the league—on paper. Santana leads a rotation of Pedro Martinez, Orlando Hernandez, Oliver Perez, and John Maine.

Money Pitcher

There can be a lot of games in the art of negotiating contracts, but in this case, when you have a brief window of time and the whole world is essentially sitting in on negotiations and knowing it has to get done by a certain hour, the leverage completely swings over to the player. Make no mistake, Santana was going to get signed. He had the Mets over a barrel, and he knew it. The Mets gave him the extra year. You can read between the lines if you wish, but the Mets had no real choice in the matter. They had to do what it took to sign him.

I can't blame Santana for wanting to get as many years and as many dollars as he could when he had that kind of leverage. I can understand the Mets not wanting to give it to him, but that's what it took to get it done. End of story.

Look at it from the club's perspective. El Duque's contract is almost up, Pedro has only one year left, and Oliver Perez is going to be a free agent. So the only guy in the rotation the Mets had under contract after 2008 who's done anything is John Maine. The Mets had to get someone else in the rotation! They didn't want to go into the season with only one starter under contract beyond this year. At least they now have two—and what a guy to have!

I am shocked that the Yankees didn't go full tilt after Santana. I would've expected them to start a bidding war

Omar Minaya, Johan Santana, Jeff Wilpon, and Willie Randolph show off No. 57 as the Mets officially welcome the ace left-hander to New York.

with the Mets. The Yankees have not addressed their pitching problems. Mike Mussina is getting old; so is Andy Pettitte. Overall, that's an old ballclub. They went with Phil Hughes and thought he was the greatest thing since sliced bread. Granted, he's 22 and comes highly rated by all the scouts and front office people, but one season does not make a career. I was worried for most of the winter that the Yankees would go hard after Santana or at least make it far more difficult for the Mets. With the way the 2007 season ended, the Mets had to do something dramatic. They needed to improve their pitching staff. They have certainly done that.

I am just flabbergasted at how this turned out. A two-time Cy Young winner in his prime for four minor leaguers? And you held your best prospect out of the deal? That's the definition of a heist.

Chapter 2

SPRING TRAINING

FEBRUARY 14, 2008

As the much-anticipated reporting date for pitchers and catchers finally arrives, there are lingering questions about the game as camps open, and many players are confronted in person for the first time by questions about the most disturbing news of the off-season: the Mitchell Report.

Former Senator George Mitchell was appointed by Commissioner Bud Selig to investigate performance-enhancing drugs in the major leagues. This came on top of the federal investigation of Bay Area Lab Co-Operative (BALCO) that revealed that athletes in numerous sports—including All-Star sluggers Barry Bonds, Jason Giambi, and Gary Sheffield—may have been supplied with various performance-enhancing drugs. In March 2006, shortly after revelations about Bonds and BALCO in a well-documented book, *Game of Shadows*, brought further stain on the game, Selig appointed Mitchell to investigate steroids in baseball.

Mitchell's 20-month, 409-page report lists 89 former and current major league players. Many of those names in the December 2007 report came from Kirk Radomski, a former Mets clubhouse attendant who reached a plea bargain on charges of money laundering and distribution of a controlled substance in exchange for his cooperation with the investigation. The report also features Brian McNamee, who stated that he injected 354-game winner Roger Clemens with steroids during a time when the pitcher's career did an about-face with the Blue Jays and then the Yankees. Both teams employed McNamee.

McNamee and Clemens sit before Congress and give their versions of the story. The dog-and-pony show settles little. It is a St. Valentine's Day Massacre for the credibility of the game and a decade's worth of record-shattering performances.

Era of Shame

I was not surprised by the Mitchell Report. I think this situation reached the point where the great majority of the players were using performance-enhancing drugs. It's hard to put a number on it. The Mitchell Report lists almost 90 names. But in truth, the report mostly covers New York. And BALCO was San Francisco. But what about Dallas? What about Houston? What about L.A.? What about San Diego? What about Chicago? Minnesota? Do you think the only culprits were Kirk Radomski and BALCO? Was Brian McNamee the only personal trainer with access to this stuff?

I think the report probably churns up more questions than it answers. The biggest question that comes out of all this is: Who is to blame?

Everybody is to blame.

The commissioner knew about it. Maybe not from the day a few players first started using the stuff, but it's not like he heard about it for the first time a couple of weeks before the congressional hearing in 2005. The effect of steroids on the game goes back at least a decade.

Baseball was in serious trouble after the strike that canceled the World Series in 1994. When the players came back after a delayed start in 1995, people weren't following the game the same way as they were before. Attendance had achieved record numbers before the strike, and it had fallen off dramatically. Ratings and revenues were down.

Then came Mark McGwire and Sammy Sosa, steroid poster boys. Everybody winked and nodded for a decade in order to get the fans back while the balls flew out of parks at a record pace. It was all about the money. Greed. Shame on the commissioner. Shame on the owners. Shame on the players. Shame on the Major League Baseball Players Association. And shame on those fans who seem to care so little about steroid use.

No one showed the slightest regard for the history of the game. Major League Baseball has been played since the late-19th century, and players are suddenly hitting 70 home runs? Babe Ruth and Roger Maris were the only two hitters to ever crack 60 home runs prior to 1998. Then that number was surpassed six times in four years by McGwire, Sosa, and Bonds.

Before the '94 strike, George Foster in '77 was the last National League player to hit 50 home runs in a season. Prior to that it was Willie Mays in '65. Cecil Fielder reached

50 in the American League for the Tigers in '90. These were major accomplishments. Then the year after the strike, balls were flying all over the place, and they blasted out of the park with even more frequency. Greg Vaughn hit 50 home runs for San Diego in 1998, and he finished third in the league. Only two other guys had hit 50 in the NL in the previous four decades, and suddenly hitting that many homers gets you only within 20 of the home-run crown? That's hard to believe. What's even harder to understand is how many people believed it. Or chose to believe it.

There was complete disregard and disrespect for the game. And all Bud Selig is doing now is trying to cement his legacy and standing in history, as if he were a modern-day Judge Kenesaw Mountain Landis. Please.

FEBRUARY 20, 2008

Today marks the mandatory date for all Mets to report to spring training in Port St. Lucie. Though most players have already arrived, a handful will be late because of visa problems. The first scheduled game is less than a week away against Mets owner Fred Wilpon's alma mater, the University of Michigan. The Wolverines will use wooden bats, but they'll go back to aluminum for games against other colleges. They're missing more than just the crack of the bat.

The Bat Makes the Man

Colleges have become the minor leagues now. Teams prefer drafting college players because they're closer to reaching the major leagues. In my day, they wanted to draft you out of high school. They wanted to teach you to play when you were 18. Today, if you come from a major college program, they expect you'll be ready for the majors in one to three years.

That's all the more reason why Major League Baseball should supply all colleges with wooden bats. MLB can afford it. It would keep colleges from playing with those ridiculous aluminum bats. I've never used an aluminum bat. Never in my life. But it's because players grow up so used to those light aluminum bats that they wind up using ultra-light wooden bats when they reach the majors. The lighter bats—such as the 30- and 31-ounce bats players use a lot today—splinter and crack more than the heavier models we used.

The lighter the weight, the worse the wood you get. The rule of thumb we followed in my day was that you never went more than 2 ounces below the length, which was measured in inches. So if you had a 35-inch bat, you never went below 33 ounces. If you went 2½ ounces less than the length, you started getting wood that was not as good. I generally used 34½ inches and 32½ ounces. A lot of players today are using 35-inch bats that are 31 ounces. It's like balsa wood—and it lasts about as long.

Maple? I think maple bats should be banned from the game entirely. Maple bats are harder and less pliable than white ash, and they do not bend with impact. They are more prone to breakage. Balls just fly off maple bats, giving an unfair advantage to hitters who use them. And when a maple bat breaks, the barrel often flies off in one piece—on to the field, the on-deck circle, the stands—like a weapon.

I always liked a somewhat thin-handled bat, which I found to be well balanced. It took me a long time to find the right one, though. I actually found the bat I used the rest of my career during the '82 World Series, after 11 seasons of playing professional baseball. I started the season with a 35-inch, 33-ounce, bat and as the season went on, I went down to 32½ ounces because the bats always felt heavier late in the year. In the first three games of the World Series, I went 0-for-11 against Milwaukee. Then I picked up Willie McGee's bat in batting practice prior to Game 4 in Milwaukee and it felt as if it were made just for me. I wound up going 0-for-4, but I hit three ropes and had nothing to show for it. I finished 7-for-12 in the Series with a World Series–leading eight RBIs, all in the last three games. I never switched from that bat after that: Model C271, 34½ inches, 32½ ounces, with a bored-out barrel at the top of the bat.

Players receive bat shipments straight from the manufacturer. I would handle the bats immediately when they came into the clubhouse. Every last one of them. The wider the grain, the better the wood and the better the bat. You can get a key and make a groove, an indentation in the grain. You can't do it between the grain lines. That's where the hard wood is. The harder the wood, the better the hitting surface. Before they outlawed it, I used to groove all my bats.

I would groove them with a key on the hitting surface above the label up to the end of the autograph on the top of the barrel—just on the fat side where you make contact. And then I'd rub it against a porcelain sink. When I was satisfied with the way the bat felt, I would take it out to batting practice and pound it for as many rounds of BP as it took to make that bat become iron. The more you hit the ball in the contact area, the more it compresses the wood. When that bat was compressed to my satisfaction, I never used it in BP again, only in a game. Then I would move on to the next bat until I had an arsenal of game-ready bats.

I would always ask for wide grain. As I got older and became a star, I always asked for—and received—great wood from Louisville Slugger. A few thin-grain bats would find their way into a shipment, and I used those solely for BP—and only after I'd already broken all the wide-grain bats into game shape.

You also need to make sure the bat is the proper weight. One season with the Mets I got a whole shipment where the bats just felt like toothpicks. I swung one of those bats for two games until I crushed a ball that wound up being caught on the warning track. I went back to Charlie Samuels, our clubhouse man, and I told him to weigh all the bats. They were all 32 ounces. I sent them all back and got a rush order of 32½s.

Louisville Slugger would send four or five dozen bats at a time. They generally don't get every single bat in a shipment right, but usually 97 or 98 percent are to the correct specifications. Bats are the tools of a hitter's trade. You wouldn't expect an artist to use a paintbrush that didn't feel right in his hand—a ballplayer is trying to hit an object going 95 miles an hour or more, so hitters tend to be particular.

FEBRUARY 21, 2008

This week's issue of *Sports Illustrated* is out and Johan Santana is on the cover. Although the Mets have had a couple of group shots on the cover since 2006, the last time a Mets pitcher graced the cover by himself was Dwight Gooden in the spring of 1993. Is there an *SI* cover jinx? Well, '93 marked the only year since 1967 that the Mets lost 100 games. Draw your own conclusions, but one first baseman went on to have a stellar career and play on two world championship teams after his lone *Sports Illustrated* cover appearance.

Covering *Sports Illustrated*

There's always some excitement when a ballplayer gets on the cover of *Sports Illustrated* before the season has even started. It's nice to see a Met on the cover, especially someone who comes with as many expectations as Johan Santana.

SI put me on the cover for the 1980 baseball preview issue with the headline, "Who Is Keith Hernandez and What Is He Doing Hitting .344?" *Sports Illustrated* interviewed me near the end of spring training that year with the Cardinals.

That was wonderful. It was the only time I was on the cover of *Sports Illustrated*. As for the headline *SI* used on the cover, I *did* come out of nowhere. The '79 season was my breakout year nationally. I won the batting title and shared the league MVP with Willie Stargell, but I had enjoyed some good years before that. In 1976, I'd hit .320 from June on, even though Philly won the division handily. I followed that up by hitting .291 with 91 RBIs in '77. The next year, I had a good first half and trailed off in the second half to finish at .255. The year after that, I was the batting champion.

FEBRUARY 29, 2008

Leap Year Day marks the first telecast of the season for the SNY crew. The Mets have already had two spring games against major league clubs. They will have 32 games against major league competition in Florida, plus the game already played against the University of Michigan and the Civil Rights Game in Memphis against the White Sox two days before Opening Day. Spring baseball is the start of a long grind.

It's All for the Pitchers

Spring training goes on for as long as it does each year for one simple reason: the pitchers need it. You have five starters and they can pitch only once every fifth day. Each starter needs five starts before heading north. There's no argument—the everyday players have to deal with it. There have been times when I haven't been ready with two weeks to go in camp and I needed those extra games and at-bats against live pitching. I never had a problem with 28 games in spring training. Of course, now there are 30-plus games on the schedule. So be it.

If you're trying to make a ballclub, all those spring training games can be helpful because it enables management to get a long look and decide if you are worth keeping, sending down, or releasing. Because the games don't count, managers can also try you at positions they might not try you at during the season.

Then there's the travel. You don't play series or have many days off, so each visit to another team's spring training site is a bus trip. You always play the teams located closest to you. For most of my career, I trained in St. Petersburg—the shared home for both the Cardinals and the Mets for my first 15 spring camps.

We would travel to Bradenton to play the Pirates, who were 45 minutes away. The Reds were 45 minutes away in Tampa. Lakeland was an hour away for Detroit. Winter Haven was an hour and a half away for the Red Sox. Minnesota was two hours away in Orlando. It was about an hour to Dunedin for Toronto. Forty-five minutes to Clearwater for the Phillies. And if you went to the White Sox in Sarasota or Fort Myers for Kansas City, that was a long way. If you traveled to the East Coast of Florida, you usually played three games in the area and stayed overnight twice. You'd hit the Yankees in Fort Lauderdale, then go to West Palm Beach to play the Braves, and follow it with the Orioles, who were in Miami at the time.

Those longer trips don't happen that often in spring training because you don't want your players to travel three hours on a bus and get off of it stiff, which increases the chance of a muscle pull. I really think that all of the spring training sites should be centralized and closer together, like the teams are in the Phoenix area. I spent only one spring training in Arizona, when I was in the last year of my career with Cleveland, and we trained in Tucson. Every road trip was a two-hour ride each way to Phoenix. It was a pain, but you do what you've got to do.

Who winds up going on most of those spring training road trips? The rookies and guys who are trying to make the club. You make every trip until you're a veteran. Then the manager starts taking care of you and you miss a lot of those long bus rides. Everyone rides enough buses coming up in the minors—and no one is nostalgic about that part of the baseball life.

Whitey Herzog had a rule for his Cardinals teams: no one could leave the bench in spring training against a National League team. If you were playing an American League team, you could get your work in and then go home. If a National League team was in for a game, you'd get your work in, take a shower, and come back to the dugout. You'd stay for the whole nine innings; you might learn something about the competition.

MARCH 8, 2008

Though it does not involve the Mets, the talk of spring training is an event between the Yankees and the newly rechristened Tampa Bay Rays. A home plate collision between a pair of marginal prospects, Tampa Bay's Elliot Johnson and Yankees catcher Francisco Cervelli, results in Cervelli breaking his wrist to put him out of action for about two months. New Yankees manager Joe Girardi says that that type of play in a spring-training game is uncalled for, while Rays manager Joe Maddon backs up his player and his effort.

Tampa Bay adviser Don Zimmer, who was playing in major league spring training a decade before Girardi was born, who chose hard-nosed rookie Girardi to be a Cub in April 1989, and who worked closely with him when they both wore Yankees uniforms in the late 1990s, differs greatly with his protégé on this matter.

"You block the plate," Zimmer tells the *New York Times*. "If I slide into him and break a leg, nothing is said. Instead of breaking my leg, I bowl him over and it's not the right play? Well, to me it's the right play, spring training or no spring training. Play the game the right way."

The Rights (and Wrongs) of Spring

I agree with Don Zimmer. There's a certain way to play the game, and that kid from Tampa Bay, Elliot Johnson, did it the right way. If he had been a veteran, he would not have knocked the catcher down. If it had been a veteran catcher involved for the Yankees, he never would have gotten in the way and tried to block the plate. You've got young players on each side trying to make their ballclubs. Both kids played it the right way. It was a clean play. I thought Joe Girardi overreacted.

If I'm trying to make a ballclub and a catcher is blocking the plate, I'm going to knock him down. It's that simple. Baseball is much more of a gentlemen's game now. It's taken on the old American League style. When I played we used to laugh at how the American League was the country club league. The players would never take anyone out with a slide. The National League was a lot grittier. You'd take someone out in the double play, and you'd knock the catcher over if it meant scoring a run. Now the great majority of players in both leagues don't knock anyone over. "Oh, did I hurt you? I'm sorry. I won't slide so hard next time."

MARCH 12, 2008
The rematch between the Yankees and Tampa Bay in St. Petersburg results in a brawl after Yankee Shelley Duncan spikes Rays second baseman Akinori

Iwamura. Like most baseball fights, it will soon be forgotten. The site of the brawl, Al Lang Field stirs up memories for Keith Hernandez, who spent his first 15 spring trainings in St. Pete, first with the Cardinals and then with the Mets (the two clubs shared the facility from 1962 until the Mets moved to Port St. Lucie in 1988). The 2008 season marks the last year of Al Lang Field, which has hosted spring games since 1922.

A 25-player All-Time Al Lang Field Team chosen by the Rays during spring training includes four Mets who trained in St. Petersburg: Tom Seaver, Nolan Ryan, Gary Carter, and Darryl Strawberry. First base is occupied by the legendary Lou Gehrig and Stan Musial.

Auld Al Lang Syne

I love St. Petersburg much more than the east coast of Florida. Al Lang Field was always special for me. The setting there was ideal for spring training.

For my first few years with the Mets, we still shared Al Lang with the Cardinals. We had to work out in the morning over at Huggins-Stengel Field, around three miles away from Al Lang. I don't have a lot of wonderful memories of Huggins–Stengel Field because it was a pretty bad facility, but Payson Field, on the other hand, was rather nice. Payson Field, named after the original Mets owner, Joan Payson, was the minor league complex; that's where we'd start spring training before the minor leaguers showed up. But when the minor leaguers arrived in camp, it became too crowded and we had to move over to Huggins–Stengel Field (it was named after 1920s Yankees manager Miller Huggins and Casey Stengel, who spent nearly two decades training in St. Pete with the Yankees and Mets).

The biggest problem with Huggins–Stengel Field was that it was too small. We spent a lot of time there with the Mets because the Cardinals, who'd trained in St. Petersburg longer, were given seniority and had their morning workouts on Al Lang Field. You really need a complex so you can coordinate drills, methods, and coaching as an organization.

The Mets made the switch in 1988. We had one owner, Fred Wilpon, who invested in real estate in Port St. Lucie. And Nelson Doubleday, the other owner, had his winter home on Jupiter Island, 45 minutes from Tradition Field. That's why we eventually moved to Port St. Lucie.

I'd spent every spring training in St. Petersburg from when I was a teenager until I was 34. I wasn't thrilled with the change, but as it worked out, we won 100 games and a division title after our first year training there. The problem during those early years in Port St. Lucie was that Mets spring training was just about the only attraction in town. There was nothing for us to do. We called it "Port St. Lonesome." It's grown a lot, but there still isn't a whole lot going on. If you want to have any fun, Palm Beach is an hour and a half away. It's not worth the drive.

MARCH 20, 2008

Johan Santana, the prize of the winter, has gone about his spring work like the seasoned pro that he is. He is getting accustomed to the increased media scrutiny that comes before and after every outing. Though Florida is a far cry from the back-page pitched battles of New York, spring training is all about building up stamina. He doubles and scores and later draws a walk at Tradition

A few weeks after being traded to the Mets and signing the biggest contract ever by a pitcher, fans in Port St. Lucie ask Johan Santana to sign a few much less expensive items.

Field. But most important, he tosses six shutout innings as the Mets blank the Orioles 7–0 in a Thursday night broadcast back to New York on SNY.

Domain

Johan Santana is very soft-spoken, polite, and reserved. I like him. There are a lot of passive personalities on this team, but Santana isn't passive—he's just quiet. He knows who I am; a lot of guys today don't.

I try to avoid the players in the clubhouse. There's so much media, and I like to stay out of their way as much as possible. I recall what it was like as a player, and these guys deserve some space. I don't go out to dinner with the players, just like I didn't go out with the coaches or the press when I played. There's a line there that you just don't cross.

In my day, the clubhouse was a place for the players and the manager and not really anyone else. The reporters were there before and after games—that's their job—but it never was the job of the front office to be in the clubhouse beyond just passing through. I played for several general managers in St. Louis: Bing Devine, John Claiborne, Whitey Herzog (though Whitey also managed, so it wasn't your usual player-GM relationship), and Joe McDonald. Frank Cashen was the general manager during my entire time with the Mets. I very seldom saw Frank. He would have a meeting once a week with Davey Johnson, usually on Sunday.

Frank was a good guy. We liked Frank, but he would just say hello and keep on walking. Frank seldom mingled with the players—just like all the GMs I had with the Cardinals. The message seemed pretty clear: the clubhouse was the domain of the manager, not the general manager. Frank even confirmed to me years later that he felt that way.

There is a whole new attitude today. General managers spend a lot more time with the players in the clubhouse. I've noticed it for the last 10 years or so. I don't agree with it. I don't think you can be in charge and be everyone's friend simultaneously. It doesn't work in the business world, and it doesn't work in a major league clubhouse, either. There's a chain of command. The front office makes the decisions on personnel and how to build a team. When I played, I felt like the team was a cohesive unit trying to attain one goal: winning. To use an analogy, as players we're like soldiers. We take orders. The front office is in command. Generals don't discuss orders with servicemen; they just give them. The player's job is to carry those orders out.

MARCH 24, 2008
One week before the season opener, the Mets look ready for the games to start counting. John Maine throws six one-hit innings against Baltimore, lowering his spring ERA to 1.78 with just one earned run allowed in his last 20⅔ innings. The 1–0 win puts the Mets' spring record at 17–9.

Spring Ahead
You throw away the records in spring training. Five minutes after it's over, it's forgotten. But players can certainly leave an impression at camp.

Everyone's in love with the left side of this infield. They should be. Manager Willie Randolph can write down Wright and Reyes on the lineup card 160 times and never think twice. The right side of the infield has questions. Delgado's coming off a bad year. Will he bounce back? At second base you've got Luis Castillo. He turned 32 at the end of 2007 and had knee surgery over the winter, yet the Mets gave Castillo a four-year deal at his age. That was a shocker.

Castillo was a fine player for many years and he was one of the best second basemen in the game, but he's starting to break down. That's a warning sign, especially for someone who uses his legs like Castillo. He was certainly a fine player. Maybe he still is. But a four-year deal is a little questionable.

Just about the whole team has been banged up in Florida. In the outfield, we've seen almost everyone this spring except the guys who'll be out there when the season starts. Carlos Beltran is coming off 30 homers and driving in 110 for the second straight year. He's a Gold Glove center fielder, no question. After having surgery on both knees during the winter, he's taking it slow this spring. He'll be there when the season starts.

Who's going to play next to him? Moises Alou was hurt the majority of last year, and he's been out for most of camp with a sore hip. Ryan Church is going to be the right fielder, but he collided with Marlon Anderson early in the spring and suffered a concussion. He's made it back to the lineup. The ones who've benefitted the most from all these injuries are Endy Chavez and Angel Pagan. Endy is going to be the fourth outfielder regardless of what happens in Port St. Lucie, but Pagan might have a chance to make the club. He was originally drafted by the Mets in 1999 and was acquired from the Cubs over the winter. Pagan has been playing every day because everyone else has been hurt. And he has played well.

Brian Schneider, the catcher, came over with Church from Washington in the Lastings Milledge trade. He's been dealing with his hamstring for most of camp. Ramon Castro has been suffering from the same injury.

It looks as if Duaner Sanchez will open the year on the disabled list again. The Mets are counting on him coming back before long. The other guys in the 'pen are already familiar: Aaron Heilman setting up; Pedro Feliciano coming off a real breakout year; Jorge Sosa, now a full-time reliever; and Scott Schoeneweis, who has a lot to prove in the second year of a big contract for a situational left-handed reliever. They're still looking at some other arms for the middle innings: Joe Smith, Nelson Figueroa, Matt Wise, and Steven Register.

There's still a spot to be won on this starting staff. El Duque's toe is still bothering him, and he's trying a new windup. It looks pretty doubtful that he'll break camp with the club. Mike Pelfrey might get the chance, even though I don't know that he's ready. Pedro has looked good in a couple of starts, and he will follow Santana in the rotation. Oliver Perez and John Maine both had strong years in '07 and are ready to prove that they're major leaguers to be counted on. It'll come down to the end of camp to see who follows them in the rotation.

MARCH 29, 2008

There are always tough decisions made during the last days of spring training. The Mets, though enduring numerous injuries during the spring, have a relatively healthy squad as they prepare to start the season. Despite elder statesmen Moises Alou and Orlando Hernandez beginning the year on the disabled list, there are still more players than the Mets have spots for on their 25-man roster.

Veteran Fernando Tatis, who has played only 28 major league games since 2003 and reported late because of visa problems, is seen as a solid candidate for the big club because he has power and bats from the right side. Switch-hitting Ruben Gotay, who was hitting .350 and playing regularly when the Mets traded for Luis Castillo at the end of July 2007, is on the bubble to make the team in 2008.

But neither Tatis nor Gotay survive the last cut. Journeyman outfielder Brady Clark trades in his St. Lucie number 93 for 44 with the big club. Tatis is sent back to New Orleans, and Gotay, out of options, is released and winds up in Atlanta. Outfielder Angel Pagan makes the club with ease, hitting .329—and in more at-bats than any Met in camp. Journeyman Raul Casanova, whose three home runs were the most by any Met in the spring and whose 10 RBIs tied Pagan for the club lead, makes the team as the backup catcher in place of the injured Ramon Castro.

Gotay Goes, Clark Continues

With today's 12-man pitching staffs, there is room for only five bench players. That makes the final spring cuts even tougher. Willie Randolph wants a versatile player who can play several positions and fill a need on the bench.

The Mets are overloaded with left-handed hitters. Otherwise, Ruben Gotay probably makes the ballclub. Endy Chavez and Marlon Anderson are both left-handed hitters, they're veterans, and there was never a doubt that they'd be on the team—so that leaves Gotay as the odd man out. He's a switch-hitter who's much better batting from the left side, and he's not a great fielder. You're not gaining anything by having Gotay on the bench—the immediate need is for a right-handed bat off the bench. That's why Brady Clark made the team. He was a Met back when Bobby Valentine was manager in 2002. Since then, he put together a few nice years in Milwaukee. He's become a bench player, a fifth outfielder.

If Fernando Tatis hadn't been held up by visa problems, maybe he would be the extra righty bat.

Angel Pagan had a great spring. He's a lifetime .250 hitter—and he played more than anybody in spring training, got more hits than anyone, and tied with backup catcher Raul Casanova for most RBIs (10). Not that anyone really cares about spring stats, but it's important to have positive statistics when you're trying to make the club. So Pagan and Casanova will go north. They made the most of the opportunity in spring. When Castro and Alou are healthy, Pagan and Casanova will both probably be sent down to the minors, but as a player, you want to be on that Opening Day roster.

All the injuries the Mets had in the spring entered into the Mets' thinking about those final roster spots. One player they sent down a little early before they could be tempted to keep him was the 19-year-old in camp who got everyone's attention every time he came up: Fernando Martinez, the outfielder the Mets held out of the Santana deal with Minnesota. I like the kid's swing. He goes the other way naturally. I think he has the chance to be a pretty good player; I just hope the Mets don't rush him. I was rushed up at age 20, and it almost ruined my career.

My first year making the club out of spring training was with the Cardinals in 1975. I stayed in St. Louis until early June. They sent me down to Triple A Tulsa after I barely hit .200 in the majors. I submit to this day I wasn't ready for the big leagues emotionally; I was too young.

That extra time in Tulsa in '75 helped me. It was the third time I'd hit .330 or better at Triple A. When the Cardinals called me up again at the end of that season, I hit .350 in September. And I never played in the minors again.

MARCH 30, 2008

The final cuts for the pitching staff also provide tension until the lucky winners are revealed the day before the season opener. Two of the more disappointing young pitchers in camp wind up making the team.

Joe Smith has options and can be sent down without going through waivers—the method required to option players to the minor leagues after their third year on the 40-man roster—but Smith still has a season beyond 2008 before the Mets have to worry about this. More worrisome is Smith's 6.43 Grapefruit ERA. Still, he beats out Brian Stokes, Ricardo Rincon, and Nelson Figueroa for the last spot in the bullpen.

Likewise, the club's 2005 first-round pick, Mike Pelfrey, also has options and takes a spring beating (35 hits and 10 walks in just 21 innings), but he gets the nod to come north. Orlando Hernandez, who had an erratic spring and suffered foot problems that caused him to alter his distinctive motion with a decrease in velocity and effectiveness, remains in Florida on the disabled list. Pelfrey takes his spot.

Roster Roulette: The Pitchers

I was surprised they kept throwing Joe Smith out there in spring games after he had a horrible first 4½ weeks. He made the club because of the last 10 days of the spring season. A submariner is nice to have; it makes it hard for right-handed batters—in Smith's case—to pick up the ball. Joe takes over the role that submariner Chad Bradford had with the Mets in '06. The upside to this is that Joe is young and has a bright future ahead of him, while Bradford is on the backside of his career.

The Mets had hoped that El Duque would be healthy enough to make the rotation. He's not. El Duque's had to alter that signature high leg kick of his. He doesn't look like the same pitcher. This calls for patience. Let his foot heal, and maybe he'll be able to help the team later. If that happens, imagine a rotation of Santana, Pedro, Perez, Maine, and El Duque. I'll take my chances with them.

So Pelfrey takes El Duque's spot heading north. If Pelfrey had been around in our day, he would have been in Triple A, pitching with no pressure, honing his skills, and not throwing under a spotlight in New York. I think they may have rushed him up here too quickly. He certainly has enormous potential.

Unfortunately, teams have to rush young pitchers to the majors today because of the lack of big-league talent. Every team has pitching problems. The hope is that the Mets have fewer pitching problems than everyone else. We'll see about that soon enough.

Opening Day Roster

If you're lucky, the 25 you break camp with will last a while, but the Mets already have Moises Alou, Ramon Castro, and Duaner Sanchez on the DL—they're scheduled to come off in a couple of weeks. They may have to wait a while longer on Orlando Hernandez. The roster is always changing. That's baseball.

Starting Pitching Rotation
Johan Santana
Pedro Martinez
Oliver Perez
John Maine
Mike Pelfrey

Bullpen
Billy Wagner
Aaron Heilman
Pedro Feliciano
Jorge Sosa
Matt Wise
Scott Schoeneweis
Joe Smith

Catchers
Brian Schneider
Raul Casanova

Infielders
Carlos Delgado
Luis Castillo
Jose Reyes
David Wright
Marlon Anderson
Damion Easley

Outfielders
Angel Pagan
Carlos Beltran
Ryan Church
Endy Chavez
Brady Clark

Chapter 3

APRIL

MARCH 31, 2008

The season has arrived and the Mets remain in Florida. When it comes to nostalgic notions of Opening Day, Miami doesn't conjure up any sepia-toned images of baseball's grand tradition. Warm? Yes. (And humid.) Fuzzy? No. Dolphin Stadium doesn't make you think about baseball, but it at least sounds better than its previous naming-rights incarnation: Pro Player (a failed spinoff of an underwear manufacturer).

Still, it's Opening Day, 38,308 people have purchased tickets, Johan Santana is on the mound, and the Mets enter the opener having gone 8–1 in Florida in 2007. (What doomed '07 was a horrible 3–6 mark against the last-place Marlins at Shea.) The Mets enter the season at 18–9 in Miami in Willie Randolph's first three seasons at the helm.

Mets 7, Marlins 2. Record 1–0.

For Openers

Opening Day is Opening Day. No matter what, you're always going to have those Opening Day butterflies. Whether you're home or away, you just want to get out of spring training and start playing games that count. It was a boon for the Mets to open in Miami because the Mets have beaten them soundly in Florida over the last three years.

When you look at Opening Day from a veteran player's point of view, the fewer of those you have to play in a season, the better. I've been on teams where the schedule has worked out that we played three Opening Days. They're a pain in the neck. Usually you're going to have play two: one at home and one on the road. Maybe you get lucky and you open at home, hit the road, and miss catching someone having their own home opener. But that doesn't happen very often. As a visiting player, Opening Day just kind of gets in the way. What you want is to get into the flow of the season.

Johan Santana got the season going the way the Mets wanted. Now he has one under his belt and looks pretty sharp. He made a bad pitch that Josh Willingham hit out of the park, but the offense put together a six-run inning, and David Wright cleared the bases with a three-run double in the fourth. The Marlins made it a little interesting by loading the bases in the eighth, but Schoeneweis and Sosa each got outs with two men on to end the threat. Otherwise it was pretty cut and dried. A win is all any team wants on day one.

APRIL 1, 2008

It's no April Fool's joke. Pedro Martinez, who had proceeded cautiously in spring training, doesn't make it through the fourth inning in his first start. For the first time in his career, he allows home runs in both the first and second innings; but it is the "pop" he hears in his left leg that abruptly ends his night. (It turns out to be a hamstring strain.) After the Mets sadly watch him exit, they rally to tie the game but lose in ten innings on the first major league home run by Robert Andino, surrendered by Matt Wise.

Marlins 5, Mets 4. Record 1–1; 1 game behind Washington.

Pall Over Pedro

Bad news tonight. It's been tough for Pedro since he became a Met. They signed him to that four-year deal just after Omar took over as GM, the deal that announced that the Mets were ready to step back in the hunt. A month after that, Carlos Beltran signed. The whole identity and direction of this team changed after the Mets landed Pedro. It's now the last year of his deal, and he's had one good season: that first season, 2005. In '06, when the Mets ran away with the division, Pedro pitched well during that great start but spent a lot of time on the disabled list because of problems with his legs—*before* the rotator cuff tear in September. Last year he came back in the last month and got progressively better with each start.

It's just a shame. You have the high of Santana's Mets debut on Opening Day, and a day later you get a punch in the gut watching Pedro get helped off the field. The president of the Dominican Republic, Leonel Fernandez, was there to see him pitch, too. Pedro is a hero in his home country. It's a rough night all around.

Best Days at Shea
SEPTEMBER 22, 1979

A Batting Champ Crowned at Shea

Cardinals 6, Mets 3 (First Game)
Of all the days at Shea I remember, the one I still think of first is the day I clinched the batting title with the Cardinals. Pete Rose was second at .334 and was on a hot streak. We both had double-headers. He had one in Philly that day against Montreal, and we had one at Shea against the Mets. In the opener, I got a single in the first inning as we scored four times. I got another single in the second inning for my 200th hit of the season, another first for me. My next time up I homered off Roy Lee Jackson just after Lou Brock had stolen second, one of the last steals of his great career. The Mets brought in another pitcher, Dwight Bernard, and I got a hit off of him my next time up. A lefty, Ed Glynn, finally got me out in the ninth, but I was up to .346 and I'd finish at .344.

Pete Rose didn't do much that day against the Expos, who were in contention. I came in late in the second game and we swept the doubleheader at Shea. The Mets had just played four doubleheaders in a row and were dead. Regardless of how few people were there—Retrosheet.org says it was about 8,500—I'll never forget it.

I never dreamed of being an MVP or a batting champ. It did not diminish the MVP in my eyes to share it with Willie Stargell. He's a Hall of Famer and one of the greats. And no other MVP race has ever finished in a tie, though there's been some very close voting. It'll be a trivia question for years and years because it's almost impossible, even more bizarre that it was two players at the same position in the same division. The Pirates took the East and went on to win the World Series. We were in the hunt until early August and then faded. Ken Boyer was the manager. It was the first time we'd turned it around with the Cardinals.

APRIL 2, 2008

For the third-straight year, the Mets feature what ESPN.com called "the best broadcast team in baseball": Gary Cohen, Ron Darling, and Keith Hernandez. Before spring training, Keith signed a contract to keep him in the team's booth through 2009. The trio still has a way to go to match the longevity of Ralph Kiner, Lindsey Nelson, and Bob Murphy, who spent the first 17 seasons in Mets history together. But Gary, Keith, and Ron seem to get along as if they've been together for two decades instead of two seasons. Keith has actually been a Mets television broadcaster the longest of the three, starting in 1999. Gary moved over to TV after 16 years in the club's radio booth, and Ron, a recent Emmy winner, returned to New York from the Nationals in 2006.

Mets 13, Marlins 0. Record 2–1; 1 game behind Washington.

About Our Booth

People always ask me about our three-man booth and want to know all about how Gary, Ron, and I work so well together. First of all, the broadcast team is greater than just the three of us. We have a director, a producer, and a production truck full of people who provide us with statistics and information as the game unfolds. The television audience sees and hears the three broadcasters, but our work is made possible by a whole unseen production team who help us do what we do on a daily basis, game by game, all season long.

The SNY network was formed by the Wilpons and Comcast in 2006 and took over televising the Mets games from MSG. The 2006 season was the first time that we all worked together, not just the three of us, but also the rest of the production crew. Gary, Ron, and I each had challenges to face in that first season together in addition to becoming comfortable with one another and working out our broadcast style as individuals and as part of the three-man team.

I was a color analyst for MSG from 1999 to 2005, but I never worked more than 50 games per year, and in the MSG three-man booths, the color analysts worked only six innings per game. I never felt like I had enough time in the booth to get into the flow of a season. I wanted to work about 100 games so that I could have a real feel for the team and do my best job as an announcer, have a better pulse of what's really going on with the ballclub. Now I am signed on to broadcast 105 games during the regular season and 10 games in the spring. This is a perfect schedule for me.

Gary came to SNY to be the play-by-play man after spending 16 years a part of the Mets' radio broadcast team. Television broadcasting was a big adjustment for him that first season because he was adapting to a whole different medium, but Gary found his rhythm very quickly. Ronnie came to our booth with only one year of experience, as a color analyst for Washington. So basically, I was the guy in the booth with the most experience in television, but we all brought different strengths to the broadcast. Ronnie's strength is discussing pitching, I bring my experience with hitting and being an everyday position player, and Gary is most knowledgeable about Mets history, because he grew up a Mets fan in New York. Of the three of us, Gary has the most statistical baseball knowledge. It always amazes me how much he knows off the top of his head. He has a mind like a steel trap.

The first day we went to work together, Ron said, "How should we do this?" And I answered, "Well, Ronnie, you have pitching, I have hitting, and Gary calls the game." It's a simplified formula for what we do, but it has worked more or less perfectly that way from day one. We hardly ever step on each other's toes. We really had to get comfortable with each other and get used to each other's idiosyncrasies and styles that first year, as Gary made the transition to television, Ronnie refined his style, and I adjusted to an expanded schedule.

2006 was a big period of growth for all three of us, but when we went into spring training in 2007 after not seeing each other all winter, it was like we never stopped. We just stepped right back into it. We're so familiar with each other now and so much more comfortable than we were at the beginning. This was to be expected, of course, but it still feels good.

The rest of our broadcast team also came together for the first time when SNY was created in 2006. Our award-winning director, Bill Webb, was the only other person who made the hop from MSG with me. I have worked with Bill for my entire broadcasting career, so the two of us have a shorthand with one another. Otherwise, the whole SNY production staff had to get used to working together.

Our producer, Gregg Picker, had worked at ESPN before joining SNY. He had produced a lot of tennis broadcasts, but he came to the job with enthusiasm and many good ideas that helped us transform our broadcast from the more conventional, conservative baseball broadcast that MSG had preferred. Gregg likes a lighter approach and encourages us to come up with ideas for how to make the broadcast more interesting and quirky. The fans all seemed to enjoy the games we broadcast from different locations in the stands, and those were some of Gregg's additions to our production. That's the only real difference between our SNY broadcast and the way the Mets had been covered previously. You can't do *too* many things differently—you're still doing a ballgame, and the game is the most important thing. People turn on the TV to watch the game and watch the players, but we also hope that our team in the booth can add to the enjoyment of our viewers.

The role of a good baseball producer like Gregg is to be a baseball fan who listens intently to the broadcast and asks us questions. If we're talking about something and we leave it hanging in the air without fully explaining it, he'll say, "Well, what do you mean by that?" or "Why did you just say that?" We can hear him, but obviously the viewer can't. Gregg wants us to expound on whatever issue we're addressing, and that helps us give the viewer the best and most informative broadcast. Gregg listens to every word, and most important, if we ever forget names or we can't find the right word to express what we're trying to say, our producer is right there in our earpiece with the right name or word so we never stall out or interrupt the flow.

The production team in the truck helps us there, too. If I'm saying that Willie Mays hit blank-blank-blank in 1964, the production guys will be right in my headset saying that Willie Mays led the league in home runs and was third in

RBIs and walks. They have computer access and help with statistics from the Elias Bureau, and they feed us information as we need it, in real time, so we can provide the viewers with the best information. We just talk around it and bring it into the broadcast. Believe me, these guys make us look good!

People ask if I feel pressure as a broadcaster. First of all, I hate the word "pressure" when it is used with a negative connotation. To me, as a player and in life as a whole, pressure is something that motivates you to meet a challenge and perform at your best. That being said, I have nothing to feel nervous or tense about in the broadcasting booth. The players are the ones out there on the field. They're the ones making the news; we're reporting it. I'm not up there at the plate in the ninth inning of a tie ballgame with two outs and a chance to win the game. I don't have that kind of challenge anymore. I'm up there in the booth purely as an observer. Why would I be nervous? Or tense? Or have any anxiety? I love what I do.

APRIL 8, 2008

After taking two of three in Florida, the Mets drop two in Atlanta. (A third game at Turner Field is rained out.) As the Mets arrive home with a 2–3 mark going into their last Shea opener, they are without their left fielder (Moises Alou, out—again—this time because of hernia surgery), set-up man (Duaner Sanchez, still working out in Florida after missing nearly a year and a half due to shoulder surgery), and number two starter (Pedro Martinez, who left the second game against the Marlins with a strained left hamstring). Oliver Perez, who

It's not your average plane passing over Shea Stadium. Fans react to the flyover by two military jets at the final home opener at Shea.

threw a combined shutout in Florida in his season debut, is still unscored upon in 2008 when he is removed with two outs in the sixth inning of the Shea opener. The Mets get out of that jam but not one the next inning. It marks the Mets' ninth straight loss to the Phillies and the seventh in a row against them at Shea, dating back to the disastrous climax of the 2007 season.

The Shea name is officially "retired" with a pregame dedication near the retired numbers in left field, but the most noticeable feature about Shea Stadium is how Citi Field dominates the field of vision and seems to hang over the old park.

Phillies 5, Mets 2. Record 2–4; 1½ games behind Florida.

Not–So-Grand Opening in New York

Home Opening Days are great. You love playing in front of the home folks, especially on a sunny day, the bunting flapping in the breeze and a full house getting its first chance to welcome a star like Johan Santana. There was great anticipation for this game because it's the last Opening Day at Shea and also because of Santana, even though it was a little subdued and tempered by the loss of Pedro in Florida.

Oliver Perez had some shaky moments—he walked Jamie Moyer, the pitcher, trying to sacrifice in the fifth, for Pete's sake—but then he got out the one and two hitters in the Philly lineup. Perez got the first two outs in the sixth and then walked a couple of guys and he was gone. Joe Smith got the last out. Was it a quick hook? You could say that, but it all points to the pitch count. The manager and pitching coach look at his total—94 pitches—see he's in a jam, and leave it to the bullpen. The 'pen didn't save this one. The defense let them down, too.

Pitchers are not trained today to strengthen their arms. A lot of starters are five- or six-inning wonders. "Five and fly" or "six and fly," we used to call them. You can't call them that today because they're all on pitch counts. If they string a few innings of 20-plus-pitches together, they're out of there—even if they've got a shutout going or have been successfully pitching out of trouble. That's the mentality they're brought up with as professionals today.

Pitchers come up from the minor leagues without ever having thrown 100 pitches in a game. Then they come to the big leagues and suddenly they're going to throw 120 pitches?

Unlikely. And then you have today's relievers, who are asked to throw only one inning per appearance. They get tired in their second inning of work. It's unbelievable to those of us who played before there were strict pitch-count limits.

It was a tough loss today. And there's a lot of disappointment because it happened against Philly, with last year very fresh in everyone's mind. But it is only one game. And it's the sixth game of the year, 156 to go.

APRIL 9, 2008

What day could be more ripe for spinning a story than the usually irrelevant second home game of the year—the first night game in the April chill, minus the crowd and excitement of Opening Day—and what more quintessentially irrelevant New York topic is there than *Seinfeld*? Although being an All-Star baseball player gets a man noticed in sporting circles, appearing on a hit television show gets the attention of people who don't know a double play from a double latte. With Jerry Seinfeld having been in the house for Shea's last Opening Day, an otherwise routine April win affords a look at Keith Hernandez's memorable star turn away from the diamond: a guest spot on *Seinfeld*.

At the time the one-hour show aired (February 12, 1992), *Seinfeld* was far from being one of the most popular programs in television history. "The Boyfriend" was only the 34th episode of the comedy series that would stay on the air for 180 episodes until it signed off the air voluntarily with enormous fanfare in 1998. *TV Guide* ranks "The Boyfriend" as the fourth-best episode of any show in television history. Jerry Seinfeld also claimed it was his favorite episode in the show's run. Many other Mets fans concur.

Mets 8, Phillies 2. Record 3–4; 1½ games behind Florida.

So Scott Boras Says, "Ever Heard of This *Seinfeld*?"

That episode was Jerry's idea because he is a Mets fan. He loved the '80s Mets, and I was his favorite player. He concocted a storyline that involved the two of us randomly meeting and quickly becoming friends, but he didn't know how to find me to ask me to be on the show. I had never met him. I was retired from baseball, it was 1991, and he wound up finding me through my agent, Scott Boras, whom I really didn't need anymore because I was no longer a player. Scott

Jerry Seinfeld takes in the final Opening Day at Shea.
(Photo by Dan Carubia)

called me out of the blue and said, "Have you ever heard of this *Seinfeld* show?" I said, "No, what is it?" He said, "Well, it's a sitcom." *Seinfeld* had been on regularly for half a season with a few scattered episodes the year before that. It hadn't caught on yet. Scott said, "We got a call from the *Seinfeld* people, he's a big fan—a Mets fan, a fan of yours—and they want you to do a half-hour show playing yourself."

I asked how many lines of dialogue, how much money, etc. He said it was probably very light work, they'd put me up for a week in Los Angeles at a hotel, pay me $15,000, and fly me there and back first class. I agreed.

They sent me the script, and I realized that this was not going to be a show in which I would have minimal lines. I was going to be a principal character. I'd never done anything like that before in my life. I called my old friend Marsha Mason, the actress, who was living in New Mexico. I told her, "Marsha, I need help. I just agreed to do something here, and I thought I was going to have maybe five lines, and it turns out I'm the guest star, and I have a ton of lines." She told me how to memorize lines: read line 1, memorize it; go to line 2, memorize it; say line 1, line 2; go to line 3. I had about a week to memorize it all. I was terrified!

Television shows change the script all the time during the week of taping. Over the course of the week we rehearsed, they kept adding lines, taking away lines, changing things to make it better. It was a true creative process, which was very interesting for me to watch.

There were Jerry and Larry David, the principal writer, and the main characters, played by Julia Louis-Dreyfus,

Jason Alexander, and Michael Richards. There were three other writers in there, and we all sat at this long rectangular table to go over the script, and everyone was adding input to make it better. We started out Monday morning at the table with the script and in the afternoon went on the set to do all the tracking, the lighting, the blocking, and the camera work. There is a whole lot that goes into making an episode at the production level. A lot of hurry up and wait. It takes forever.

On Tuesday we worked all day, read every scene with the script in our hands and kept on making changes. On Wednesday there was no more script—you had to know your lines. There was a lady with a copy of the script and if you got into the middle of a sentence and you forgot what you were supposed to say, all you had to say was "line" and she'd prompt you to the line you forgot. She also had a stop-watch, because everything had to be timed to the precise second to get to the commercial break. Thursday was more of the same, but the team was still making changes, altering the script, making it funnier, making it better.

On Friday after 5:00 PM we did a complete run-through for about eight NBC executives. They had to give their approval and deem that it wasn't too racy. Around 8:00 PM, we went on the soundstage and performed the episode in front of a live audience. Then we came back the next morning and did it all over again on the soundstage without an audience. The director and producer chose the best takes to edit and dub. Everyone involved in the show made it clear to me that it was important to really do well in the live version on Friday night. They felt it was a funny show, and they didn't want to have to put in a tape of fake laughs ("laugh tracks" as they are called in the TV business). They would rather have real laughter. Saturday's taping in studio was a relief—everything went smoothly without the pressure of a live audience. I really was stressed out and scared stiff of doing it in front of 300 people on Friday night.

On Sunday, it was all over. I was relieved to have completed the show, but at the same time I was very happy that I'd been able to do it. I'd come in not knowing anything about the process, and I handled it pretty well, if I may say so myself. It was a whole new experience for me, and it was one of the great experiences of my life.

I still hear about the "I'm Keith Hernandez" line from *Seinfeld*. My delivery of that line took only one take. It was a voiceover. We were in the middle of one of the sets and Larry David said, "While we have the boom mic here over Keith, let's just do the voiceover in that scene with Elaine." When it came to that line, I have to admit, I didn't know how to say it. So I basically asked Larry, "How do you want me to say that? How would you say it?" He said it and I told him, "Get everything ready with the tape. You say it, I'll wait a beat, and then I'll say it just as you said it." So he said it, then I said it, and they were happy with it.

Jerry and Larry told me later that they had written two versions of the episode: a half-hour episode and an hour-long version with added scenes. They loved the script, they knew it was a winner, and they wanted to use it during sweeps. They told me that everything hinged on whether I was good enough to make the show an hour long. If I wasn't, the show would just have been shorter. They were satisfied with my performance, so they used the long version. The rest is television history. Seventeen years later, people still ask me about that show nearly every day.

APRIL 10, 2008

The Mets are back to .500 after taking the series from the Phillies. It isn't easy, though. The Mets have a 3–0 lead with John Maine shutting out the Phils through six innings. Then he allows a Pedro Feliz home run to start the seventh and is removed after a double by Chris Coste. Pedro Feliciano pitches out of trouble in the seventh, but Aaron Heilman allows two runs to tie it in the eighth. Billy Wagner, Joe Smith, Scott Schoeneweis, and Jorge Sosa combine to hold the Phillies off the scoreboard through the twelfth inning. It looks as if the game will extend to thirteen innings after the first two Mets are retired by Tom Gordon, but Jose Reyes rips a double. Angel Pagan, considered a long shot to make the team when spring training began, singles up the middle. Jayson Werth makes a superb throw home to Coste, but Reyes is ruled safe by umpire Ted Barrett on a bang-bang play. It is the first break to go New York's way against Philadelphia in what feels like a century.

Mets 4, Phillies 3. Record 4–4; 1½ games behind Florida.

Sliding Past the Phillies

That was a very close play at the plate. It could have gone either way. Gary, Ron, and I had all the great camera angles in the booth, and it was still very difficult for us to tell for sure. Werth made a very strong and accurate throw. If you have a guy out there with a popgun arm, he's safe, easily.

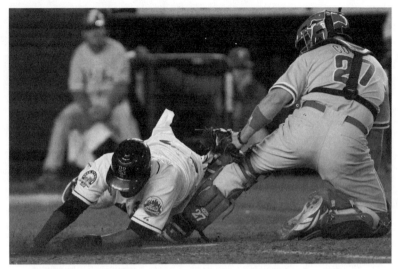

A bang-bang play at the plate goes to Jose Reyes and the Mets as they beat Chris Coste and the Phillies in twelve innings at Shea.

That's an aspect of the game you don't see as much with the new stadiums today.

The new parks don't have those rounded fences that get deeper as you move away from the foul lines into the gaps. No more symmetrical dimensions; the new fences go straight out at right angles from the foul line. So where are the gaps? There *are* no gaps. No one has 380-foot gaps anymore. Those tiny new parks like the ones in Philadelphia or Cincinnati have dimensions like Wrigley Field. The only difference is that Wrigley is a great old-time park built more than 90 years ago, and the wind off Lake Michigan usually dictates how the ball will carry.

The result is one-base-at-a-time baseball. A runner on second can't score on a single 20 feet from the left fielder's left in the gap because the shortened gaps allow the corner outfielders to play shallower. Guys can't score from first on a double off the wall. All that takes away from the excitement of the game. There's nothing better than watching someone trying to score from first on a double in the gap with a close play at the plate. It's all gone with the new parks. Now everything is for the home run.

Beating Philly that way was an important win for this team. The Mets lost the home opener in disheartening fashion, then took a laugher behind Pelfrey on Wednesday, and won the rubber match in twelve innings on a bang-bang play. This was great ballgame to watch.

It's only the eighth game of the year, but these two teams have clearly developed a rivalry since the middle of last season. Winning the first series is big, especially for the Mets, given the way 2007 ended.

APRIL 12, 2008

Johan Santana makes his first start at Shea. Fans greeted him very warmly during pregame introductions on Opening Day, and they now cheer him wildly as he takes the mound against Milwaukee's ace, Ben Sheets. The Mets stake Santana to a 2–0 lead in the first inning, but the Brewers hit three home runs off Santana, including a long blast in the seventh by Gabe Kapler, who has come back after a year's retirement as a minor league manager. When Santana walks off the mound trailing 5–2, a loud chorus of boos follows him. The reaction is far more disturbing than a loss in an April game.

Brewers 5, Mets 3. Record 5–5; 1½ games behind Florida.

Tough Crowd

I don't think it's right. Nothing is worse than getting booed at home. When you get booed on the road, it's fine, you kind of like it. It fires you up. But getting booed at home makes it very lonely out there. To put it simply, I just don't think good fans boo their own team.

The game has changed in a lot of ways in recent years, and the fans have changed, too. When I was growing up, my dad would not let me boo an opposing player. And if an opposing player made a great play, you clapped for him. If a visiting pitcher left the mound after eight innings and he pitched a great game, he always got applause from the audience. You don't get that today. It's a lack of class, in my opinion.

Santana is a hell of an acquisition, one of the biggest trades the Mets have ever made. He's as important as any man on this team. But he's not going to go out there and go 34–0 in all his starts.

It's crucial to have a stopper. He's there to stop the bleeding.

APRIL 20, 2008

A five-game winning streak comes to an end with a Sunday night game in Philadelphia. One complete turn of the rotation sees only one starter fail to pitch into the seventh inning, and four of the five earn wins. The one who didn't get a victory kept the Mets in a game they went on to win in fourteen innings to finish a three-game sweep of Washington. Mike Pelfrey, winner of his first two starts of the season (a great beginning considering he didn't win at all until his 10th start in 2007) is roughed up Sunday night in Philadelphia. The Mets take him off the hook with four runs in the sixth, but Pedro Feliz homers off Pedro Feliciano for the lead. The game ends with Philadelphia shortstop Eric Bruntlett, filling in for injured Jimmy Rollins, robbing Carlos Beltran of a hit that would have tied the score.

Phillies 5, Mets 4. Record 10–7; ½ game behind Florida.

Bad Ending, Good Run

The Mets showed something by winning four in a row against the Phillies after losing on Opening Day at Shea. The players, the fans, the media, everybody is thinking about what happened at the end of last year each time these teams play. The Mets pitched well in this series, which isn't easy in that little bandbox in Philly.

The Mets also got a little lucky playing the Phillies minus Jimmy Rollins. He sprained his ankle and missed the last two games of the three-game series at Shea and the entire series in Philly. He pinch hit, but without Rollins in the lineup, the Phillies were at a severe disadvantage. He's a Met killer. Without Rollins, the Mets won the last two games at home and two out of three in Philly.

Rollins missing those games is worth noting, but what's most important to take out of this is that the Mets played well against their rival and won both series.

APRIL 27, 2008

The Mets take two of three from the Braves at Shea, but as has been the case early in the season, even when the team plays well other news overshadows it. Today it is about whether the previously slumping Carlos Delgado should have acquiesced to a long ovation by coming out for a curtain call following his second home run of the game. After the game he said that he had come out of the dugout only twice in his career: once in Toronto, when he hit four home runs in a game on September 25, 2003, and after he clubbed his 400th career home run at Shea on August 22, 2006.

"I've got a great deal of respect for the game," he said after the win. "I don't think that's a place for a curtain call." His decision—and fan reaction—was back-page material in the tabloids and a source for endless yammering on sports call-in radio shows.

Mets 6, Braves 3. Record 13–11; 1½ games behind Florida.

Curtain Falls

As I said earlier, I feel that fans boo more today than they ever have before. Whether it's the money the players are making or the steep ticket prices, I don't know, but it's counterproductive. It came to a head today when Carlos Delgado didn't come out and take a bow after his second home run. I don't blame him one bit.

In all my years with the Mets, I do not remember the majority of the team being booed like this when players don't perform or get big hits or get big outs. It's been happening with disturbing frequency this year. Guys have been booed here before, from time to time, but not the whole team. Just about the only Met they don't boo these days is David Wright.

There wasn't much to boo about in that game against Atlanta. It was a nice performance by Nelson Figueroa, and the Mets played very well defensively. The Mets did get a little bit lucky because Chipper Jones didn't play, nor did

Yunel Escobar. Chipper played only the first game, and Escobar got hurt at the start of the first game of the series, Friday night. John Smoltz had to come out early in the third game, and he wasn't himself. Without Chipper in the lineup, the Mets are 2–0 against the Braves. With Chipper, they're 0–3. So the Mets got a little fortunate with the injuries to Chipper and the other Braves much like they did earlier with the Phillies and Rollins.

APRIL 30, 2008

Billy Wagner blows his first save of the year against the Pirates, but the unearned run that ties the game keeps his ERA at a perfect 0.00. The Mets wind up winning in eleven innings on David Wright's walk-off hit, but it costs Johan Santana his third victory, forces Wagner to throw two innings, and results in the Mets using seven pitchers.

The next day is a Wednesday matinee, and it is delayed nearly an hour because of a water main break. When the game begins, the Mets play as if the power's been shut off. Pirates pitcher Tom Gorzelanny comes up with the bases loaded in the second inning and hits what looks like a double-play grounder, but Luis Castillo boots it. Oliver Perez responds by walking his fourth batter of the inning to force in another run and then allows two hits and a sacrifice fly. He exits the game after 27 balls and 28 strikes, leaving behind plenty of outs to be gotten by a spent bullpen that's about to head across the country on a road trip to Arizona and Los Angeles. Wagner lets Perez—and every media outlet in New York know—that the starter's quick disappearing act did not go unnoticed and wasn't appreciated by the bullpen.

Pirates 13, Mets 1. Record 14–12; ½ game behind Florida.

One Month in the Books

So at the end of April the Mets find themselves two games over .500, ½ game behind the surprising, division-leading Florida Marlins. It is not a great month, but they are holding their own despite the loss of Pedro. On the upside, Angel Pagan and Ryan Church have played wonderfully. Pagan, subbing for the injured Moises Alou, has been in the middle of every Mets win, getting several clutch RBIs and being on base to score a few other key runs. But Ryan Church has been the Mets' player of the month.

I cannot say enough about Ryan Church. He has hit the heck out of the ball and has played great defense with an incredibly strong and accurate arm. I have never seen a quicker release from an outfielder as I have from Church. Most important, Church has been hitting left-handers well. That was one of the many big questions coming into this season regarding Church. In the opening series in Florida, Cookie Rojas (ex-player, former Mets coach, and a current member of the Marlins' Spanish–language radio team) told me that Church is a heck of a player who just needs a chance to play every day. He told me that he liked that trade as much as the Santana trade. Everybody now is beginning to shut up and stop criticizing Omar's trade that sent Lasting Milledge to Washington for Church and Schneider.

Here are Pagan's and Church's numbers for the first month (including that one game in March), covering 26 games apiece:

- Pagan: .278 batting average, 10 runs, 7 doubles, 12 RBIs

- Church: .316 average, 21 runs, 4 doubles, 3 HRs, 19 RBIs, .385 OBP

Ollie and Billy

That's definitely not the way you want to end what had been a good homestand. They'd had a poor ending to their last trip, getting knocked around in Chicago and then splitting two games in Washington with Ollie taking a loss after one of his classic blow-up innings. The Mets came home and beat the Braves twice, got rained out Monday against the Pirates, and then Billy Wagner had his first blip Tuesday night. A Reyes error set up his first blown save and forces Willie Randolph to use more of the bullpen than he might have liked. But the Mets won the game, so the next afternoon they were still trying for four in a row on the homestand.

Your starter has to go six innings minimum in a day game following an extra-inning night game in which everybody was used in the bullpen. Instead, Perez walks the ballpark. He walked five of the first 10 batters he faces. Then the Pirates started hitting, and he was done in the second inning. Twelve Pirates came up to bat in that inning, and it's not as if it were Dave Parker or Willie Stargell in the middle of that Pittsburgh lineup.

Perez became unglued after the error by Castillo. If they had turned the double play, the Mets would have been out of the inning in a scoreless game. Instead, it was 7–0 by the time Nelson Figueroa finally got the third out.

For Perez, it was an awful start. After the game, Billy Wagner's comments weren't much better. Wagner told the reporters that Oliver Perez needs to "step up," find a way to stop the bleeding, and give the bullpen a little breather. Billy's right, but he doesn't need to say it to a room full of reporters who are looking to write anything other than a boring blowout story. Billy helped them fill the papers with his rant, but it's not as if Perez isn't out there trying.

Chapter 4

MAY

MAY 10, 2008

The month of May begins with the Mets' first West Coast swing. They manage a 3–3 trip out west, winning two of three against the first-place Diamondbacks and dropping the first two in Los Angeles against a Dodgers club that had won 10 of 11. The Mets take the Wednesday matinee at Dodger Stadium 12–1. John Maine becomes the first Mets pitcher since Oliver Perez almost a year earlier to pitch into the ninth inning. Like Perez in 2007, Maine is removed just shy of the complete game despite a big lead. More important, outfielder Angel Pagan dives into the stands to snag a foul ball in the first inning; he then aggravates his injury with a headfirst dive in the third. The team's Opening-Day left fielder will not play again in the majors in 2008.

The Mets head home in fourth place behind Florida but only two games out in the standings. The first game of the homestand is rained out, forcing a day–night doubleheader, only the third separate-admission Shea Stadium twin bill with the Mets hosting both games. It makes for a long day and is not a favorite of the manager, the players, or the announcers.

Mets 12, Reds 6. Reds 7, Mets 1. Record 18–16; 3 games behind Florida.

All Day and All of the Night

Rainouts are part of the game, but I wish that they had called the game earlier on Friday and saved everyone from coming out to the park. Everyone just sits at the park fiddling around. Waiting. Players do understand that there's a gate that teams have to worry about. When a game is officially called, you go home and you're always a little happy. But you always regret it later when you have to play that makeup doubleheader somewhere down the road. Unfortunately for the Mets, "down the road" turns out to be the very next day, because this is Cincinnati's only trip to New York.

So why, you ask, is there a three-hour gap between the last pitch in the first game the first pitch in the second game? It all hinges on where the owners of those seats would sit if everyone came to the ballpark. For weekend games, there's a big advance sale at Shea, and all those seats are sold. So when a game is rained out and has to be made up, it creates a big problem. The advance sale for future games is so good that the team is forced to have a split doubleheader. What seats are you going to give people as a rain check? If the stadium has been sold out, how can you tell, if you're management, who's going to come to your game and use a certain ticket for a seat and who's not? If you have 20,000 or even 10,000 people coming with rain checks on top of the large crowd already expected for the scheduled game, there won't be any place to put them. Particularly at Shea this season, with the construction of the new stadium and the lack of parking, it would be tricky. There would be unbelievable traffic with people going out and more people coming in.

They had day–night doubleheaders when I was playing in the minor leagues. They wanted (and needed) the gate. In the minors, this is understandable. But at the major league level, they're making plenty of money, so I do think it's kind of greedy. Give out rain checks to a variety of other games to increase the number of options and reduce the need for a split doubleheader. That could solve the problem. Or else offer refunds.

Playing two games in one day creates a major headache for pitching staffs. Even with Johan Santana scheduled to pitch in the first game, you can't rely on one pitcher going all the way in one of the games to save your staff. You want to get length from your starters in a doubleheader, and starters today don't give you enough length. Everyone leans on the bullpen, even teams that don't have a very good bullpen. That's why most teams carry 12 pitchers.

When I played, there were 10-man pitching staffs and more doubleheaders—always with just 30 minutes in between games. You generally used your long guy—we usually called him a "swing guy"—as a starter in one of the games so that we could go through a doubleheader with just four relievers. We played anywhere from three to nine twin bills every year during my Mets career. We managed to get through it.

Best Days at Shea
SEPTEMBER 17, 1986

Clinching Night at Shea

Mets 4, Cubs 2

I was really sick, so I didn't start the game. I used to have horribly bad sinuses—I had to get sinus surgery after I retired. If I have a cold it takes 10 days to go away. I was 12, 13 years old when I broke my nose playing Pop Warner football. It was a Saturday workout before the game, just a walkthrough on plays without pads and helmets. I forget the kid's name, but he had just moved from Oklahoma and was overly exuberant. He came charging at me from his defensive position—I was quarterback—and I thought he was going to put up his hands. Instead we knocked noggins and he broke my nose. He was a big knucklehead.

But I sat the night we wound up clinching the division in '86 against the Cubs. Dave Magadan made his first major league start in my place and got three hits. It was important for me to be on the field when we clinched. So I asked Davey to put me in for the ninth and I caught the last out. I would have started, but I was in such a bad way, we were 20-something games in front, and it was such a cold night. I said to hell with it, and I rested. But I played many a game ailing, and I'd be out there playing and miserable.

I was expecting the fans to come on the field, and they did. Someone actually tried to steal my glove! One of the fans tried to pull it off my hand when we were on the mound. I had to squeeze my hand to keep him from pulling it off.

The Mets had made the playoffs only twice before then, in '73 and '69. We were thrilled to celebrate after having lost a couple on the road when we were on the verge. It was quite a feeling. It was quite a year.

In the opener against the Reds, Johan took care of business. Santana didn't have his great stuff, but he pitched out of trouble and the Mets beat up on the Reds' relievers to win the first game by six runs. I always bring my computer to the ballpark, and between games in a doubleheader I play Strat-O-Matic Baseball, the game. And I try to find a place to take a nap. Split doubleheaders are more difficult on the road. A lot of times I can't find a place to sleep between games. At Shea, I can go to one of the suites and take a snooze. Today, I take an hour-long nap between games against the Reds.

Big Pelf's Nightcap

It's hard to win twice in one day. The Mets couldn't against the Reds, though Mike Pelfrey deserved a better fate. The bullpen let a close game get away, but Pelfrey threw a good game, though he does have more hits allowed than innings pitched at this point. I've said time and time again on the air that I feel the Mets have rushed him to the big leagues too quickly. I think Pelfrey has a chance to be a very good pitcher. He throws hard, but right now he should be in Triple A, honing his secondary pitches.

A couple of years ago the Mets convinced him to start throwing a slider. This is only his second year throwing that pitch. He's thrown a curveball his whole life. Pitching coach Rick Peterson thinks that a slider is a better pitch to go with his sinking fastball. OK, but to expect him to refine this new pitch on the big-league level, that's a tall order. To top it off, they are teaching him another new pitch: a change-up! And they'll force him to learn command of *this* pitch on the big-league level, too! I am sorry, but I think he should be in Triple A perfecting these two new pitches, away from the scrutiny of a demanding press and impatient fan base. He's getting pounded, and I worry about his confidence. This could shatter most mere mortals.

MAY 13, 2008

After taking two of three from the Reds, the last-place Nationals come to Shea. The Mets swept the Nats in their first trip to New York in April and split a short series at Nationals Park to take four of five overall. Washington, however, wins the opener of the four-game series and pounds Nelson Figueroa. Figueroa, a Brooklyn native, pitched superbly before family and friends (including a game at Shea against Washington) in his first major league starts since 2004. After that early success in '08, however, he has been hit hard. Following his 10–4 loss to the Nationals on May 12, Figueroa and Jorge Sosa (who was at the time tied for the club lead with four wins but sporting a bloated 7.06 ERA) are both designated for assignment. They are replaced on the roster by Matt Wise, returning from the disabled list, and Claudio Vargas, an 11-game winner in 2007 who was cut by the Brewers in spring training.

As Washington rallied against Figueroa, several Nats choreographed cheers in the dugout, including coach Lenny Harris. The visibly annoyed Figueroa mimicked their cheers as he left the mound and later called the Nats "softball girls." The first batter the next night, Felipe Lopez, is hit by John Maine's opening pitch of the game. The Mets go on to win with Ryan Church knocking in four runs as Maine wins his fifth game to take over the club lead.
Mets 6, Nationals 3. Record 20–17; 2 games behind Florida.

Bush Payback

I thought those dugout cheers by Washington were bush league. I've have never seen that in all my years in baseball. I blame the manager, Manny Acta. That's just a lack of control over your team. Lenny Harris, the hitting coach, was doing it, too—and he should know better. It's outrageous behavior!

Obviously it upset Figueroa. He got out of the inning, but I think he lost his cool from that point on. The Mets dropped Figueroa after the game. It didn't take the league long to catch up to Figueroa. He wasn't throwing hard enough. They realized he was a breaking-ball pitcher. For the Mets, he was Plan B after losing Pedro in the second game of the year. Claudio Vargas is Plan C. He's a serviceable veteran, and they're hoping to get some length out of him. This all stems from—and we certainly have mentioned this on the air—Pedro and El Duque being on the shelf. Omar Minaya will have to change his philosophy regarding older players. Guys today are not going to play into their forties anymore.

John Maine showed something out there. He's had to step up a little with all the uncertainty they've had in the rotation, and today he stepped up and took charge. I don't know if Maine drilled Felipe Lopez on purpose to start the game, but it certainly was appropriate given all the foolishness on the Washington bench the night before. Retaliation definitely went on in our day. If you showed someone up, you got drilled. I don't have any problem with that.

The Mets bounced back from a poor game Monday night and did what needed to be done. Washington is not a good-hitting club. It is a last-place team, not an upper-echelon team. You've got to beat that team.

MAY 15, 2008

A Thursday matinee at Shea turns into one of the flash points of the season. It begins as a perfect afternoon to see a game from the upper deck. After talking about it off and on for a few weeks, the broadcasting trio of Gary Cohen, Ron Darling, and Keith Hernandez sit together in the first two rows of the upper deck. The trio welcomes several special guests during the broadcast, but the fast-moving game provides a storyline far more unique than an open booth in the top deck: the team that has gone longer than any other without ever throwing a no-hitter has Mike Pelfrey holding the Nationals hitless through six innings. Aaron Boone singles to start the seventh and kill the no-hitter, but the game remains scoreless. Jason Bergmann, called up from Triple A Columbus to make the start, keeps the Mets off the board on just three hits. The Nationals break the deadlock in the eighth on a double by Jesus Flores, a bunt, and a sacrifice fly.

In the ninth, Carlos Beltran leads off with a single and Ryan Church lifts a fly ball down the left-field line, but Willie Harris comes all the way over from left-center to make a spectacular catch. Beltran steals second and moves to third when the throw goes into center field. With the tying run 90 feet away and the infield in, Carlos Delgado drills a liner right at Boone, who throws across the diamond to complete the second first-to-third double play in as many innings. That ends the game as well as the homestand and leaves the Mets with three losses in four days against the same struggling team that had beaten them five times in late September 2007, contributing to the worst collapse in the game's history.

Closer Billy Wagner admonishes teammates he thinks have hurried out of the locker room. "Someone tell me why the ———you're talking to the closer.

I didn't even play. They're over there, not being interviewed." After a pause, he adds, sarcastically, "I got it. They're gone."
Nationals 1, Mets 0. Record 20–19; 2½ games behind Florida.

Wagnerian Opera

You have to look at the whole thing in context. Billy Wagner had already chastised Oliver Perez when he got knocked out early against the Pirates at the end of April. If you recall, Wagner said Perez needed to step it up. I think Wagner is trying to take a leadership role, but teams in general don't look for leadership from the bullpen pitchers. They just don't play in enough games to command that kind of respect.

The comments were inappropriate. Billy had good intentions, but he aired dirty laundry in public.

I think it was handled wonderfully at the time by Willie Randolph, who told him to keep it in-house next time. Wagner and Perez talked, and Wagner came out the next day saying it would be kept in-house in the future. OK. Fine. I'm sure the comments weren't appreciated, but it was smoothed over. So everything was fine. Right?

And then we come to the Nats matinee game, the 1–0 loss. It's two weeks after Wagner's first outburst, everything is forgotten—and then Wagner makes another set of comments that I thought were inappropriate. This is not a happy clubhouse. There is an undercurrent of resentment on this team because only a select few stand up and answer to the press on a daily basis after a tough loss or a losing streak. There is a feeling that some of the Latin stars don't take their share of this responsibility. I have talked to Mets beat writers, and they say that most of these players do stay after-ward and opine, but unfortunately, whether intentionally or not, they don't offer much that is insightful or interesting for the next day's story. Wagner's statements clearly open up some old wounds, which is not good.

Willie forced the issue by calling a club meeting and telling the players not to go through the media to air their complaints in the future. I will say that Beltran and Reyes did answer questions after the 1–0 game. Delgado did not, but he had a prior obligation that Willie knew about and so he left after the game ended. So for Wagner to make a blanket statement against his teammates was wrong.

The media problem has been festering on this team. It's a growing cancer, and I partially blame the front office for letting this happen. Everybody is paid well to play at this level. But it doesn't matter if a player is making minimum wage or $20 million a year—answering questions from the media is part of your job, in both good times and bad. I think the Mets have always sheltered their players far too much. It bears repeating: it is a player's job to talk to the media. And it is also a player's job to consider very carefully how his statements might be interpreted, both inside and outside the locker room.

Still No No-No

It would have been wonderful if Pelfrey had thrown a no-hitter and we were in the upper deck calling it. Throughout all of those years with all of those great Mets pitchers in a pitching-oriented organization, they've never had a single no-hitter. On the other hand, Boston, with its whole great history as a slugging team, has nearly 20 no-hitters. Go figure.

I've participated in three no-hitters. I was on the field for Bob Forsch's two no-hitters in St. Louis and also for Tom Seaver's no-hitter when he was with the Reds and I was with the Cardinals.

A no-hitter is different. It has a different level of intensity than other games. After the fifth inning, you go out for defense aware that you need to be on point. The last thing you want is to have a ball get by you that costs your guy a no-no. Most important, you never mention it to the pitcher. Baseball players are superstitious, and you don't want to jinx your pitcher by informing him of his potential no-hitter.

The Upper-Tank View

Sitting in the upper deck was a lot of fun. It was a beautiful day for it. It was a great time; I loved it. But I wouldn't want to watch a game up there all of the time. Gary Cohen did it a lot as a kid, so that's the reason we were in those seats. It's too high, though—I wouldn't pay to sit there. Maybe I'm spoiled.

I didn't really sit up in the upper tank as a kid in San Francisco at Candlestick Park. My family didn't go to a lot of games. My dad was a San Francisco fireman, and we didn't have a lot of money to spend on entertainment. But when we did go to a game, my father bought box seats behind the third-base dugout. We went to maybe five games a year, but we always sat in those box seats. You'd get a good view of the left-handed hitters there.

I did sit in the upper deck with my brother in '71 for the American League playoffs at Oakland when the Orioles swept the A's in three games. They lost the first two in the best-of-five in Baltimore. They came home, and there were limited seats available for Game 3. We went over and bought tickets. Uecker seats, down the right-field line, upper tank.

Reggie Jackson was in right field and hit two home runs that day. Bert Campaneris, Joe Rudi, Sal Bando—that whole crew was ready to win. That was the first year they won the division. The '71 season was the big year for Vida Blue and Catfish Hunter. The Orioles won that day with Jim Palmer to take the pennant, but then they lost to the Pirates in the World Series.

The Giants were by and large terrible in those days, and the A's were up and coming, but it was not the kind of crosstown rivalry you have in New York. It was basically East Bay versus West Bay. The East Bay was more blue collar than the West Bay. As far as I'm concerned, the Oakland Coliseum was a better place to play and watch a game than Candlestick.

I was never a big Giants fan. I was too young to recall what it was like before the Giants moved from New York to San Francisco, but I do remember when they arrived. I was very happy about that. Major League Baseball in San Francisco—and Willie Mays to boot! I'm sure most New Yorkers weren't as happy as I was.

MAY 18, 2008

As the Mets stumble to Yankee Stadium across town in apparent disarray, rain clouds descend and the Friday night game is rained out in the Bronx—but not before the players address what happened the previous afternoon.

Then on Saturday, in front of a national audience, Johan Santana beat Andy Pettitte 7–4. On ESPN *Sunday Night Baseball*, Oliver Perez cruises. Even a ridiculous reversal of a Carlos Delgado three-run home run can't prevent a drubbing of Chien-Ming Wang. As the Mets get ready to head to Atlanta, however, the talk is all about an article by the *Bergen County Record*'s Ian O'Connor, to whom Randolph thought he was speaking off the record before Sunday's game. The quote that causes the most trouble concerns how the manager feels he is viewed by others—Randolph even mentions the camera angles used to portray him on SNY—and why traits that are respected in the case of Joe Torre are seen as flaws in Randolph. The manager asks, "Is it racial? Huh? It smells a little bit."

Despite winning both games of the shortened two-game set in the Bronx to give him the best career record of any Mets manager against the Yankees (11–9), Randolph comes under extreme scrutiny and criticism. For someone whose future was uncertain the day after the season-ending collapse the previous fall, this is unwanted controversy in a job that comes with plenty built in. *Mets 11, Yankees 2. Record 22–19; 1 game behind Florida.*

H-Bomb Lands on Train

After Wagner spoke out yet again, he met with Delgado on Friday. I'm sure they had a heated exchange, and I thought the Mets came out and played with fire on Saturday against the Yankees—a terrible Yankees team with A-Rod and Posada both on the DL—but the Mets did what they had to do. I watched both days and thought, "Oh good, here they

Oliver Perez was superb as the Mets won both games in the Bronx in May.

finally have their hats on. Let's get on this train and get it out in the open." A fistfight, something to break the tension; those things happen in a clubhouse on occasion. Just ask those three-time champion A's from the early 1970s. A fight between teammates sounds divisive to fans, but it can sometimes clear the air and get the players' focus back on the game.

Nothing like that happened this time, but I think the Mets are on their way. There was a clearing of the air on Friday after the Wagner incident, followed by a rainout, and then the team came back and played with an intensity they hadn't shown since 2006. Then Willie drops a hydrogen bomb on this team with his astounding remarks.

He said it on Sunday, before the second game against the Yankees—I want to make that clear. He made those comments *before* the Mets completed the two-game sweep at Yankee Stadium. The story didn't come out until Monday, so the Mets had no idea about it when they played the Yankees Sunday night. They were all fired up, playing solid baseball, sweeping the Yanks—and then this. As a result, all the wind was taken out of their sails. I'm shocked that Willie brought up race, particularly since the Mets' organization, at every level, is one of the most ethnically and racially inclusive in baseball.

On top of everything else, I've never heard a manager complain before about how he was being covered on camera by a TV network. I'm stunned!

MAY 21, 2008

The day–night doubleheader in Atlanta that follows the sweep in the Bronx turns into a complete disaster. In the afternoon makeup of an April rainout at Turner Field, Tom Glavine pitches against the Mets for the first time since his horrific one-third of an inning on the final day of 2007 that ended the Mets' season in agonizing and pitiful fashion. This time Glavine wriggles out of a first-inning jam on two line-drive outs with the bases loaded. He retires the last 17 batters he faces to improve his career record against the Mets to 17–7. (The Mets went 5–14 against

Atlanta in games started by Glavine over his five seasons in New York.) The second-game loss turns tragic on the final play. While unsuccessfully trying to break up a double play in the ninth inning, Ryan Church is kneed in the head by Yunel Escobar. Church suffers his second concussion since spring training.

The Mets, now in fourth place in the NL East, take a 1–0 lead in the third game of the series only to see it turn into a lopsided defeat. It is Atlanta's 12th win in their last 13 games at Turner Field and Mike Pelfrey's fifth straight loss overall. Before the game, Randolph appears on his weekly radio spot on WFAN and apologizes to Mets ownership, SNY, and his players for creating an "unnecessary distraction" with his comments and for implying that he might be treated differently than white managers.

Braves 11, Mets 4. Record 22–22; 3½ games behind Florida.

Storm Gathering

For a team that does not like the media glare, Willie's remarks have only added to it. Since his comments, the Mets have been blown out in three straight games by their arch rivals in Atlanta. It seems to me that the team's spirit collapsed. They are playing like a team that has lain down and died. There have been too many recent distractions for the Mets. If Santana goes out and loses the Thursday night finale in Atlanta, it will be one long flight to Denver. The team is scheduled to arrive in Denver at 4:00 AM eastern time. We'll see what they're made of. Santana needs to pitch another big game.

That is essentially what this whole series has been about. Claudio Vargas—Plan C—is not the answer. The Braves were going to clobber him. That was pretty plain to see. Pelfrey can't get his change-up over; he can't get his slider over, either. He threw a nice three or four innings, but the Braves had their way with him the second and third time through the order. That has been the difference in this series. The Braves are a team that doesn't swing at bad pitches—they waited out Maine and Pelfrey while clobbering Vargas in between. The Mets, on the other hand, came down here dejected and deflated. In the first three games of this series, the Braves just poured it on.

The Braves did just what they had to do. They took the early lead and never let up. They just buried the Mets. With a team that is down, you put your claw right on its throat and just tear them up. A good team presses its advantage and doesn't let up. It's war out there.

If Santana wins tonight, salvages a game in Atlanta, and then the Mets take two out of three in Colorado, that will buy Willie some time. But if they have a 2–5 road trip…

MAY 26, 2008

Johan Santana can't hold a seventh-inning lead in Atlanta, Billy Wagner can't protect a ninth-inning lead the next night in Denver, and one bad pitch on getaway day costs John Maine at Coors Field. The Mets finish the road trip at 1–6. Willie Randolph spends Memorial Day afternoon inside Shea meeting with Mets ownership and Omar Minaya, who had flown to Denver after the Atlanta disaster. The meeting ends with neither Randolph's dismissal nor a commitment to him as manager for the rest of the season. That night, Mike Pelfrey loses his sixth straight decision. At three games under .500, it is the club's worst mark of the year. The Mets also continue to play without right fielder Ryan Church, whose condition worsened after flying to Denver on the previous road trip. He

A slow start on top of a nightmarish end to 2007 increases the pressure for a change at the top.

remains on the active roster but is not physically able to perform because of his two concussions.

Amid the speculation over Randolph's future during the brutal road trip, Hall of Fame catcher Gary Carter, who was Mets co-captain with Keith Hernandez during their last two years together at the end of the 1980s, was asked on the *Mike and Murray Show* on Sirius radio whether he was interested in the managing job with the Mets.

"Boy, I'll tell you what—I would love that, guys. When I saw that on ESPN today [that Randolph's job might be in jeopardy]...I got on the phone and I called [Mets VP of Media Relations] Jay Horowitz and I asked Jay, 'Should I try to call Mr. [Fred] Wilpon?' If there is this going on, I just want them to know of my availability. I'm only a phone call away, because my contract [managing the independent Orange County Flyers] allows me to leave the ballclub. I could be in New York tomorrow, if necessary, because if there's anything at the major league level I can leave this job."

Keith Hernandez is among the loudest voices speaking out against his former teammate's poor timing and judgment.

Marlins 7, Mets 3. Record 23–26; 6½ games behind Florida.

Nothing Is Easy

Santana did not pitch one of his best games in Atlanta. His final line was seven innings pitched; 12 hits; four runs, three earned; no walks; and one strikeout. He was in constant trouble throughout the game, but he battled his way out of numerous jams. With a 2–1 lead in the bottom of the seventh, his luck ran out. Give the Braves credit—they hung in there and finally got to Johan for three in the seventh. It was a very tough loss, a four-game sweep against the Bravos, and, as if to pour more salt on the wound, the team had a late night four-hour flight to Denver that won't arrive until 4:00 AM EDT, with no off-day. Hey, mama never said it was gonna be easy!

Church In and Out

Ryan Church hasn't started a game in almost a week because of the concussion he suffered in Atlanta. It is his second concussion since March.

It's a shame. So far this season, Church has been the best hitter on the team. He's excelled batting second, fifth, sixth, seventh; wherever they've put him, he's produced. He's batted well over .300 since Opening Day. He's also given the

Mets solid defense and a strong arm at a position where both have been lacking in recent years.

In a game like baseball in which timing means everything, a concussion can completely alter your performance. I had a concussion in 1980 with the Cardinals and lost the batting title that year to Bill Buckner, who was with the Cubs. Coincidentally, I had a collision with Buckner who was leaping for a bad throw at first base on a ground ball hit by me at Wrigley. His leap carried him into the base path, it was a close play, and we had a vicious collision. We both have facial scars from that collision to this day. I was knocked out. It took five days for me to be able to shake the cobwebs out, but I missed only two games. If I had sat out five or six days, I would've won my second batting title in a row. Buckner wound up at .324. I finished at .321.

On Managing

Regarding Gary Carter's comments, I feel that Gary did a classless, inconsiderate, insensitive, and tasteless thing. You just don't say that you're ready to take someone's job when that man's job is on the line. If you want to manage, you wait until the manager is fired, and *then* you say, "I would love to manage the club." You shouldn't be picking at the flesh while the carcass is still out there alive.

My name is always tossed around in the media whenever there's a perceived shakeup in the Mets manager's chair. The fans seem to think that I'll come manage, and all I have to do is snap my fingers and it'll be 1986 all over again. I just don't think that's realistic.

Would I like to manage? This isn't something I'd ever say on the air, especially now with Willie's situation ongoing, but because this isn't appearing in print until after the season is over, I'll share my feelings. It would be intriguing for me to manage. It would be another challenge—the ultimate challenge—and another chapter in my baseball life, but managing today is different than it was in my time. The job is more of a fishbowl existence than it's ever been. Everything you say in the press is broadcast both before and after the game as well as dissected in the papers, on the Internet, and on the radio call-in shows. It's a 12-hour daily commitment and all-year 'round. I know I wouldn't be able to give that—though I'd be lying if I said I wouldn't be interested to see how well I'd do.

So while managing would be a great challenge for me, "no" is my answer, unequivocally. I'm very happy with where I am these days in the booth, and I hope the Wilpons are happy with me there, too.

MAY 28, 2008

Just as the Mets hit their lowest point, the club rebounds with a strong effort by Johan Santana plus solid bullpen work to even the series. The next night features two dramatic comebacks in the rubber game against the first-place Marlins. Endy Chavez hits his first home run of the year—and his first-ever pinch-hit homer—to tie the game in the ninth inning. After Alfredo Amezaga hits his first home run of the year to break the tie in the top of the twelfth inning, David Wright walks, and then Carlos Beltran singles to start the bottom of the inning and put men on the corners. Damion Easley strikes out, but Fernando Tatis—

recalled from the minors two weeks earlier—doubles into the left-field corner to plate the tying and winning runs. It marks the first win by the Mets this year when they trailed after eight innings.

Mets 7, Marlins 6. Record 25–26; 4½ games behind Florida.

Walking Off Happy

The team sleepwalked through Denver. The Rockies have no business taking two out of three from the Mets, but that's exactly what they did. The Mets limped home at 1–6 for the week—their worst road trip since 2001—and opened up the homestand with a three-game series with the first-place Marlins. The Mets had better get their act together, or it could be *Adios, amigos.*

After the meeting between Willie, Omar, and the management on Memorial Day, the team didn't perform well that night. It's the same old Mets story—they get ahead and the Marlins come right back with four runs in the third. A smack in the nose, and the Mets lay down and die.

Willie changes the lineup for game two against the left-hander. He benches Delgado and puts Castro in to catch. I think they're going to go with a platoon now behind the plate. I don't know what they're going to do with Delgado. Through almost 50 games, Delgado is hitting .215 and he's knocked in only 25 runs—Reyes has one fewer RBI. Obviously, Jose's off to a good start and Delgado isn't, but you've got to have a better differential in production than one RBI between your first- and fifth-place hitters if you're going to be successful. Willie's decision is to give Delgado a couple of days off with two left-handers coming up for

Florida. Right-handed Damion Easley starts at first base in his spot.

Then the Mets played two very, very good games. They showed energy, life, and resolve. It was sparked by the guys off the bench: Easley, Castro, Endy, and Tatis. I thought the Santana win on Tuesday was the best all-around game the team has played all year. They're a different club right now. The main difference I notice is that they're not simply trying to hit home runs. Base hits to right field with fewer than two outs advancing runners into scoring position? It's called situational hitting. That's something the Mets haven't done all year, but they're doing it now.

And then Wednesday night in the rubber game against a first-place club, the Mets went out and played a game they really needed to win—to show that they can indeed put together solid performances on successive nights. It's not easy, though, because the bench was short as a result of Church's concussion. He's in uniform but can't play, so Willie's bench is only four players deep, a serious managerial handicap.

It would have been such a disheartening loss, although I think in their present mind they would have bounced back from it. We'll never know, because they pulled it off. It is obviously a huge win in extra innings.

And it was the bench again that winds up winning this game for Willie. Chavez hit the huge pinch-hit home run to tie it in the ninth. The Marlins eventually took the lead in extra innings, but Tatis came through again with the double into the corner to bring in the tying and winning runs.

Tatis has seen only a few dozen at-bats in the majors since 2004. He is hoping to get more playing time so he can get into the groove of the season. He had retired from the game and the main reason for his return is his desire to raise money to build a church in his hometown in the Dominican Republic, which is a very nice story. Tatis is essentially starting over at the major league level. He's getting a chance to play right now, because Church is sitting out. Tatis was a big-time power hitter when he was in his prime with the Cardinals almost 10 years ago, but the power's not back yet for him. He's hustling his butt off, going from first to third on hits and taking the extra base. Fans want to see a little hustle. The last two nights they've had it, and they like what they see.

Strategy Session

In the rubber game with Florida, I thought Willie should have pulled out Oliver Perez after the fifth inning. I would not have left him in to pitch if he'd gotten into any trouble in the sixth. He just was not having a good game. He was Perez the Erratic, the bad Oliver Perez. I would've brought in a righty to face Cody Ross, who wound up hitting his second home run of the night off Perez, to give the Marlins a 5–4 lead.

It's easy to second-guess after the fact, but look at *when* Willie implemented those changes in the course of a game. To begin with, Willie had to manage differently because he was limited to only a four-man bench. That affects decisions you make with your pitching staff, and it clearly limits when you can send up a pinch-hitter or make other in-game switches. You've got to save your bullets, as they say.

Winning the game was important enough for Willie to say, "OK, I've got to pull out all the stops." When the Mets fell behind on the Ross homer in the sixth, Willie had to manage to win, and it meant from that point on he just had to throw in the kitchen sink, even it meant using his entire short-handed bench.

- After Perez finishes the sixth, Scott Schoeneweis comes in to pitch the seventh. Willie uses his first bench player—Raul Casanova—to bat for Schoeneweis in the bottom of the seventh. The Mets are carrying three catchers, so Schneider is still available, along with Endy Chavez and Delgado, all left-handed hitters. Result: pop-up.

- Aaron Heilman throws two shutout innings. It gets the Mets to the bottom of the ninth still trailing by only one run—those two scoreless innings may also build up Heilman's confidence.

- Chavez bats for Castro in the ninth and homers. It's an electrifying moment for the crowd, this club, and Endy, who had come through as a pinch-hitter just once all season prior to the at-bat.

- Willie tries to win it right then, as he should have. He sends up Delgado to bat for Heilman; Carlos walks. With two outs, Luis Castillo also walks. Now with the winning run at second and David Wright up to bat, Willie gets more speed on the bases by pinch-running John Maine for Delgado. Maine is a good athlete, and he runs much better than Delgado. He represents the winning run. Davey Johnson always used to pinch run with Ron Darling in similar situations back in the '80s. Schneider—the backup catcher—is now the only man left on the bench, and he's not any more likely than Delgado to score on a base hit. Wright flies out, but Willie's given it his best shot. The best laid plans of mice and men...

- The Mets have a new battery for the tenth inning with Schneider, the last bench player, and Billy Wagner, his closer. The Marlins go down quickly, and the Mets have four-five-six in their order due up in the bottom of the inning.

- The Mets go down in order, and Willie opts to take out Wagner after an inning, in favor of Duaner Sanchez. He retires the Marlins in the top of the eleventh and helps himself with a sacrifice in the bottom of the inning, but Castillo makes the last out with two men on.

- The Marlins take the lead in the twelfth when Alfredo Amezaga hits his first home run of the year against Sanchez. Justin Miller, a journeyman reliever, comes in to try to close it—something Kevin Gregg couldn't do three innings earlier. Miller makes Marlins manager Fredi Gonzalez pull out his hair when he walks his first batter, David Wright. Carlos Beltran singles to put men on the corners with no one out. The Marlins opt to not fill the bases intentionally for a force at any base, and it pays an immediate dividend when Miller fans Easley. Now Miller is a ground ball away from a game-ending double play that would hand the Mets another excruciating loss, but Tatis comes through and Beltran scores all the way from first to win the game.

Meaning to the Mets

It was just two days after Memorial Day, but that was a win the Mets may look back at a few times over the year. The Mets have to prove to the division—and to themselves—that they have the grit to win. Philadelphia has certainly shown that. The Braves have beaten the Mets like a drum in Atlanta this year. The Marlins have a payroll about *one-sixth* the size of what the Mets have to work with, yet they came into this contest with a 5½-game lead.

The problems are far from over for the Mets, but they fought back twice in this game when they were bloodied and on the ropes. The bench players sparked the team and turned it around. The Mets came home 5½ games behind and off of a horrendous road trip. If they would have lost the rubber match of this series, they would have fallen to 6½ games behind. Instead they showed lots of spark to close that margin to 4½. That is a huge two-game swing. The big question is, can this club sustain this type of play? To be honest, I just don't know.

MAY 30, 2008

The Mets win their third-straight game—their longest winning streak in a month—as Claudio Vargas beats Dodger Brad Penny, whose 6.38 career ERA against the Mets is the highest all-time mark by any starting pitcher with at least

20 starts against a club (and his career record at Shea is 1–10). Dodgers skipper Joe Torre also drops his first game managing in New York after a dozen seasons with the Yankees. The next night, Chan Ho Park, who made one horrible start for the '07 Mets before being released, holds the Mets at bay after wildness plagues Dodgers wunderkind Clayton Kershaw. The Mets take the lead in the seventh and bring in Aaron Heilman with the tying run on base in the eighth. Thirteen pitches and four hits later, the Dodgers run away to a 9–5 victory.

Dodgers 9, Mets 5. Record 26–27; 4½ games behind Philadelphia.

Bad Day

The Dodgers are situational hitters. They put together four-straight hits to right field off Heilman in the eighth inning, each with the first baseman holding the runner on first. That's how it's done. That's a missing component in today's power-dominated game. But look what it did: first and third every time. The Dodgers applied pressure and forced Willie to bring the infield in: sound fundamentals by the Dodgers.

With the Mets up by a run, a man on first, and nobody out in the top of the eighth, why didn't Willie use Sanchez against the Dodgers instead of Heilman? The Mets are going to be careful with Sanchez's arm; he missed more than a year with two major shoulder surgeries. My feeling is that if the Mets are going to win, they will have to win with Heilman, too. If you recall back in 2006, even when Sanchez was pitching great, Willie often used Sanchez and Heilman in tandem. Willie would throw Sanchez one day to bridge to Billy Wagner, and then the next day he would go to Heilman. And if a left-hander was due up, he would use Pedro Feliciano. Willie is praying that Aaron Heilman can find his old 2006 form. But Heilman is a lot like this Mets team as a whole: Jekyll and Hyde. Will the real Aaron Heilman please stand up?

I agree 100 percent with the move to bring in Heilman. He threw two strong innings the other night in the win against Florida. He was angry when he pitched that night against the Marlins. He was throwing hard, hitting spots, and when he came back to the bench he was as fired up as I've seen him all year. But it seems that every time you think Heilman has turned the corner, he goes out there and gets shellacked.

Heilman has been beaten up this year and has allowed five home runs in just 28⅓ innings, but he has talent. I always say that you can feel sorry for yourself, but no one else is going to feel sorry for you. Lou Brock came up to me once when I was struggling at the plate in St. Louis and said, "What are you feeling sorry for yourself for? Why are you getting mad at yourself? You should be getting mad at the pitcher. He's the one that's getting you out, and you might have to go home and not fulfill your dream of being a major league player because of the pitcher. Channel your anger toward the pitcher." That was some of the best baseball advice anyone ever gave me, and it's just as true today.

Heilman needs to focus his anger and frustration at the hitters. He did that against the Marlins at a crucial time on Wednesday, but last night, the Dodgers just served everything he threw to right. And that was the ballgame. He has to take stock from both of those experiences—the good and the bad.

Stranded

The eighth inning was the obvious turning point in the game, but look at how many runners were left on base: Mets 11, Dodgers 2. That's why Los Angeles won. They had four big hits in a row while the Mets had trouble all game long with men in scoring position.

It's worth noting that Willie put Delgado back in the lineup against Clayton Kershaw, the left-handed starter for L.A. Delgado was put back in the lineup the night before against righty Brad Penny and had one hit off him and another off lefty reliever Joe Beimel. Willie said he's not going to platoon Delgado; he just gave him two days off. They have no one else to play first base. What can he do, have Damion Easley or Marlon Anderson play first base on an everyday basis? That's not going to happen, even if Delgado is hitting around .220. You need to have that threat of the longball or the hope that Delgado breaks out of this two-year slump.

Chapter 5

JUNE

JUNE 3, 2008

The Mets complete a rousing come-from-behind win over the Dodgers on Saturday, and then Santana puts on a Sunday night pitching clinic and Ryan Church hits a home run in his first start since his concussion on May 20. Both games against the Dodgers at Shea are nationally televised. After the Sunday-night contest, the Mets make a late-night trip across the country. They stumble to a 10–2 loss to the Giants on Monday as Oliver Perez retires only one batter in the shortest outing of his career. (His ERA stands at 5.70.) With Pedro Martinez back from a hamstring injury and making his first start since April 1, the Mets look much more refreshed the next night in Keith Hernandez's native San Francisco.

Mets 9, Giants 6. Record 29–28; 4½ games behind Philadelphia.

Waking Up in San Francisco

I work about two-thirds of Mets games each year, but I always make the San Francisco trip. My brother lives there, and I usually stay at his house in San Carlos. This year I was able to fly in a day early because SNY did not broadcast the Sunday night game at Shea; instead, it was aired on ESPN's *Sunday Night Baseball*. That game should never have been scheduled as a night game with the Mets scheduled to play 3,000 miles away the following night. On the schedule issued at the start of the season, that Sunday's game was originally listed as a 1:10 PM start. ESPN intervened and switched it to Sunday night, so the Mets did not leave LaGuardia until after midnight and arrived at their hotel in San Francisco after 5:00 AM—Pacific time. It's no wonder that they played like they were sleepwalking on Monday night at AT&T Park. Normally when teams travel coast to coast, they have a scheduled off-day for travel or R&R. Not so this time for the Mets, unfortunately.

Game 2 of the series on Tuesday night was an important game for the team, with Pedro Martinez making his first start since his injury two months ago during the first week of the season. It was only natural for Pedro to be rusty. He didn't have command of his fastball, and he could not get his change-up over. He had great movement, but he couldn't put the pitches were he wanted them. After the game, he told me that it was a little chilly and the air was dry, and that prevented him from getting the feel of the ball on his fingertips for his change-up.

All great pitchers make the necessary adjustments with each start, and Pedro certainly falls into that category. Even when he doesn't have his best stuff or isn't 100 percent physically, Pedro is constantly making adjustments to be as effective as possible in the particular start. It is always fascinating to talking to Pedro after a game: finding out what he had, what he didn't have, or what he was thinking on the mound in a particular situation facing a particular hitter. Pedro is highly intelligent and articulate regarding his trade. That's why he's a Hall of Famer. Talking to him is like having a conversation with Tom Seaver.

I was surprised that Willie kept Pedro in for as long as he did: six innings, 109 pitches. In the fifth and sixth innings he started getting his curveball over, and Pedro ended his start on a high note. He gave up a five hits those last two innings, but he finished with a classic Pedro moment: first and third, no one out, and he kept dropping curveballs in there to end his night with strikeout, strikeout, ground ball. Neither runner budged that inning. Bravo!

The Mets scored plenty of runs for him, and Pedro even had two hits himself. That's great, but he's not paid to hit; he's paid to go out there and pitch. And if he pitches like he did in San Francisco, he'll win. This is all very encouraging.

Barry Zito, on the other hand, had nothing on the night—absolutely nothing. The Mets should have clobbered him. That eight-run fifth inning was just waiting to happen. It was a shock to see how Zito has diminished. And *diminish* is the word to use. I've seen him pitch in his prime. Now he's throwing only 83–84 miles per hour! How could anyone possibly be fooled by his breaking stuff? He can't throw the ball by you at that speed. I don't want to beat up on Zito, but let's be honest here: 83 miles per hour is getting close to the realm of batting-practice speed.

Best Days at Shea
SEPTEMBER 11, 1974

The Longest Night

Cardinals 4, Mets 3 (25 innings)
It was my first game at Shea. I'd been in the major leagues with the Cardinals for less than two weeks, and we rallied to tie the Mets in the ninth. I came up in the twelfth inning against Harry Parker to pinch hit. Dave Schneck robbed me of a home run, right by the bullpen gate in right field. A line drive against Harry Parker—it would've been my first home run in the big leagues. Instead, I had to wait until the next year in L.A. I got my first major league hit in '74 in my hometown San Francisco. I was 20 years old.

That game at Shea was the game in which Claude Osteen came on in relief and went nine innings–plus of four-hit shutout ball and he didn't get the win. Bake McBride scored from first in the twenty-fifth inning on the wild pickoff throw. The ball rolled down the right-field line.

When the game was over, there was no beer for the guys who played. Manager Red Schoendienst had used everybody on the roster, so the clubhouse was filled with players who were out of the game and they drank all the beer. The game went seven hours, the longest game at Shea. It is also the longest night game the National League has ever had, the longest NL game, period, that didn't end in a tie. I wasn't sure it was going to end, either.

JUNE 7, 2008

The Mets win the rubber match in San Francisco and then head to San Diego. Coming into the four-game series, the Padres own the second-worst record in the National League. San Diego win the first three games of the series against the Mets by the same 2–1 score. Counting a win in their previous game by that same score against Chicago, the Padres are the first team in history to win four consecutive games by a 2–1 count. Their meager average of 3.7 runs per game—second-to-last in the NL—actually goes down during their winning streak. Two of the wins against the Mets come in San Diego's final at-bat. In the series opener, Scott Schoeneweis hits Paul McAnulty with the bases loaded in the ninth. On Saturday night Scott Hairston homers off Pedro Feliciano to end the game in the tenth inning.

Padres 2, Mets 1. Record 30–31; 6½ games behind Philadelphia.

Going Once, Going Twice...

It's as if we suddenly traveled back in time to the deadball era—three games in a row with a 2–1 score. The Mets have never lost three straight by that score, not even those lousy Mets teams in the '70s. San Diego's Triple A lineup scores only six runs in the first three games, but the Mets lineup scores only three. Three runs!

The Mets score only once on Saturday against Cha Seung Baek, a pitcher who was designated for assignment a week and a half ago by the Seattle Mariners, the worst team in baseball this year. Baek is throwing watermelons up there, and the Mets still can't get good wood on the ball. It is shocking.

Just a couple of days ago, I really thought that the Mets were building something. They had rebounded after that horrible trip to Atlanta and Denver, followed by the meeting between Willie, Omar, and ownership on Memorial Day. They had a 5–2 homestand, taking two out of three from Florida and then three out of four against the Dodgers. The Mets lost the first one in San Francisco after getting to town at dawn, but the team came back by winning the next two against the Giants. Then at San Diego, a fourth-place team, the wheels come off the bus—yet again.

Greg Maddux pitched for the Padres against the Cubs the night before the Mets came to town—another 2–1 San Diego win—so the Mets didn't have to face Maddux in this series. Jake Peavy and Chris Young, both All-Stars in 2007, are on the disabled list. Despite playing (and losing) the opener Friday night to veteran lefty Randy Wolf—who is now 10–5 lifetime against the Mets—they missed Peavy, Young, and Maddux. They faced a bunch of Triple A pitchers and inexplicably scored only one run per game.

JUNE 8, 2008

With Pedro Martinez pitching in the Sunday finale, the Mets finally score multiple runs in San Diego. The club clings to a 6–4 lead until two are out in the eighth. Then Billy Wagner comes out of the bullpen and allows a run-scoring single to Jody Gerut and a three-run, pinch-hit home run to ex-Met Tony Clark. It marks the first four-game sweep of the Mets in San Diego since 1980.

The depleted Mets lineup has Damion Easley and Endy Chavez in the corner outfield positions because Ryan Church, still suffering the aftereffects of his second concussion in less than three months, sits out after the opening game with severe headaches. Ramon Castro, scheduled to catch the Sunday game, oversleeps and is late arriving to Petco Park. Raul Casanova takes his place in the lineup.

It is the second time in less than three weeks that the Mets have been swept in a four-game series on the road. Willie Randolph, whose club had won seven of nine games and three straight series after his Memorial Day meeting with management, finds himself under more intense scrutiny as the team heads back to New York. It is important to note how many games the Mets have fallen behind Philly at this very low point in the season.

Padres 8, Mets 6. Record 30–32; 7½ games behind Philadelphia.

A Petco Mauling

It was a regression, a major step backward for Pedro in Sunday's finale in San Diego. He gave up 10 hits—all singles—but balls hit by Brian Giles and Khalil Greene just missed reaching the seats in that big ballpark. It was only his second start since returning from the hamstring injury, so I'm still optimistic about him. It was clear from the start of the game that Pedro didn't have great stuff, and he pitched out of jams in just about every inning. Nonetheless, he was still in line for the win when he left the mound after five innings.

The Mets just couldn't get out of the eighth inning. Duaner Sanchez got a strikeout and came out for Billy Wagner, pitching in the eighth inning for the first time this year. Jody Gerut greeted Wagner with a single, and Tony Clark followed with a three-run, pinch-hit home run, and it was officially a lost weekend. That series will stick in a few people's craws even more than the Atlanta sweep two weeks ago.

San Diego's bench is as thin as any team's in baseball, yet their reserves picked them up in this series. On the other hand, with Church dressed but unable to play, Willie was managing with a short-handed bench himself. I think he has done a terrific job managing without a full complement of players. He also has handled the bullpen well in this series, putting the right pitchers in at the right times. All a manager can do is make the moves that put his team in a position to win. It's up to the players to execute, and this time the Mets just didn't succeed. The bullpen (the left-handers in particular) was terrible in this series. Granted, the Padres scored only two runs per game in the first three games, but in that first game Schoeneweis hit a batter with the bases loaded; Feliciano allowed a home run on Saturday night; and Wagner (who did not even appear in the first three games) came in with two men on in the eighth and gave up a three-run homer. All of these plays are game-losers, and they make for a very long cross-country plane ride home to New York. This is the lowest point of the season thus far—and it has been a season marked by low points.

Regarding Church, I am afraid the doctors have mishandled the entire situation. The only recourse at this point is to put him on the disabled list and give him time to heal. If he stays on the roster in the vain hope that he may be able to contribute, the manager is left a player short over an extended period of time.

Collapse Follows Them

At this point in the season, the question now has to be asked, and with great import, *How much of this relates to last year's collapse?* And the word "collapse" is very kind. If a team had a late-season implosion like that in my day, the media would have relished calling it a "choke." I remember very clearly that the 1964 Phillies season was dubbed "the Choke of '64."

What is the residual effect of the end of the 2007 season? I don't know, but right now this team looks as if it has lost all confidence. The players seem shell-shocked. This game is a great humbler. As the old baseball saying goes, *Just when you think you have it all figured out, this game will crawl right out of the weeds and bite you hard on your butt.*

Willie's on the hot seat again. Let's face it, if the Mets have a bad homestand, he might be fired. And if the team continues like this until the All-Star break, he's gone without question.

JUNE 12, 2008

The Mets need to play a solid series against NL West leader Arizona and instead let two games get away from them. The one game they win comes in thirteen innings after a devastating, game-tying home run by Arizona's Mark Reynolds in the ninth inning. In the opener, the Diamondbacks rally from an early 5–1 deficit against John Maine and the bullpen. Billy Wagner blows two saves in an 18-hour span, costing victories for Mike Pelfrey and Johan Santana (neither of whom get a decision despite leaving with shutouts and multiple-run leads). Coupled with the crushing series finale in San Diego, Wagner has the worst week of his career: three blown saves in as many appearances. In his first 23 games of the season, he had a 0.36 ERA, one home run allowed, and 13 saves in 15 tries.
Diamondbacks 5, Mets 4. Record 31–34; 7½ games behind Philadelphia.

Blown Away

The Mets really needed to bounce back after that horrific series in San Diego. Instead, they returned home and things actually got worse. In all three of the games at Shea, the Mets were in a position to put away a first-place Arizona club, but the Diamondbacks came back late in each game. No lead seems safe at this point.

John Maine had a 5–1 second-inning lead against Arizona in the opener and couldn't hold it. Claudio Vargas, pitching in relief, gave up the lead, and Joe Smith allowed a home run to take the loss. The Mets scored five runs in the

Billy Wagner blew three ninth-inning leads in a span of four games, increasing the frenzy surrounding Willie Randolph's job security.

first two innings but didn't score the rest of the way. The offense just shut down after an early burst, and the bullpen couldn't hold the lead. It seems to have become a pattern for this club.

In the second game, Wagner blew a second consecutive save. He had two strikes on the hitter, and then he hit Mark Reynolds in the foot with a pitch—but the umpire didn't call it. Then Reynolds hit a game-tying home run! You could see the looks on the Mets' faces: complete exasperation.

Beltran won it in the wee hours of the night. He is a high-ball hitter, and he drilled an upstairs pitch to send everyone home in the thirteenth. With that win, the Mets ended a five-game losing streak.

However, the next afternoon's rubber match may have been the hardest loss to swallow among a week of devastating defeats. Johan Santana went seven beautiful shutout innings in the matinee, leaving with a 4–0 lead. Arizona again woke up when they saw the Mets' bullpen; they scored two in the eighth, two in the ninth, and won in the tenth. Joe Smith did his part to get the Diamondbacks back in the game in the eighth, Wagner coughed up his third straight lead, and Heilman lost it in extras.

The Mets left eleven in scoring position: David Wright stranded five, Beltran four, Easley three, Delgado one, Castro four, Tatis two, Marlon Anderson two, and Chris Aguila—the player finally brought up to take Church's spot—left four on base. Wright and Beltran both popped up with the bases loaded in the seventh when the Mets could have put the Diamondbacks away. Everyone's face had the same look—on the field, in the dugout, in the stands—that says one thing: *When is this going to stop?*

The Mets could have won all seven games in the past week. Instead, they came away with one. They had the lead or were tied in the ninth inning in four of them. What do they do about Wagner? He's their closer. This team has no other options for that role. He simply has to work through this. Until a week ago, he had been picture perfect; he would come in, and it was pretty much game over. Now all the wheels are coming off this bus at once.

JUNE 15, 2008

Interleague play brings the Texas Rangers to Shea Stadium for the first and last time. A rainout on Saturday night and a flight to California on deck for Sunday night brings about an old-fashioned single-admission Father's Day double-header. Jim Bunning threw a no-hitter 44 years ago on Shea Stadium's first Father's Day game, but the two struggling teams in this 2008 twin bill are far from perfect. The Rangers nearly blow a six-run lead but hold on to win the opener. Billy Wagner pitches a one-two-three ninth for his first save in four tries this week to split the twin bill.

Ryan Church is finally put on the disabled list, joining Moises Alou, who comes off the DL, bats twice and goes back on. With outfielders now at a premium, veteran Trot Nixon is acquired from the Diamondbacks. Robinson Cancel, just up from New Orleans, gets his first major league hit since 1999 to snap a sixth-inning tie in the nightcap. The patchwork Mets take two of three from Texas, but the newspapers, radio, and TV are swirling with stories of Willie Randolph's imminent firing.

Rangers 8, Mets 7. Mets 4, Rangers 2. Record 33–35; 6½ games behind Philadelphia.

Texas Twin Bill

This Texas club reminds me of the American League teams from my generation. They hit with power but they have lousy defense and absolutely horrible pitching. Howie Rose said on the radio, "This is the perfect recipe for 3½- to 4-hour games every day." Their pitchers don't throw strikes, but their offense can score plenty of runs.

It was an embarrassment how poorly Texas played in the field. With a five-run lead in the eighth inning, the third baseman, Ramon Vazquez, backhanded a ground ball down the line (a tough play) and tried to turn a double play instead of getting the sure out at first. He made a bad throw—though the error is somehow charged to the second baseman—and set up a Mets rally that nearly won the game. The third baseman has to understand what the situation is before executing the play. With a five-run lead, he needed to make sure of one out. It's that simple.

Pedro got the win in the nightcap, and Billy Wagner finally got through an outing unscathed. The Mets got a split of the doubleheader, won the series, and actually wound up with a .500 homestand after an inauspicious beginning. Yet Shea was nearly empty when the second game ended, and the hostility among those who remained was obvious as the club prepared to head back out to the West Coast for the fourth time.

The Theory of Negativity

Mets fans don't seem to like this team. It was never that way with us in the '80s. They were tough on George Foster, they

Willie Randolph endures a doubleheader split in what will be his final day at Shea Stadium.

killed George Foster, but I've never seen them collectively boo a team like they do now.

In my opinion, East Coast fans—Philly, Boston, and New York—are the toughest fans in the country. They fall in love with their team, but they will turn on a club when it does not win. Maybe Mets fans feel as if the team has taken on the spendthrift ways of the Yankees, and they don't like that. I think that Mets fans pride themselves on rooting for the New York team that doesn't throw money around. The Mets have had more bad times than good in their history, but they were always the blue-collar team in town. Now the Mets have a payroll of almost $140 million (one of the highest in baseball), and I don't think it sits well with the fans. Then again, if the Mets were running away with their division, people would be fighting their way into Shea to cheer this team.

The Red Sox had a similar image, not as lovable losers, but as a team that would find a way to break a fan's heart. All that has changed now that the Red Sox have won two world championships, and the fans have changed with it. Boston fans were starved for a championship for so long, but now they rank right there with some of the most arrogant, obnoxious fans in the game. Red Sox Nation? A lot of people are just sick of hearing about it.

JUNE 17, 2008

The team's fourth western swing in eight weeks begins with a strong effort by Mike Pelfrey in a 9–6 win over the Angels, the team with the second-best record in the American League. It is the Mets' third win in four days, but with the club

6½ games out of first place and around-the-clock speculation about the future of the team—not to mention constant harping on its past failures—general manager Omar Minaya fires Willie Randolph after the game. The time of his dismissal is not lost on the New York press; the news is released via an e-mail sent at 3:14 AM eastern time.

Fans who did not stay up for the late game see the news scroll the next morning of the Mets win followed by news that Randolph, pitching coach Rick Peterson, and first-base coach Tom Nieto have been fired. Bench coach Jerry Manuel is appointed manager for the remainder of the season. Two coaches are summoned to the big club from Triple A New Orleans—pitching coach Dan Warthen and Zephyrs manager Ken Oberkfell—while minor league field coordinator Luis Aguayo is elevated to third-base coach. Oberkfell is named first-base coach, and Sandy Alomar Sr.—whose namesake is also a coach on the team—is moved from the third-base box to bench coach.

Even fans who had taken to shouting "Fire Willie" at Shea and the members of the media, who updated the macabre "Willie Watch" on a near-hourly basis, are stunned at the timing of the dismissal. Randolph is a sympathetic character as he leaves the club that he rooted for as a kid growing up in Brooklyn, played for in his final major league season, and managed to a 302–253 record to become the fourth-winningest manager in Mets history.

Firing him in California when it could have been done in New York before the team left Sunday had even Randolph's many detractors up in arms. Randolph told the *New York Times* that he asked Minaya on Sunday night, "If I'm not the guy to lead this team, then don't let me get on this plane." Minaya said he made up his mind on Monday and flew out to California to do it face-to-face before word of the decision leaked out in the press.

SNY launches all-day live coverage with Keith Hernandez in the SNY studios in Manhattan (he was not scheduled to broadcast during the trip). That night, the Mets start the Manuel era with Jose Reyes grabbing a tight hamstring after a single to open the game. Then he refused to leave the field. Manuel sent Reyes to the clubhouse, and the shortstop threw his helmet. Reyes later apologized to Manuel and his teammates. Johan Santana and the Mets fall 6–1.

"We looked very tired. I know I was tired," the new manager said. "Maybe they were going through what I was going through."

Angels 6, Mets 1. Record 34–36; 6½ games behind Philadelphia.

Change of the Guard

I heard about the managerial change on ESPN. I was surprised because Willie was on that plane to the West Coast. I thought if Willie had a bad trip, he'd be fired in Colorado this weekend at the earliest. After winning three out of four, I didn't think the axe would fall in California. The firing caught a lot of people off guard.

It's almost like watching a Shakespearean tragedy. In this 24–7 news cycle, news gets gnawed like a bone, dissected, rehashed, and told over and over again. Then suddenly there's nothing left, and everyone moves on to the next topic. It is what it is.

You could see that Omar was really torn during the press conference in Anaheim. This was clearly the most difficult decision he's made since he joined the Mets in the fall of 2004. I really think Omar spoke honestly, and that it was tough for him to let Willie go.

It was Willie's first managerial job—his dream job. He weathered everything well initially. There were some growing pains in 2005 when the Mets fell out of it in mid-September, but the team finished strong and I think that carried over to 2006. The Mets were finally able to end

Amid much sound and fury from the fans and media, Jerry Manuel took over as Mets manager after the team's 34–35 start.

Atlanta's era of complete dominance over the NL East (the Braves won the division title every year from 1995 to 2005 and three straight NL West titles before that). The Mets were never really challenged in 2006, and then they rolled over the Dodgers in the division series. Things fell apart in the 2006 NLCS against St. Louis. The Mets lost in seven games to a team they probably felt they should have beaten, but you don't get rings or trophies for being the better team on paper.

I don't think that the Mets have been as cohesive as they were in 2006. The 2007 Mets held a comfortable lead until deep into September, but then came the September collapse—the result of a thin starting staff, a porous bullpen, a worn-down Wagner, a defense that made errors in critical games, an offense that stopped hitting in the clutch. They blew the lead and handed the division to Philadelphia.

Has the 2007 collapse carried over to this year? I think so. You can blame any player you want, or you could point to several of them, but the reality is that when a team underperforms and the ownership is unhappy, it's the manager who's in the hot seat. The Mets took the additional step to fire pitching coach Rick Peterson. The pitching staff has regressed over the past two years, and ownership felt it was time for a change there, as well.

Am I surprised that Omar made the move when he did? Yes. I thought that Willie's dismissal wasn't handled particularly well. But am I surprised that they changed managers during the 2008 season? No. Teams change managers all the time. The 2007 collapse, combined with the sub-.500 record this year, and, perhaps most important, evidence that the players did not respond to Willie's leadership, make it difficult to think back to 2006 and how close this team was to a World Series.

Looking at the standings now, the Mets are 6½ back and in third place. That's not a good position, certainly, but it's not like being 10 games back. We're not even at the All-Star break; there's more than half a season of baseball still to play. The Wilpons and Omar rightfully believe that this team has a strong chance to win the division under a new manager.

Most Managerial Wins in Mets History

Manager	Years	Postseasons	Record
Davey Johnson	1984–90	2	595–417
Bobby Valentine	1996–02	2	536–467
Gil Hodges	1968–71	1	339–309
Willie Randolph	2005–08	1	302–253
Yogi Berra	1972–75	1	292–296
Joe Torre	1977–81	0	286–420

O Come, Manuel

The first part of the press conference seemed overly dramatic. Omar was on stage for a long time, but the only thing I really learned was that he doesn't like to fire a manager in uniform. Jerry Manuel broke the heaviness a little by joking that he plans never to take off his uniform. "Don't look at me just in terms of an interim manager," he added. That is a strong statement from Jerry. He wants to manage again, and with those words he let management and ownership know how much he wants to manage this particular team.

Jerry gave a very good press conference. New Yorkers have not had a chance to get to know Jerry during his time as bench coach with the Mets. He's a highly intelligent man and he was Manager of the Year with the Chicago White Sox. Jerry Manuel knows baseball. Most important for the Mets, he knows this team. He has been with them through the entire Randolph era, and he knows every player's strengths and weaknesses.

Nothing is etched in stone now; Jerry wants to make his own evaluations of the players. "My cleanup hitter right now might not stay my cleanup hitter," he said. I'm curious to see what he will do with that spot in the batting order. Beltran has been the cleanup hitter throughout the first three months of the season, but maybe Jerry will move him to number two. Maybe he moves Wright out of the three hole. I'm not sure that there's a true third hitter in the lineup.

It will be interesting to study this situation and see how the club responds to its new manager. The Mets have yet to demonstrate the ability to pick themselves off the floor when they've been smacked in the mouth.

Along the Coaching Lines

With Tom Nieto and Rick Peterson fired from the coaching staff, the Mets needed to fill those positions. Dan Warthen is the new pitching coach in New York. Ken Oberkfell was the manager in New Orleans, and he will be the new first-base coach. Luis Aguayo takes over at third. Sandy Alomar Sr. moves from third-base coach to bench coach.

Ken Oberkfell and I were in the same infield on the 1982 world championship team in St. Louis. He was a smart player and he is a good baseball man. I haven't talked to Ken yet, but I look forward to congratulating him at the beginning of the next homestand. I know that Ken is considered managerial material at the major league level, so I think he has been promoted in part to assess the talent on this ballclub. He is definitely one of the top candidates for the NY Mets' manager next year. The competition is on for the manager's job.

Humble Beginnings

It was an inauspicious start in Anaheim for the new manager. The Mets had won three out of four, with their ace set to take on the mound. They needed a big game out of Santana, but they didn't get one. The whole team came out flat. I just didn't see the fire. Maybe it will take a while for the dust to settle from the Randolph firing and the media circus that led up to it.

Reyes started the game with a hit, but he grabbed the back of his leg rounding first. Every Mets fan—and it's been a long day for anyone following this team—felt his or her heart flutter when Jose pulled up lame at first. The fans remember those hamstring problems that Jose had when he first came up. Everyone knows the Mets are a different team without Reyes. He's the catalyst.

Jerry does not want to take any chances with Reyes' hamstring. He's too important to the club to risk losing him for any length of time. And Jose wanted to stay in the game. You have to like a player who wants to stay on the field for his team. But when Jerry came out to check on Jose and took him out of the game, Reyes gestured wildly with his arms and then threw his helmet to the ground. Jerry was having none of it. He followed Reyes into the clubhouse and had a few words with a very apologetic Jose, we found out later. I think there is a new sheriff in town, and it is high time.

We're going to find out what this team is made of. They're facing a very tough team here in Anaheim, but they still have a chance to take the series. Going to Colorado is always tough, but when the Mets return home they will face a very bad Seattle team. After that, it's the Yankees. The Bombers got their clocks cleaned by the Mets in the last series in the Bronx. The upcoming Yankee series includes a two-stadium, two-borough, day–night doubleheader, followed by the most daunting part of the schedule so far, four in St. Louis and four in Philly. That eight-game road trip ends the first week of July. They will either be out of it by then or they'll have turned it around.

JUNE 18, 2008

In the ninth and down to their last out against the top closer in baseball, the Mets finally do what's been done to them repeatedly: they get the big hit. After a K-Rod wild pitch advances the tying run into scoring position, David Wright singles to tie the game, snapping Francisco Rodriguez's club-record string of 25 consecutive saves. In the tenth, Damion Easley homers for the game winner. The bullpen even chips in, allowing just one hit over four innings to get the 501st win of Jerry Manuel's career, which comes more than four years after his last victory, when he was manager of the White Sox.

Mets 5, Angels 4. Record 35–36; 5½ games behind Philadelphia.

501 in Pocket

The Mets held an early 3–0 lead in the rubber match, but Oliver Perez let it get away in the fifth. In a move not usually employed by Willie Randolph, Jerry Manuel kept the pitcher in after a bad fifth inning. Perez threw a scoreless sixth, exiting after 104 pitches and saving a beleaguered bullpen. Damion Easley hit the game-winning home run in the tenth inning, and the Mets beat the AL West leaders in two out of three in Anaheim. They have to feel good about that. They could have easily lost that series.

I don't see K-Rod enough to know him as a pitcher, but if he's given up only two runs in his 25 saves, that's impressive. That wild pitch just before David Wright's hit cost him, though.

I like that Jerry is playing Easley more. It is too bad that he's 38; he's very professional and is playing great this season. He is not a power hitter, but his game-winning home run is the most important hit of the season so far. On the plane to Denver, Jerry allows the team to celebrate by playing music as loud as they like on the late-night flight. Under Willie Randolph, there was a headphones-only music policy during air travel. I don't have a problem with that, but I like that after all the team has been through this season, Jerry made a special exception to the rule after this big win. Unlike the somber Mets flights of the past, this one is a raucous affair.

JUNE 22, 2008

The Mets take two of three from the Rockies. Jerry Manuel finishes his first road trip as Mets manager with a winning record. When the Mets ended a trip in Denver less than a month ago, Willie Randolph's club had just a 1–6 mark on the two-city trip with hordes of reporters and a meeting with management awaiting him in New York. The road won't be as rocky now that the Mets' schedule shows no more western swings and just seven games outside the eastern time zone in the rest of the season.

Mets 3, Rockies 1. Record 37–37; 3½ games behind Philadelphia.

What Fans Want

Mets fans want what every fan wants: for their team to be out there hustling and playing with spirit. Since Jerry took over as manager, he certainly has challenged this team to play at a higher level, and so far they have responded. It's the same cast of characters that have been out there all year. I think it is Jerry's quiet and understated manner and firmness that has effected this team's recent rejuvenation. Jerry has stated publicly, "If guys don't perform, they won't play." In my mind, that's just how it should be.

Jerry showed his change in managerial philosophy from the very first batter. The way he handled Reyes during that first game in Anaheim sent a strong message to the entire ballclub. Reyes responded. The entire team has responded.

I have to believe that Jerry sat on the bench as a coach for the last two years seething at what he saw transpiring on this ballclub: underperformance, lack of drive, and in the end, a lack of results. In my baseball experience, I have seen players who would lie down and quit if they didn't like a manager. I don't think that will happen here. The Mets like Jerry. More important, they respect him. The fans are warming to him, too.

A Prediction

We are a week away from the mid-season mark of 81 games, and I don't feel that Philadelphia, Atlanta, or Florida have enough pitching to win the division. On paper, the Mets have been the best team since 2006.

The old baseball wisdom says, *The only games you can control are the games in which you are playing*. The Mets can't worry about who Philly, Atlanta, or the Marlins are playing. If they win, no one can catch them. I will go out on a limb right now and make a prediction. If the Mets stay away from injuries, I think they'll win the division.

JUNE 23, 2008

Jerry Manuel's first day in New York as manager centers on something he said that looked peculiar in print. After the series finale in Denver, he said in reference to the fans, "It's very, very fertile ground for growth in Shea Stadium...sometimes fertile ground has fertilizer." That comment became a back-page story in the New York tabloids and not a positive one. Addressing the press at Shea before the opener of an interleague series with Seattle, Manuel explained, "What I meant was that this was fertile ground, a good thing.... I said this is the most fertile ground in baseball," according to Mark Hale in the *New York Post*. Then Manuel admitted, "I have to be me. It'd be difficult for me not to be honest, and if things are taken differently, then I'll have to live with that or I'll have to deal with that."

A pitch from Johan Santana to Felix Hernandez proves far too fertile, resulting in the first grand slam by an American League pitcher since 1971. The runs are unearned, and Johan Santana's ERA drops to 2.93, even though the Mets haven't won in four straight starts by Santana (7–6).
Mariners 5, Mets 2. Record 37–38; four games behind Philadelphia.

Jerry's Mouth

Jerry Manuel made a comment about Mets fans booing Aaron Heilman, and he called them fertilizer. That is basically a nice way of calling them, let's just say, "manure." Then Jerry had to backtrack. Beware of the New York media circus!

I think the fans like Jerry very much already. They have had a week to get a feel for him during the road trip as well as in his articulate, insightful pre- and postgame interviews and conferences. The fact that the Mets had a good road trip helped, too.

With all of the anticipation coming into this homestand, the team's first game back in New York was a flop. In my experience as a player, the toughest games were always the first ones at home after a West Coast swing. Traveling out west always seemed easier than coming back. I always felt flat after the trip back to New York, and today the Mets are playing the same way. David Wright made an error to keep an inning going and then Johan made a bad pitch to the Seattle pitcher for a grand slam. The Mets were never in this game from the beginning. It is a big disappointment for Mets fans. But there's an old baseball axiom, *Turn the page*, which is exactly what this team must do.

JUNE 27, 2008

The rainout in May makes for a one-city, two-stadium doubleheader in June. The last game between the teams in Yankee Stadium is like the first the two teams played there back in 1997: a Mets win—although this one ends up a bit more lopsided. Carlos Delgado homers twice, setting a franchise-record nine RBIs in the game. Delgado had just 11 home runs and 35 RBIs entering the game—though he did have a three-run homer at Yankee Stadium on May 18 that was negated when the umpires botched the call (Jerry Manuel, then the bench coach, was ejected for arguing the decision). Mike Pelfrey gets the win in his first career start against the Yankees. The Mets take all three games in the Bronx this season, a first for the Mets.

After a speedy commute to Queens at the height of Friday rush hour, the Mets bats go silent. Retread Sidney Ponson and several relievers blank the Mets and Pedro Martinez in the night portion of the doubleheader. It is the fourth time in 46 days that the Mets have played twice in one day. Their overall record on those days is 3–5.

Mets 15, Yankees 6. Yankees 9, Mets 0. Record 39–40; three games behind Philadelphia.

The Bronx Bombers

Baseball teams play 162 games in approximately 180 days. It is a long season, to say the least. Sometimes you have to examine the schedule and figure in the travel and the fatigue factor that can come with it. Professional baseball players are well-conditioned, well-compensated athletes, of course, but even they can't play the game at the major league level without some rest.

Earlier in the month, the Mets had a Sunday night game in New York followed by a Monday night game in San Francisco. They limped into the hotel at dawn, only to head

David Wright is the first to congratulate Carlos Delgado after the first baseman sets a club record by driving in nine runs in a game against the Yankees.

to the ballpark later that afternoon. Oliver Perez couldn't get out of the first inning, and Mets were pummeled. Today, it was the Yankees who didn't get any favors from the schedule, and they looked just as bad as the Mets did at AT&T Park.

The Yankees played the previous night in Pittsburgh, getting in just three innings before it started pouring. There was a three-hour rain delay before the game was ultimately canceled, and the Yankees didn't get in to New York until 3:00 AM. And they had to make up a game with the Mets the following afternoon from *their* previous rainout. It came as little surprise that the Mets kicked the Yankees' butts in that first game.

Still, Pelfrey labored on the mound. I think he threw well today, but the Yankees have a good left-handed lineup, and lefties tend to give Mike more trouble. He needs to pitch lefties inside to be more effective. It was not a good pitching line for him: five innings, eight hits, four earned runs, five strikeouts, and four walks. The one thing you really can't overlook is those four walks. Pelfrey needs to improve his control if he's going to be successful. But he shows a lot of mental strength out there, and he's also had great games where he came away with nothing and even taken a loss despite pitching well. He's made of strong stuff, this Pelfrey kid.

Even though Pelfrey wasn't dominant this time out, he wound up with the win because the Mets' offense had a big day. The Yankees were winning 4–3 until the Mets tied it in the fifth on a Carlos Beltran RBI. Delgado put the Mets ahead with a two-run double to make it 6–4. Then Delgado's grand slam iced it the next inning and he crushed a three-run bomb in the eighth. It was a great day for Delgado, who has struggled throughout the season. Met fans are happy to see him finally breaking out of it.

Up in the booth, Gary Cohen looked through the Mets' record book for most RBIs in a game, and I was one of the Mets that Delgado surpassed with his big day at the plate. My good friend Dave Kingman held the club record for RBIs in a single game with eight back in 1976. My biggest day came in April 1988 in Atlanta, when I drove in seven runs. I hit two homers, a two-run shot and a grand slam on the day after my divorce was finalized. What a way to celebrate, right?

What Rush Hour Traffic?

The bus ride after the first game of the Bronx-Queens double-header was just amazing. We got on the road at around 6:15 PM, smack in the middle of Friday afternoon rush-hour traffic. It is the height of summer and everyone in the entire city seems to be trying to get out of town. Neither team showered. Everyone went straight to the bus in their game uniforms. The second game was scheduled to start at 8:00 PM. And guess what—it takes us only 30 minutes to go from stadium to stadium. A New York miracle!

The Major Deegan and the Grand Central were completely shut down, except for our caravan. I looked down at the FDR from our perch, and traffic is stopped for as far as the eye can see, past the 59th Street Bridge. The police had shut down all the expressways to and from both stadiums 30 minutes prior to the end of the first game. It was like a presidential motorcade, an absolutely amazing sight.

A sea of Mets fans were tailgating as we entered the parking lot at Shea. We had not eaten all day, and some of those barbecues were looking good as we passed by. The cheering was deafening when the fans saw their victorious team arrive at the ballpark. Everyone was exhilarated by the big win at Yankee Stadium. The whole experience was unforgettable; I've never been a part of anything like that, and I won't forget it anytime soon. It is a great reminder of how much baseball means to this city.

The Yankees' Turn

The Yankees showed grit coming back to win the second game, considering their late-night trip home from Pittsburgh and the pounding they took from the Mets in the afternoon's first game.

Pedro simply didn't have it tonight, but he still regained velocity on his fastball. He gave up two runs in the fourth, two in the fifth, and couldn't get out of the sixth. He's had five starts since coming back from the DL, and his ERA is over 7.00. The win in Texas was the only decent start since his return. After tonight's game, Pedro said that he will review the film, because he thinks he may be tipping his pitches, particularly his change-up. It remains to be seen whether Pedro will return to old form or if this is who he is now.

Sidney Ponson threw well in his first start as a Yankee. He came into the game with a 4–1 record—not bad for someone designated for assignment earlier this month by a team as desperate for pitching as the Rangers. The Mets had two on in the first and didn't score. Then they loaded the bases in the second and third innings, once with no outs and once with one out. They failed to score in both of those opportunities, always a bad omen. Ponson went on to retire eight of the last nine batters he faced. By the time the Yankees pinch hit for him in the seventh, it was a 9–0 rout. Counting Tuesday's 11–0 pounding by Seattle, the Mets have been shut out at Shea twice on this homestand.

JUNE 29, 2008

After two straight losses to the Yankees, Oliver Perez takes the mound with a 6.75 ERA and only one win since defeating the Yankees in May. Now he toes the rubber a little differently—from the middle instead of the left-hand side—and the results are astounding. The Yankees, keeping all but one lefty bat on the bench, barely touch him. His fourth-inning strikeout of Alex Rodriguez on pure heat is jaw-dropping considering the southpaw's recent failures. He also improves to 4–0 with a 1.52 ERA in four starts against the Yankees since becoming a Met in 2006. The Mets win the season series against the Yankees for only the second time since interleague play began in 1997.

Carlos Delgado crushes another home run and Ryan Church looks good in his first game since returning from his stint on the DL. Billy Wagner earns his fifth straight save to finish Ollie's work. One down note is an error in the seventh inning charged to Jose Reyes after his slightly errant throw is dropped by Delgado. The next batter flies out to end the inning, and Reyes throws his glove and sunglasses on the field. Our SNY cameras captured this emotional outburst.

But the win puts the team in a good frame of mind as they end interleague play and hit the road against teams that are ahead of them in both the wild-card and division races.

Mets 3, Yankees 1. Record 40–41; 3 games behind Philadelphia.

Ollie's New Groove

Dan Warthen had the opportunity to watch Oliver Perez pitch during spring training, when he was pitching coach for Triple A New Orleans. He made notes on adjustments Perez could make to his motion. Now that Warthen is in New York, he's been able to help Oliver make those changes. Under Rick Petersen's tutelage, Oliver toed the rubber with his chest facing directly toward the first-base dugout. His body was almost perpendicular to the plate, so that he had to look over his right shoulder to get signs from the catcher. When Perez started his windup, his initial step backward with his left foot went in the direction of left field. With the follow-through, he fell dramatically toward the third-base dugout, similar to Bob Gibson's follow-through. This positioning had Perez throwing across his body, a no-no for pitching fundamentalists.

When they started working together on the big club, Perez told Warthen that Peterson had him stand with his right foot on the first-base side of the rubber before starting his windup, and that he felt that he couldn't pitch right-handers inside from that side of the rubber. He would rather stand in the middle of the rubber, which is the way he had always pitched in the past. Warthen said, "You go, son!" And in this game, we saw the results.

Tonight against the Yankees, Oliver's body is squarely facing home plate when he takes his signs from the catcher. He is also rocking straight back at the beginning of his motion. Most important, Perez has significantly shortened his motion altogether. He now has a much more compact and fluid windup; there is no extra body or arm movement as he makes a pitch. I also noticed an adjustment to Oliver's follow-through. His finish is now toward home plate instead of third base.

It may sound like a lot of adjustments, but believe it or not it is fairly minor fine-tuning for a pitcher. The results, on the other hand, are nothing short of astounding. Ollie threw

85 percent fastballs tonight. More important, his fastball is back. He was clocked throughout the game in the mid-90s, and consistently threw inside pitches to right-handers. Up to this point in the season, Ollie was summarily tattooed by the righties. But tonight, facing a tough Yankees lineup stacked with right-handed hitters, he dominated them. Pitch after pitch, Perez threw a great game. Kudos to Dan Warthen!

The at-bat of the game came in the fourth inning. After Oliver gave up a hit to Jeter, he fell behind 3–0 to Alex Rodriguez. What happened next was one of those moments that make this game so wonderful. Perez did not give in to A-Rod. He kept shooting bullets inside until finally, after a multitude of pitches and foul balls, Perez struck A-Rod out swinging. What a matchup in a critical part of the game. Great stuff!

All in all, Jerry has done a good job in his first 12 games as manager of the Mets. The team is 40–41 halfway through the season and 6–6 under Jerry. Now comes the biggest road trip of the year, followed by the All-Star break and the official second half of the season.

Interleague Wrap/Rap

Once again, the American League dominated the National League in 2008 interleague play with a 149–102 record. The Yankees still have a makeup game in Pittsburgh, but otherwise interleague play is finished for the year. Only three NL teams were over .500 in interleague play: the Mets, the Reds, and the Braves. Arizona, Philadelphia, and the Cubs—the three NL division leaders—were a combined 16–29 in interleague play.

The Mets were 9–6; Cincinnati, 9–6; Atlanta, 8–7; Philadelphia, 4–11; Florida, 5–10; San Diego, 3–15; Dodgers, 5–10; Arizona, 6–9; Cubs, 6–9.

While the Phillies were busy losing eight of nine in interleague play, they let the Mets sneak in the back door and right back into the race for the division. The Mets are now only two games back in the loss column and three behind in the standings. This is pretty remarkable, considering how poorly things went for the club for most of the first half of the season.

I'll never be a fan of interleague play, but in this case it surely has benefited the New York Metropolitans.

Chapter 6

JULY

JULY 4, 2008

The Mets split four games with the Cardinals to start July, but the big story in the newspapers July 4 concerns something that happened almost a week earlier on the plane to St. Louis on June 29 after the last game with the Yankees. It started with Jose Reyes throwing his glove and sunglasses on the field the play after committing an error in a close game. Reyes confronted Keith Hernandez on the team flight about what he heard was said on the air following the shortstop's brief outburst. Reyes told Bart Hubbuch of the *New York Post*, "It makes me mad, because [Hernandez] played the game, too. He knows it is not an easy game. And he knows when you make an error, you are supposed to feel bad."

A tough loss against the Phillies in the first game of a huge series winds up putting the media focus back on the field.

Phillies 3, Mets 2; Record 42–44; 5½ games behind Philadelphia.

Plane Talk

Saturday's Subway Series matchup was the *Game of the Week* on network TV, and Gary, Ron, and I were back in the booth for Sunday's game against the Yankees. Jose Reyes made a bad throw to first base and was charged with a two-base error. It wasn't a terribly bad throw; Delgado should have been able to handle it for the out. Jose threw a little bit sidearm and the ball tailed toward home plate. Reyes was visibly upset with himself. Later in the inning, with a runner on second and two outs, Church caught a high fly ball in right field, a can of corn, to end the inning. Before Church even made the catch, Reyes slammed his glove down and, in the process, his sunglasses as well a few pieces of his jewelry fell off and landed on the field. I know it was highly unlikely, but if Church had dropped the ball, Reyes would have had to scramble 10 feet to retrieve his glove. To make matters worse, after Church made the inning-ending catch, Jose walked over to his glove with a noticeable attitude. He picked up all the stuff he threw and dropped on the field, and then half walked–half trotted back to the dugout. He got to the first-base line, and went into the dugout with a petulant attitude. If there's one thing that makes a team look bad, it is players failing to run on and off the field between innings. This is basic baseball etiquette.

Well, I criticized on him on the air for his on-field carelessness, his negative attitude, and his lack of hustle. In my opinion, Jose's behavior tonight was disrespectful to the game and set a poor example for viewers, especially for impressionable children. Little Leaguers all over the world were watching the game, kids who idolize and emulate Jose Reyes, including children in his native Dominican Republic. What are those impressionable young people going think when they see their role model behave that way on TV? What kind of message does it send to them, that poor sportsmanship is OK? In my entire life, both as a fan and a player, I have never seen a major leaguer behave that way on the field, with or without television cameras rolling. I was absolutely incredulous, and I said so on the air.

I won't go into specifics of my conversation with Jose on the plane after the game. He was upset; I was not. He said his piece; I said my piece. My criticism had nothing to do with the error Jose made. I criticized his attitude and the way he behaved after the error. Based on the comments Jose gave to the media, he still seems to think that I criticized him about the error. If that is really what he thinks, he doesn't get it and he never will. All major leaguers make errors from time to time. It's part of the game. How a player chooses to behave afterward is a different matter. We'll leave it at that.

The story of our heated in-flight conversation leaked out Friday, five days after the incident. It was an ugly back-page story in all the New York papers. There really is no such thing as a secret. I feel badly because the team has had enough distractions this season, but I also have a job to do. I refuse to jeopardize my professional reputation by being anything less than an honest and straightforward baseball analyst.

That being said, I have nothing but praise for talent whenever I see it, and Jose Reyes is certainly a truly gifted athlete and a cornerstone of this team. In my opinion, he is one of two potential Hall of Famers on this New York Mets ballclub, alongside David Wright. Mets fans have had the great fortune to follow the careers of these two fine players ever since their rookie year, when the two of them came up together. I hope that they will both remain Mets to the end of their careers. They both are extremely talented, and if they anchor the left side of the Mets infield for another 15 years, New York fans will be lucky indeed.

JULY 7, 2008

The Mets stun the doubters by winning three straight from the Phillies at Citizens Bank Park—although nothing comes easily. Following Philadelphia's walk-off win in the first game of the series, the Mets take a 3–0 lead in the Saturday night contest, only to see the Phillies tie it on a three-run Ryan Howard homer, the only hit allowed by starter John Maine. The Phillies manage just three hits off five relievers, while the Mets score three times in both the eighth and the ninth innings to overcome a one-run deficit and win 9–4. On Sunday, following an almost three-hour rain delay in the eighth inning, the Mets cling on to a 2–0 lead with two outs in the ninth when Jayson Werth homers off Billy Wagner to tie the score. The Mets persevere, and Fernando Tatis homers in the twelfth while Joe Smith, the sixth Mets pitcher of the game, allows only one hit in 2⅓ innings for the 4–2 win.

The Monday night finale, though, is the most stressful of all. The Mets have a nine-run lead by the middle of the sixth inning, but the Phillies battle back to get the tying run to second with two outs in the ninth, with Wagner again facing Werth. His soft liner is caught to the great relief of Mets fans who'd tuned in to an early laugher only to watch it become a white-knuckler. (SNY even planned to take phone calls in the booth before the Phillies intervened.) Channeling the late Bob Murphy from an alarmingly similar game against the Phillies in 1990, TV broadcaster Gary Cohen—who was Murph's radio partner back then—exclaims as the Mets shake hands, "The Mets win the damned thing by a score of 10–9." These Mets also have a winning record for the first time since June 5. *Mets 10, Phillies 9. Record 45–44; 2½ games behind Philadelphia.*

Heart-Stopping Finale

In St. Louis, the Mets looked as if they were starting to play better, and they should have taken three of four from the Cardinals instead of splitting the series. The bullpen blew the third game in that series, giving up home runs in the eighth and ninth. On they went to Philly for an important four-game series. The Mets were 4½ games behind the Phillies in the standings, so this presented both teams with potential golden opportunities. For the Mets, it was a chance to close on the Fightin' Phils; for Philadelphia, it was a big opportunity to distance themselves even further from their archrivals.

Every Mets fan has to love the outcome of this series. After losing the opener and falling 5½ games back, the Mets turned it around and beat the Phillies in the next three games. The Mets accomplished this in fine fashion by basically kicking the Phillies' fannies to end a 5–3 road trip on an incredible high.

The Mets caught Philly at a point in the season when they were struggling offensively. Every Met victory on this trip featured a different hero. Both Easley and Reyes played particularly well during this stretch. I also liked that Jerry moved Endy Chavez to the second position in the lineup.

With all of the injuries on the team, Chavez has been seeing more playing time recently. Under Randolph, Endy usually hit in the eight hole. I always thought that Endy's assets were wasted in the eighth spot, and he hit well in the number two spot on the road trip.

Five different pitchers got wins on the trip, including three (Tony Armas, Pedro Feliciano, and Joe Smith) who had yet to win a game this year. The bullpen isn't perfect (two of the three losses were accredited to the 'pen), but they did step it up and pitched very well in Philadelphia.

These are games the Mets would have found a way to lose earlier in the season, before Jerry Manuel took the helm, so this four-game set against the Phillies will be the one they'll look back on as a turning point if they win this division. Everyone came out of this road trip feeling energized, like they're right back in this thing—which they are. They took their third straight series from the Phillies this year, winning two of them at Citizens Bank Park.

The Mets have beaten the Phils head to head, which is the one thing they must do if they are going to win the division. The Phillies can feel good about battling back from nine runs down in the series finale, but ultimately the Mets came away from these four games feeling much better about themselves as a team than Philadelphia does.

JULY 8, 2008
The Mets return home to face one of the league's top pitchers in San Francisco's Tim Lincecum. Manager Jerry Manuel, who was ejected for arguing a dubious

home-run call by the umps and wasn't in the dugout for the heart-stopping conclusion Monday night in Philadelphia, talks to the team on the field before the game about a play in the ninth inning the previous night that unnecessarily put the tying run in scoring position.

The Mets play flawlessly in the field against the Giants, Mike Pelfrey wins his fifth straight start, and Carlos Beltran's three-run home run in the first inning is the big blow. It is the club's fourth straight win. The Mets move into second place for the first time since May 18, the night the Mets completed a two-game sweep at Yankee Stadium.

Mets 7, Giants 0. Record 46–44; 1½ games behind Philadelphia.

Smart and Aggressive

Back home at Shea on the following day, Jerry implored the Mets to be more aggressive on the bases. This is a ballclub with a ton of speed. Beltran, Reyes, Wright, Church, and Endy Chavez—all of them can steal bases. Willie Randolph didn't utilize this team asset to the fullest at the beginning of the season. Manuel told his men that it's time to steal more bases and apply more pressure to the opposition.

Jerry told Beltran that he doesn't care that he currently owns the all-time record for stolen-base percentage (he is 14 of 15 so far in '08 and 264 of 300 for his career for a .880 percentage). In Jerry's eyes, Beltran has not been stealing enough bases this season. Everyone knows that Carlos had double knee surgery in the off-season, but he has stated in the press that his knees are fine. Beltran and the rest of his speedy teammates have not been stealing often enough, in Jerry's estimation. "I don't care if you guys get thrown out stealing bases, as long as you steal in the right situation. I want you guys stealing more bases," he said. Jerry's other messages to his troops were that he wants to see more situational hitting, better defense, and smarter play all around. He called the entire team together for an on-field meeting before batting practice to give them a little lesson in playing smart baseball. He wanted to address a play in the ninth inning of that wild Philly finale that particularly irked him.

With the Mets nursing a two-run lead, Eric Bruntlett rashly tried to go first to third on a single up the middle—not a smart play by Bruntlett, especially with his team down by two runs. A player never wants to run his team out of an inning in that situation. Beltran tried to throw him out at third even though Bruntlett's run meant nothing; it would not have been the go-ahead or tying run. If Bruntlett scored, it would have brought the Phillies to within a run. The more important run is the guy who just hit the single, the guy who is the tying run! If he is held on first base, he is kept out of scoring position. Beltran made a strong but inaccurate throw up the third-base line to David Wright's left. Wright tried to make the tag instead of keeping the ball in front of him so the runner rounding first couldn't advance to second. The ball got by David, and to make matters worse, Billy Wagner was not backing up third. So the run scored and the tying run advanced to second base on the throwing error. The Mets got out of this jam and won the game, in spite of the four separate boneheaded plays on that one single up the middle. To wit:

- Boneheaded Play #1: Bruntlett is overly aggressive on the bases and tries to advance to third when his run means nothing.

- Boneheaded Play #2: Beltran throws to third when he should have thrown to second to hold the tying run on first.
- Boneheaded Play #3: Wright tries to tag Bruntlett out on a bad throw, allowing the ball to get by him and the tying runner to advance into scoring position.
- Boneheaded Play #4: Wagner does not back up third base.

No wonder Jerry was miffed. That one play encapsulated a swath of the mental errors that losing teams make on a consistent basis. Winning teams simply do not make these errors.

Today Jerry stressed the finer points of playing winning baseball in a purely tutorial manner and tried to get the team to think one step ahead. This team is listening. As I have stated many times on the air, before every pitch, in every inning, a good player in the field will remind himself of the situation (the score, the inning, how many outs, how many men on base, etc.) and then make a mental plan: "If the ball is hit to me, what am I going to do?" That way, when the ball is hit to him, he is already prepared for any eventuality. Jerry delivered a similar message to the Mets today, and the team took it to heart—and onto the field.

In the first inning against San Francisco, facing All-Star pitcher Tim Lincecum, Chavez singled with one out, Wright walked, and Beltran hit a three-run home run. The Giants have a truly anemic offense, so that first inning provided all the ammunition the Mets needed to win the opener of the homestand.

As if the Mets didn't have enough injuries to deal with, Ryan Church goes back on the disabled list. The lingering effects of his concussion are not going away. He came off the DL on June 29 and batted .360 in his seven games back. Luis Castillo beat him to the DL, going on the shelf at the end of the St. Louis series with hip problems. Castillo was replaced on the roster by Argenis Reyes, a minor league free agent infielder signed in the off-season from Cleveland.

JULY 10, 2008

The Mets finally give Johan Santana a breather. He throws only five innings in the rain on Wednesday night and the Mets go on to shut out the Giants again. New York's string of 21 consecutive scoreless innings against San Francisco ends in the matinee on Thursday, but Fernando Tatis homers to snap a tie in the seventh and the Mets pick up the first sweep of the Jerry Manuel era.

There is some bad news, though. The Mets announce that an MRI on Moises Alou reveals a torn left hamstring. Alou, who turned 42 a week earlier, had endured calf problems all season, playing just 15 games and hitting .347 for the Mets. He is the last in a long line of major league outfielders in his family dating back half a century to the debut of his father—and Moises' manager in Montreal and San Francisco—Felipe Alou in 1958. Moises' uncles Jesus and Matty also had lengthy major league careers.

Mets 7, Giants 3. Record 48–44; 1½ games behind Philadelphia.

Alou No More

Moises Alou's calf injury is problematic. I know all about calf injuries from personal experience, having torn my calf in Cleveland in 1990. I did not recover fully for the rest of the season. Believe me, I tried, but every time I did, I would reinjure it in a week. It's a particularly tough injury for a baseball player. When a player has a hamstring or groin injury, he can monitor all his movements to protect the damaged part as much as possible. But the calf absorbs all of the pressure of that first step out of the box after hitting the ball. How can an athlete monitor that, when he is used to playing purely by reaction? It's a tough thing to do. An injured player wants to get back in the lineup and help his team, but at the same time he is constantly aware that taking a wrong step or straining to make a play will put him out of the lineup again. Reinjuries take at least twice as much time to heal.

This damaged calf is a tough break for Alou. He has had an injury-plagued career, and I know he is disappointed not to be able to play. I feel for him. He worked very hard in the off-season to prepare for this year. Alou is one heck of a player and he has had a wonderful career, but this is probably the end of the line for him.

Giant Pushover

The Mets lost their first game against the Giants this year and won the last five. I will say this about the 2008 Giants: they stink. They have a Triple A lineup, one of the worst lineups I've ever seen. I knew the Mets would beat Barry Zito in the day game. Zito didn't have a prayer, and then Tatis won the game against their bullpen.

The Mets also beat Tim Lincecum and Jonathan Sanchez, both very good pitchers. Lincecum throws hard and has a good future ahead of him. I also like the left-hander

Jonathan Sanchez. He has great stuff, but he needs to improve his control and command of his pitches, like most young pitchers. Nonetheless, these two were no match for Jerry's Mets, who got the sweep.

JULY 13, 2008

On ESPN's *Sunday Night Baseball*, Mike Pelfrey puts an exclamation point on a resurgent first half with his sixth straight win and the Mets' ninth in a row. The Mets hammer Mark Redman and the Rockies to sweep the three-game series. The biggest surprise is Colorado's seven hits, breaking the Mets' record string of allowing three hits or fewer for five straight games. The defending NL-champion Rockies stumble into the All-Star break at 39–57, the third-worst mark at the break for a defending NL champion (not counting strike seasons). But the Mets are suddenly making everyone look bad, and their nine wins in a row are the most by the team since April 2000, the year the franchise won its last NL title. Manuel's record is 17–9 since taking over, and the Mets go into the break a half-game out of first, picking up five games in the standings during the streak. *Mets 7, Rockies 0. Record 51–44; ½ game behind Philadelphia.*

The Perfect Homestand

Colorado came in and played terribly—they couldn't hit. Jerry's squad beat Mets killer Aaron Cook in the opener on a Damion Easley home run in the eighth to break a 1–1 tie. On Saturday, the Mets beat Ubaldo Jimenez, who had previously defeated the Mets in Denver in June. Then on Sunday night, the Mets crushed veteran Mike Redman for the sweep. Colorado never had a prayer in that game. That's the difference between the way things are going now for this team as compared to a month ago. Earlier in the year, Redman might have beaten them—or the Mets would have found a way to lose one of those games. Instead, the Mets kicked some Colorado butt and took numbers.

The Rockies fell behind early in the game, and then they lay down and died. Surprisingly, the Rockies weren't hustling. They dialed it in. That's the first time I've ever seen the Rockies do that for manager Clint Hurdle. They just looked terrible in the series.

As for the Mets, you can't do better than a 6–0 homestand.

Jerry's Town

The team is hustling. It has life. Mets fans have found it hard to root for their team because of the way the Mets played the first three months of the season. I heard this time and again from die-hard Met fans. It had very little to do with last year's collapse; Mets fans were beside themselves about the team's lifeless, zombie-like play in April, May, and early June.

What explains this recent resurgence? First of all, consider the starting pitching. Every team plays better when it plays behind solid pitching, and the Mets starters have been on a roll lately. Even with Pedro injured through most of the season and in decline, the Mets' starting rotation of Johan Santana, Mike Pelfrey, John Maine, and Oliver Perez is one to be envied by most teams in the major leagues. Jerry recognizes that his starters and his closer are the strength of his

For the third time in 2008, a home-run call goes against the Mets when New York appears to be in the right. Jerry Manuel is twice ejected for arguing these decisions in vain. Instant replay will be instituted before the end of the season to specifically deal with home-run calls.

pitching staff. He has issued a challenge to his starting pitchers: go at least seven innings in each start. The deeper the starters can pitch into games, the less the manager has to lean on middle relievers, who are almost always a weak link in any pitching staff. If starters on any pitching staff can't consistently pitch past the fifth inning, that team's bullpen will eventually wear out. This is what happened to the Mets last year. The seventh inning takes a pitching staff into the territory of the set-up men. In the Mets' case, those guys are Duaner Sanchez and Aaron Heilman from the right side, and Pedro Feliciano from the left. These three have been anything but consistent so far this season, hence the need for Mets starters to go deeper. I understand why Manuel is urging his starters to step it up.

As a personal aside, I have never understood why a six-inning, three-run outing for a starting pitcher should be considered a "quality start." To me, this recent redefinition of good starting pitching is a lowering of the bar. It sounds great in a negotiation when an agent can say that his client had x amount of quality starts so therefore he should be paid y dollars. I mean, really, with an ERA of 4.50? That is nothing to brag about!

The Stars Are Bright

It feels as if the stars are aligning for the Mets. They now have the perfect schedule remaining. They don't have another trip to the West Coast. They won five of eight on the road against two of the better NL teams (St. Louis and Philadelphia) and then came home and swept two of the worst teams in the league in San Francisco and Colorado. That's nine straight wins for the Metsies. Momentum is building. What better way to go into the All-Star break?

I told Gary Cohen after the *Game of the Week* on Saturday that I think the Mets are going to win this division. The first thing out of his mouth is, "Really? You think so? But Chicago's better." The Cubs are coming to Shea for four games in the last week of September. Wouldn't it be exciting if those games really meant something that final week? What a barn-burner that would be!

I'll take my chances any day with the Mets' four starters in a short series. Santana is a second-half pitcher, Perez has pitched great since his start, and Pelfrey has won six straight. Maine has been a little inconsistent—he's labored in a lot of his starts—but he has eight wins. Certainly, nobody wants to face the red-hot Mets and their white-hot starting pitchers right now.

JULY 17, 2008

The All-Star Game at Yankee Stadium goes on for so many innings that David Wright nearly makes his big league pitching debut in that game with Boston right fielder J.D. Drew as his mound opponent. It doesn't happen; the AL forces a run across the plate against Brad Lidge in the bottom of the fifteenth inning. Billy Wagner blew the save after coming on in the eighth, setting the marathon in motion.

The Mets arrive in Cincinnati ready for the second half, a half-game out of first place and winners of nine straight. Even though Johan Santana is pounded and Scott Schoeneweis allows a bases-clearing double in the seventh, the Mets do some heavy lifting in the ninth and are able to extend the winning streak to an even 10, the longest by the Mets since July 1991. With the Phillies on an off-day, the Mets begin the second half in a flat-footed tie for first place.
Mets 10, Reds 8. Record 52–44; tied with Philadelphia for first place.

Back in the Flow

As a player, I always worried that I might get out of sync after the All-Star break. After three days off, it would always take me a couple of games to get back in the rhythm of the season. Clubs always schedule a mandatory workout on the day after the All-Star Game for that reason; they don't want any rust to take hold.

I would have picked Jose Reyes for the All-Star Game. I think he deserves to be an All-Star. David Wright was a late replacement for Alfonso Soriano, who was voted in as a starter but is recovering from a broken hand and can't play. NL manager Clint Hurdle opted for another closer in Billy Wagner, so the New York Metropolitans are represented by two of their best players in the mid-season classic.

Cincinnati Comeback

The come-from-behind-victory was a big win for the Mets for two reasons. First, teams always want to generate good momentum after the All-Star break, Second, the win catapulted the Mets into a tie for the NL East division lead, a place they have not seen since April 19.

Santana did not pitch well in the second-half opener in Cincinnati. The Mets gave him a 2–0 lead in the fourth, but he coughed up five, including back-to-back home runs by Adam Dunn and Edwin Encarnacion. Santana basically gave up a cycle in that inning: a single, double, triple, and two home runs. His pitches were up in the strike zone and all over the place.

Jerry wanted to get a couple of innings out of Carlos Muñiz in middle relief, so he put Nick Evans out there in the ninth position in an early double-switch. Evans wound up getting a base hit and scoring in the fifth inning when David

Wright hit a two-out single to drive in two. That rally got them back in the game. Then Tatis hit *yet another* big home run to give the Mets the lead in the sixth.

Coming into this game the Mets bullpen had been excellent, riding a scoreless streak of 19⅓ innings. Muniz and Feliciano added two more shutout innings to bring the streak to 21⅓. Then Aaron Heilman pitched the seventh inning, protecting a 6–5 lead. He got two quick outs and then, before you could bat an eye, Edwin Encarnacion doubled. Manuel played percentages and intentionally walked the hot-hitting Joey Votto, who represented the tying run.

I've always felt that intentionally walking a tying or go-ahead run should be avoided at any time in a game. Jerry could not have possibly had Schoeneweis ready for Votto unless Scott had been warming up at the beginning of the inning, which he was not. Heilman completed his rapid breakdown by walking the light-hitting David Ross, Heilman's greatest sin. Exit Aaron Heilman, enter Scott Schoeneweis. Unfortunately, Scott promptly gave up a three-run, pinch-hit double to switch-hitter Javier Valentin, Jose's brother. That ended the bullpen's shutout string and looked as if it would put an end to the Mets' winning streak as well.

Argenis Reyes started the rally in the ninth, David Wright homered off closer Francisco Cordero to tie it with one of the biggest hits David has delivered on the year. Beltran and Easley both singled, and then Delgado knocked in the go-ahead run.

Earlier, in the fourth, Delgado had hit a monumental, two-run homer that probably went more than 500 feet. I couldn't see where it landed—maybe somewhere in the Ohio River. Since July 1, Carlos Delgado has been red hot, hitting .396 with four homers and 10 RBIs. He has driven in 20 runs in the last 18 games. It looks as if he has finally come out of his 1½–year hibernation.

The bullpens are rested because of the three-day All-Star break. As a result, both managers used up most of their bullpen staff in this game. Reds manager Dusty Baker called on every reliever except Jared Burton, and Jerry Manuel used everyone with the exception of Joe Smith. Jerry also employed his entire bench except for backup catcher Robinson Cancel. In sum, he used 23 of his 25 players to win this ballgame. I think Jerry managed a heck of a good game today.

Including this win, he Mets have picked up 7½ games from the Phillies since June 13 to claim a share of first place.

JULY 18, 2008

All good things must come to an end, and so ends the team's longest winning streak in 17 years. While Billy Joel takes the field at Shea Stadium for his second concert in three days, the Mets are falling to the Reds at Great American Ballpark. It is their first loss in exactly two weeks. The loss knocks the club out of first place for the moment, but the Mets—left for dead a month ago—are right in the thick of the race. And even after winning 10 of 11 and lopping 4½ games off the deficit in that span, there's always room for improvement. Keith Hernandez starts thinking about how this team might make changes for the better with its lefty-dominated lineup.

Reds 5, Mets 2. Record 52–45; 1 game behind Philadelphia.

A Modest Proposal

I feel that Carlos Delgado is ready to move back into his accustomed cleanup spot. I can see that he has made enormous advances at the plate and has sustained this for close to three weeks, during which he has hit seven home runs. He looks like the Delgado of old who struck fear into the hearts of American League pitchers. Since Delgado's amazing resurgence, he is leading the Mets with 17 home runs on the year. He has also been on tear with RBIs.

During his prolonged slump, Delgado was striding too quickly, thus committing too early and lunging. This leads a hitter to swing at bad pitches, particularly breaking balls in the dirt. Now Delgado seems to be seeing the ball much better out of the pitcher's hand. As a result, he is staying back and letting his hands do the work. Because he is no longer swinging at bad pitches, he is getting ahead in counts, taking more walks and, more important, wearing out National League pitchers.

I have said before that Delgado is the key to this lineup. He is a natural cleanup hitter and a very powerful clutch hitter. With him in the four hole, Jerry can move Beltran to the third position in the order, Wright to fifth (where I like him best), Church (when he comes back) and/or Tatis—in the sixth position. The veteran Damion Easley is perfect for the seventh position, and the platooned catching corps of Castro and Schneider eighth. Reyes and Chavez should remain in the first two spots in the order.

The right-hand hitting Wright affords Delgado all the protection he needs, particularly against lefties. Remember,

David murders left-handers. If pitchers fall behind Delgado, they will be more inclined to go after him with fastballs. The productive Fernando Tatis has been getting more playing time since Church and Alou have been on the DL. Tatis is currently hitting behind Delgado, but since Fernando has been away from the game for a few years, opposing pitchers are willing to walk Delgado if they fall behind and make Tatis try to beat them. With Wright behind Delgado, that will come to an end. With Beltran hitting third, he is protected by Delgado, and the switch-hitter adds speed to the top of the lineup along with Reyes and Chavez. Against lefties, Easley can move up to the second spot and Tatis and/or Church can hit in either the sixth or seventh positions. The lineup loses a little speed at the top against lefties, but Damion easily compensates for that deficiency by being a good bunter, a situational hitter and, most important, a great hit-and-run guy. Here are the projected lineups that I like, with the ninth slot for the pitcher. I hope I haven't confused anyone!

vs. Lefties	vs. Righties
1. Reyes (S)	1. Reyes (S)
2. Easley	2. Chavez (L)
3. Beltran (S)	3. Beltran (S)
4. Delgado (L)	4. Delgado (L)
5. Wright	5. Wright
6. Church (L)	6. Church (L)
7. Tatis	7. Easley
8. Castro	8. Schneider (L)

Look at these lineups: speed at the top, power in the middle, and a beautiful left-right, left-right balance from top to bottom. Just like the lineups the Mets had in 2007! It all hinges on Delgado hitting in the cleanup position. Now that Carlos is productive again, everything falls into place. *Voila*!

I know that Mets fans must be thinking, "They've just won 10 in a row, Keith. If it ain't broke, don't fix it!" To all of you skeptics, I say, "Do it!" No matter which of these lineups Jerry uses, every player is involved. In my career, I played for managers who pretty much just played their regulars day in, day out, and limited their bench solely to pinch-hitting. After a month of moldering on the bench, those players would say, "What am I here for, anyway? I never play!"

Whitey Herzog was the best on-field manager I ever played for. He excelled at involving all of his players in the game and making them feel as if they were contributing to the team. Jerry Manuel manages in the same way. For example, in the last game against Colorado, Jerry played Nick Evans and hit him second. He believes in resting his players and in making everybody on the roster feel as if they are helping the team. I like this very much.

The Streak Ends

The bullpen did a great job this time in spite of the loss. They went 3⅓ with only one hit, but the Mets really lost the game in the fifth. It was another game where John Maine couldn't survive the fifth. He hasn't been able to get through six in his last four starts. It's becoming a cause for concern. On the flip side, Cincinnati starter Bronson Arroyo pitched a great game—just as he did at Shea in May. He went for eight innings, giving up four hits, two runs, one walk and notching four strikeouts. He was in complete command.

The Mets left only two men on base in the game. Francisco Cordero pitched one inning for the save—an easy save, really, but he pitched a lot better than the night before. A red-hot Mets team that had been averaging 6.4 runs per game during the winning streak must tip their caps to a very, very sharp Bronson Arroyo. So now the Mets need to go out there and start a new winning streak.

JULY 22, 2008

The Mets split the last two games in Cincinnati, including another late comeback win against the Reds. After faltering at the plate in Saturday night's loss in Cincinnati, the Mets take an early lead on Sunday only to see the Reds rally to score three in the fourth and one in the sixth for a 5–4 lead. The Mets tie it in the seventh after Wright walks, steals second, and scores on Carlos Delgado's single. The Mike Pelfrey versus Endison Volquez pitcher's duel never materializes, but Big Pelf gives the Mets seven innings. Duaner Sanchez throws two frames, and after the Mets take the lead on a throwing error in the tenth, Billy Wagner saves it, retiring the Reds in order, despite arm stiffness throughout the inning.

Wagner is unavailable when the Mets and Phillies, tied for first place in the NL East, open a key three-game series at Shea Stadium. Johan Santana goes eight innings, but when he leaves after 105 pitches with a 5–2 lead, the Mets' bullpen, reverting to their old ways, give up six runs in the ninth, allowing Philly to take the series opener and regain first place.

Phillies 8, Mets 6. Record 53–47; 1 game behind Philadelphia.

Stiff and Sore

The story line of this game goes back to Sunday's win in Cincinnati, when Wagner couldn't get loose and later said that he "felt a little cramping in the shoulder, a little tightness." Jerry came out to the mound to check on him. Wagner said he was OK and went on to strike out the side to end the game.

But Wagner was unavailable in the Santana game against Philly, and the Mets lost. Sanchez, who's been very good lately, gave up three base hits. The bases were loaded with no one out in the ninth, and Jerry brought in the submariner Joe Smith in the hope of getting a ground ball double play. Smith did his job and induced the ground ball to Reyes' left. Jose initially hesitated, then decided to start a double play by tagging second base for the unassisted force out. The hustling Philly base runner beat him to the bag, and everyone was safe. Reyes' mental error was the big play of the inning. A combination of things went wrong for the Mets in that ninth inning, but it all hinged on not getting the first out of the inning on that grounder. With a four-run lead late in the game, Jose should have made sure of one out.

Taguchi was the next batter, and I noticed that Endy was playing shallow in right field. I understood what he was thinking. Chavez wanted to have a chance to cut down the tying run on a base-hit. But we know all about those swirling winds at Shea, and tonight the wind was blowing out to right. Endy was taking a gamble with Taguchi, who is not a power-hitter. The odds of hitting one over his head were very slim, but that's exactly what happened. The gusty wind carried the ball over Endy's head for a game-tying double, and the Mets went on to lose a tough one against their division rivals.

JULY 24, 2008

After what is arguably the toughest loss to date—and there are several to choose from already—the Mets rebound against the Phillies to take the series. John Maine and Oliver Perez both pitch solid games and the Mets get some timely hitting late to recapture first place. Billy Wagner is back on the mound for the ninth inning and nails down the save in both games. Conspicuously missing from the Thursday matinee is Jimmy Rollins, who arrives late to the ballpark and is benched by Phillies manager Charlie Manuel.

Mets 3, Phillies 1. Record 55–47; 1 game ahead of Philadelphia.

Bouncing Back

The Mets came back to win the next two and take the series. Maine threw a good game on Wednesday night—not a great game but better than his recent starts. It was easily his best start in his last five or six games. He gave up two solo home runs to Victorino and Jenkins, but all in all, Maine battled to give the Mets the performance they needed, going seven solid innings and getting the win.

Brett Myers is just back from a demotion to the minors. He was in trouble throughout and issued five walks in five laborious innings. Unfortunately, the Mets stranded too many men on base to take full advantage of the situation, and Myers left the game with it tied 3–3.

David Wright reacts after scoring right behind Robinson Cancel on Carlos Delgado's tie-breaking hit against the Phillies.

Reyes had Wednesday's big hit, a late three-run home run off Ryan Madson. Philly has one of the best bullpens in the league, but the Mets socked it to their 'pen in both wins.

Perez threw his best game of the season in the Thursday afternoon game. His body language and demeanor on the mound exuded confidence. What impresses me most about his performance was how calm, cool, and collected he looked on the mound. Today he pitched like a 15-year veteran. I've never seen that before from him before; maybe he's maturing.

You have to give a share of the credit to Dan Warthen—as a coach, he is more practical and less philosophical than

Rick Peterson. I think that Peterson emphasized too much psychology and not enough fight with his pitching staff. Pelfrey was already starting to come around under Peterson, so you can't give Warthen complete credit, but there is a different approach to pitching at work under Warthen, who has clearly made the necessary adjustments with Perez. Tonight we witnessed the results.

Perez matched up well against the Phillies, with their abundance of left-handed hitters. Utley has been in a bad slump, and Howard can be pitched to. Oliver overmatched both of them. In his four starts against the Phillies this year, he has a 0.35 ERA, and the Mets have won three of those games. Interestingly, the only Philly in this game who really stung the ball was Eric Bruntlett, Jimmy Rollins' replacement at shortstop, who went 3-for-4.

Where *was* Jimmy Rollins? That was the question. He was late arriving at the ballpark because his car was stuck in traffic, and as a result he was benched by Charlie Manuel. There is no excuse for a player arriving late to a game. I don't care if it's a day game after a night game or if traffic is backed up for 10 miles. Punctuality is expected of a professional ballplayer, and that's all there is to it.

It's especially unacceptable considering that the Phillies were playing their main division rival...for first place...and Rollins is their team leader. Still, I think Charlie Manuel did the right thing by benching Rollins, no matter how important the game.

Delgado Does It Again

Delgado came through with an opposite field, two-run double in the eighth against tough lefty reliever J.C. Romero. He continues to hit more than .400 for July, and today he was in the prestigious cleanup position for the second straight game. Jerry feels that Carlos has made the necessary adjustments at the plate and that this is not just a flash in the pan. I could not agree more. Delgado will probably not hit .400 the rest of this season, but he could very well stay consistent for the rest of the year and be the cleanup hitter this team sorely needs. We shall see.

The Mets have taken all four series against the Phillies this year. They came back to win both of the July series after losing the openers. The team clearly continues to respond to Jerry. They're playing hard for him. They're hustling!

JULY 27, 2008

The Mets take two of three at home from the Cardinals. The bullpen makes Mike Pelfrey's win in the opener a little scary in the ninth, but they keep the Mets in the middle game until they eventually lose it in fourteen. No reliever is needed at all in the rubber game.

Santana's win, the 15th in New York's last 19 games, is the first complete game by the southpaw since 2007—against the Mets at Shea Stadium when he was with the Twins. It is the first nine-inning complete game by a Met since Oliver Perez shut out Atlanta on September 6, 2006. That span includes 290 regular-season games—plus another 10 postseason games—and two wins termed complete games in 2007 that were rained out well before reaching nine innings. Given that the Mets used eight pitchers the previous night and the fact

that their spotty 'pen has endured a heavy workload all year, Santana's performance means more than just the end to a statistical anomaly.

Despite being in first place, the Mets have questions as they hit the road and
prepare for the trading deadline. They have several needs but relatively few
trading chips because of the four top prospects they sent to Minnesota for
Santana over the winter.

Mets 9, Cardinals 1. Record 57–48; 1 game ahead of Philadelphia.

Omar's Dilemma

It was a good homestand. The Mets went 4–2 against two of
the best teams in the National League. More important, they
are atop the National League East with a one-game lead over
the Philadelphia Phillies. It builds on the team's success at the
beginning of the month with the winning trip to St. Louis
and Philadelphia. Now the Mets head to Florida to play a
surprisingly feisty third-place Marlins team that is just two
games behind the Mets. With the trade deadline just four
days away, Mr. Minaya has a very tough decision to make
indeed. *To trade, or not to trade? That is the question.*

What should he do about Ryan Church? Church is still
suffering severe headaches as a result of those two concussions. No one knows when he will be able to play again, but
he is not currently on the DL. He was the Mets' best player
for the first 7½ weeks of the season, and the Mets are hoping
that he can return to play soon. Does Minaya take a chance
on Church in the hopes that he can come around, or does he
make a move to shore up the corner outfield? Moises Alou is
out, too. Jerry Manuel has been playing Marlon Anderson,
Endy Chavez, and Fernando Tatis in both corner outfield

Best Days at Shea
OCTOBER 25, 1986

Three Men in a Room

Mets 6, Red Sox 5 (10 innings)
I remember every game in the playoffs against Houston. I kind of want to forget the first two games against Boston, but I definitely want to remember the last two.

In Game 6, I was angry. It looked as if we were going to lose the game and the World Series. I flew out in the tenth for the second out and went down into the locker room. When we started rallying, I said, "There are hits in this seat." And I didn't move until Mookie hit that grounder.

That story's been told so many times. The only thing I can add to it is that Jay Horowitz, the Mets' media director since before I got there, came up to me many years later and said, "Keith, remember that story you always tell about Game 6, how it was just you and Darrell Johnson? I was there with you. We all three watched it together." I totally forgot about that.

Darrell Johnson was our advance scout, and he'd managed the Red Sox in the '75 Series. He gave us great advice on playing the Green Monster at Fenway: the Red Sox assumed that on balls hit off the Green Monster, the throw would go to the lead base. In Game 3, we were down two games to none but had a 3–0 lead in the middle innings. Rich Gedman hit a ball off the wall with a man on first. Mookie grabbed it and threw to second and got Gedman trying for a double, to end the inning. That's as good of an application of advance scouting as I've ever experienced.

Johnson managed Game 6 at Fenway when Carlton Fisk hit that home run in 1975. Eleven years later, he was in a room with me at Shea watching the end of another great Game 6. And don't forget Jay.

positions. Anderson and Chavez cannot be expected to play on a day-to-day basis for the remaining two months, and Tatis has been away from the game so long that it is unclear how he will hold up playing every day.

So perhaps Omar will try to acquire a right-handed out-fielder just as a stopgap measure for the rest of the year. Another option could be the organization's top prospect, Fernando Martinez, who is currently in Double A. This kid has a bright future ahead of him. I love his swing, but he has been injury-prone so far in his young career. Should the Mets rush him up and let him play every day?

Or should Omar go after another late-inning reliever because the bullpen has been so erratic? There is certainly room for improvement in that department. If Omar decides to strengthen the bullpen, he needs to find a pitcher who can pitch in the seventh or eighth, bridging to Wagner—someone similar to the Phillies' Chad Durbin. Colorado's closer, Brian Fuentes, is on the block, and the Mets are interested, but I personally think that the Rockies are asking for too much. They are insisting on Fernando Martinez. I am not completely sold on Fuentes, and the Mets already have a fine closer in Wagner. Maybe Omar is looking toward the future, because Wagner isn't getting any younger. As I see it, those are Omar's options. Although any of those additions could help the Mets land a division title, there's no guarantee in any scenario. Too many GMs have mortgaged their teams' futures in the hope of winning in the present, with disastrous effects. One example that comes to my mind is when Boston traded minor leaguer Jeff Bagwell to Houston for middle reliever Larry Andersen in 1990. Andersen helped Boston for only the remaining two months of the season. As for the Astros, well, everyone knows how the Bagwell story ends.

One thing is clear: the Wilpons want to win in this final season at Shea. Fred Wilpon addressed the club in spring training and said that nothing short of a world championship would do. Ownership has facilitated this by giving Omar Minaya *carte blanche* to assemble the best possible team. The Mets now have one of the highest payrolls in the game. If the Mets do not play baseball in October, it will not be for lack of effort from ownership.

Chapter 7

AUGUST

AUGUST 1, 2008

After an 18-8 July, the dog days of August arrive, and the Mets do not make any deals. There are plenty of other trades that do happen, including Ken Griffey Jr. going from the Reds to the White Sox, Manny Ramirez from the Red Sox to the Dodgers (with Jason Bay going from Pittsburgh to Boston), ex-Met Xavier Nady and Damaso Marte from the Pirates to the Yankees (one of two AL East deals that sent a parcel of prospects packing for Pittsburgh), Ivan Rodriguez to the Yankees from the Tigers for Kyle Farnsworth, Mark Teixeira from Atlanta to the Angels, and Casey Blake from the Indians to the Dodgers. Earlier July deals had seen Jon Rauch go from Washington to Arizona, Randy Wolf from San Diego to Houston, Ray Durham from San Francisco to Milwaukee, and Joe Blanton from Oakland to Philadelphia. The two biggest deals had occurred within one day and 100 miles of each other: the Brewers getting CC Sabathia from Cleveland and the Cubs answering the next day by acquiring Rich Harden from Oakland.

The Mets come into the weekend empty-handed having dropped two of three in Florida to fall out of first place after six days in the lead. Things don't start out any better in Houston. Pedro Martinez pitches for the first time since July 12—he has been out with tightness in his groin and his shoulder and also missed time when his father passed away—yet he pitches decently against the Astros. Aaron Heilman, however, does not.

Astros 7, Mets 3. Record 58–51; 1 game behind Philadelphia.

Dealing with No Deals

I'm not surprised that the Mets didn't pull off a trade. Every team wanted Fernando Martinez, but Minaya said no to losing the team's best prospect. Omar decides to stand pat, so with two months left in the season, the Mets must play the hand dealt to them. I still think they are going to win the division.

Of all of the trades that did happen around the league, I am surprised that Griffey is going to the White Sox. It is a big gamble by the White Sox because Griffey is a shadow of the player he used to be. I knew that Manny was going to get traded—it was just a matter of where. Off he goes to the Los Angeles Dodgers. Do you think Joe Torre had something to do with that?

It would be an understatement to say that this hasn't been a good road trip for the Mets' bullpen, which reared its ugly head again in both Florida and Houston. In the first game in Florida, John Maine left the game in the fifth inning, nursing a 2–1 lead. From the booth, it was obvious to both Gary and me that John was hurting. Jerry Manuel and trainer Ray Ramirez went to the mound to assess the situation, and we

Best Days at Shea
OCTOBER 27, 1986

Rolling Sevens

Mets 8, Red Sox 5

We came back from nowhere to win the '86 World Series. We'd won 108 games, and the press would have murdered us if we lost that Series. We lost the first two games at home and then won four of the next five against a good Boston team. Since I've been counting, there have been only two world championships in Mets history, and we're one of them.

In the sixth inning of Game 7, with runners on second and third, we were down 3–0. Bruce Hurst pitched around Tim Teufel; he pitched to him very carefully and walked him. Hurst threw two breaking balls to him after falling behind in the count. I was very surprised that he pitched around Teufel to get to me, even though I gave him a lefty–lefty matchup. I said, "Here we go again." It was the same situation as in 1982, when I came up against lefty Bob McClure with the bases loaded in Game 7 of the World Series. I got the hit that tied the game with Milwaukee on a full count. Two World Series, two Game 7s, and I come up in a critical situation in the sixth inning both times with the team behind—what are the odds of that?

I was behind in the count to Hurst, 0–1, and I stroked the pitch to left-center to make it 3–2 and Teufel went first to third. That was the hit of the game. That was our opportunity. Gary Carter followed and drove in the tying run.

Orosco throwing his glove was one of the greatest moments in World Series history. Think about Jesse, how he was feeling, after being with the team through all of those years when they just stank. Did he ever think it was going to turn around? Did Mookie? The guys who were there during the lean years? It was very special for me that I was an integral part of turning around a perennial loser. But for those guys, who had been in last place all those years, it had to be a really special moment for them.

saw Maine clearly gesture toward his right shoulder. Not willing to take any chances, Jerry lifted John from the game. Jerry used five relievers to finish out the game, and Joe Smith and Scott Schoeneweis gave up five runs in the eighth for the loss.

The Mets won the second game behind yet another wonderful performance from Oliver Perez. It was Oliver's seventh win of the year, and this one put his record over .500 at 7–6. This time the bullpen got the job done, with Wagner collecting his 27th save. Delgado again came through with an eighth-inning, two-run bomb off the tough lefty Renyel Pinto for the game clincher.

In the rubber match, the Mets fell out of first place when Joe Smith gave up a couple of late runs—yet again. Pelfrey was hit hard; it was his first loss in 11 consecutive starts dating all the way back to May 26. During those starts, Mike went 7–0 with a stellar 2.57 ERA.

Surprisingly, Mike's last loss came at the hands of this same Marlins squad, which seems to have Pelfrey's number thus far in his burgeoning career. Mets management is starting to voice concern regarding Mike's workload so far this year. During this start, he eclipsed last season's mark of 152⅔ innings pitched. In today's game, pitchers are carefully monitored not to exceed 100 pitches per game. The Mets are concerned about their young pitcher hurting his arm with this season's extra workload. Again, I feel that if pitchers were allowed to strengthen their arms by going deeper into games in the minor leagues, this simply would not be an issue.

Even though July ended on a sour note, the Mets can look back with overall satisfaction. They started the month two games under .500 and in third place, 3½ games behind the Phillies. On July 31, after going 18–8 on the month, the Mets are eight games above .500 and in second place, one game behind Philly. The Marlins are in third place and only 1½ games behind Philadelphia. July has not been so kind to the Braves, who have lost five games in the standings, dropping to nine games back.

Without Tatis and Delgado, the Mets would be right there with the Atlanta Braves: very far behind in the rearview mirror. In the month of July, Delgado hit .357 with nine home runs, 24 RBIs, an on-base percentage of .455, and a superlative .714 slugging percentage! Tatis' production in July is nearly identical. He hit .397 with six home runs, 18 RBIs, a .463 on-base percentage, and an even more superlative slugging percentage of .767. Both men are strong candidates for National League Player of the Month.

In the series opener in Houston, Pedro Martinez had his first start since July 12th. He gave up three solo bombs— one to much-maligned ex-Met Kaz Matsui, one to Carlos Lee, and one to the Astros' starting pitcher, Brandon Backe. It's hard to say which long ball ticks off Mets fans the most.

He is far from superb in this outing, but he kept the Mets in the game, exiting after five with the game tied 3–3. That is, until Aaron Heilman entered in the eighth. The Astros teed off against Heilman with a grand slam from Mark Loretta and took the game away from the Mets.

Jerry Manuel keeps running Aaron out there in the hope that he can get it together. Aaron has been one big tease this season. The Mets have done everything they can think of to help Heilman recover his 2007 form. But every time he has a couple of good days and Manuel thinks he is coming around, Aaron breaks everybody's heart by getting shellacked. It's approaching the point where Aaron might be better off somewhere else—away from the critical glare of the New York media and Met fans. With just 7½ weeks remaining in the season, Aaron may have pitched himself out of being used in any meaningful situations for the rest of this season. I have a hunch the Mets might trade him in the off-season. Heilman has good stuff, no question. Maybe he'll get the chance to start with another team. I know that even though Heilman loves being a Met, deep inside he would welcome the chance to be a starting pitcher again.

These are the dog days of August, no question about it. It's hot at every ballpark, and there are very few off-days. Teams have been playing every day for four months. It's one day at a time, and the players have to grind it out. Teams can look at it only one way: *Let's get on a hot streak*. With 53 games remaining, the National League East is a three-team horse race between the Phillies, Mets, and Marlins. One streak from any of these teams could make the difference. Right now, none them are taking charge—they're all treading water. I am looking forward to seeing how things unfold in this month.

AUGUST 3, 2008

Things get uglier on Saturday night after Billy Wagner allows a bases-loaded single with the Mets clinging to a 4–2 lead. One runner scores immediately after another as Mark Loretta jars the ball from Ramon Castro's grasp and Hunter Pence crosses the plate moments later—like a lead block opening a hole for a running back to score a touchdown. (The game is, after all, in Texas.) Castro is injured on the play and is forced to leave the game. The Astros go on to win it in the next inning and Heilman is again tagged with the loss.

John Maine, who left his last start in Florida in the fifth inning, skips his Sunday start because of a sore shoulder. Maine heads for the disabled list—and is replaced by the team's 2007 first-round pick, reliever Eddie Kunz—while Wagner will be on the DL soon. Marlon Anderson also jumps in the crowded DL line with a pulled hamstring while Daniel Murphy arrives from Double A to replace him.

Oliver Perez, who won New York's only game on the trip, pitches on short rest and takes the loss as Randy Wolf gets his second win for his second team against the Mets in 2008. (Wolf was part of the devastating four-game San Diego sweep in June.) The Mets score just seven runs in three games as Houston sweeps New York for the first time since 1993. It is also the first sweep of the Mets since Jerry Manuel took over. The Mets slip to third place.

Astros 4, Mets 0. Record 58–53; 3 games behind Philadelphia.

Astros Pluck Mets

The Mets have started the month of August with a pretty tough trip. The Marlins and Astros are both better than expected. Houston really swings the bat and has some pluck in that little bandbox called Minute Maid Park. The Astros can throw three or four runs on the board in a New York minute. They're better at jogging around the bases than running them. In this three-game sweep of the Mets, the 'stros displayed some of the most egregious base running I have ever seen.

During his last outing in Miami, John Maine left the mound early because of shoulder stiffness, and he skipped this last one as a precautionary measure. He said that this discomfort has been going on for several weeks. This is alarming, because the Mets cannot afford to lose any of their starting pitchers, particularly with less than two months to play.

On short rest, Oliver Perez started in John's place in the final game of the series and did not have a good outing. After giving up three runs in the fourth, Ollie settled down and stopped the bleeding. He threw two more scoreless innings after that bad fourth—which is a good sign. In the past, Oliver has had trouble settling down after a problematic inning. Perez has always been a pitcher with an outstanding arm and tremendous power stuff. His main weakness is a tendency to lose focus. How many times have we seen Ollie cruise through five innings, only to look like a completely different pitcher in the sixth? This didn't happen today, which is further evidence of Perez's maturation.

Oliver could have gone deeper into this game. He threw only 78 pitches, but the Mets were trailing, and Manuel needed to lift him for a pinch-hitter. Eddie Kunz, who had just arrived from Triple A New Orleans to make his major league debut, threw a scoreless seventh inning.

Carlos Beltran is in a slump; David Wright is in a deeper slump. Five games into this six-game road trip, Carlos is

4-for-17, and David an ice-cold 3-for-20. Both hitters have been unproductive, with only two RBIs apiece.

With Beltran and Wright struggling, Jerry experimented with the lineup by moving Beltran into the two hole. Manuel moved Tatis up one to the fifth spot, followed by young Daniel Murphy, just up from Double A and also making his major league debut tonight. Unfortunately, the experiment ended up being the most feeble lineup that the Mets had put out there all year. I understand that Jerry is trying to get Beltran going again by hitting him ahead of David. He is hoping that Carlos will get more fastballs. Unfortunately, it didn't work.

To make matters worse, the team's hottest hitter, Delgado, got absolutely nothing to hit without Beltran batting behind him. Instead, Houston was willing to walk the rampaging Delgado in any potentially damaging situation. The league has finally started to notice that Carlos Delgado is once again the Delgado of old, the guy who hits 30+ home runs and drives in 100+ every year.

The Mets can withstand the right-ankle injury that Ramon Castro sustained during the collision at home plate on Saturday night. Because of injuries, the Mets have carried three catchers more than a few times throughout the course of the summer. Jerry has kept all three sharp with enough playing time. So Robinson Cancel is ready to step right in and play. It is unclear whether Castro will go on the disabled list, but Schneider and Cancel will carry the load until Ramon returns.

Castro has been hurt so often during the last few years that the Mets have learned to make do without him. Ramon is a good guy to have on the team because he keeps the team loose. He is to the 2008 Mets what Roger McDowell was to our '86 bunch: a great practical joker. This kind of chemistry on a team is one of the intangibles that can bring a team together and help it win. It doesn't hurt that Castro is also a darn good player, of course. He is a good defensive catcher with a strong and accurate arm. He can hit, and he has power. The only problem with Ramon is keeping him in uniform and off the DL.

What might prove more problematic for the Mets is losing Marlon Anderson, who has pulled a hamstring. Without Marlon, the Mets' left-handed hitting bench is weakened. It looks as if Jerry may play the youngsters Daniel Murphy and Nick Evans, which would send Endy Chavez back to his customary role as a pinch-hitter and help shore up the depleted left side of the Mets' bench.

AUGUST 5, 2008

The Mets stumble back to New York and send Mike Pelfrey to the hill to start the homestand against the mediocre San Diego Padres. Fernando Tatis homers twice and the Mets take a 6–2 lead into the ninth. Now working with Billy Wagner on the DL (strained left forearm), the Mets realize how much they miss someone who answers to the name of "closer." Jody Gerut's three-run homer in the ninth off Aaron Heilman makes a lot of throats tight, but Joe Smith gets the second out and Scott Schoeneweis procures the last out as the Mets beat the last-place Padres for the first time in five tries in 2008.

Mets 6, Padres 5. Record 59–53; 2 games behind Philadelphia.

Slightly Fortunate Mets

Eight days ago, the Mets left New York with a one-game lead. Well, that is all kaput! During that 1–5 road trip, the Phillies went 5–1 during the same period. So the Mets come home in third place three games behind the division-leading Phils and a half-game behind Florida. It could not have been much worse.

Bullpen Blues

The Mets have suffered a lot of injuries and have generally done a good job of getting through them, but losing their All-Star closer could spell the end of the road for the team. This is a real test for this Mets ballclub and its leaky bullpen. The Mets can only hope that Billy will be back soon—for the month of September, if not sooner.

Until Wagner returns, what is Jerry Manuel going to do? He told the ever-inquisitive New York sports media that he may use anyone, including the recent rookie call-up Eddie Kunz. In baseball parlance, this is called "bullpen by committee." It does not reflect well on this Mets 'pen that the manager is considering a young pitcher fresh out of college as his closer during a tight pennant race.

Given the way the bullpen has performed throughout the season, it is not inconceivable to entertain this notion. Give the ball to Kunz, see what the kid can do—throw in a wild card, throw the joker into the deck! It is similar to what has been asked of Daniel Murphy and Nick Evans since they were called up, and Daniel and Nick have so far been pleasant surprises. They both have been in the thick of things, contributing daily to the Mets' cause. It may be up to Kunz to do the same thing on the mound. Jerry is willing to employ any strategy that can help his team overcome losing Wagner.

Those three kids will learn in a hurry playing in New York. Being a professional athlete is different here than it is anywhere else. There is a lot more media attention in this town, and not a lot of patience from the fans. My advice to these guys is to not read the papers. It is very tempting to read the glowing articles written by beat writers when a player is doing well, particularly when he is young. But if he goes through a bad stretch, the same writers who penned those glowing columns will turn on him.

It is only natural for a player to want to read about himself after a good day, but he has to bear in mind that good days are only part of the story. Bad days often make juicier stories than good days, and it's easy to get disheartened by negative press. I read the papers when I was a young player, and I read them later in my career when I was already highly successful. As a seasoned veteran, I could handle the bad along with the good much more easily than when I was younger. As a vet, a player is better equipped to let it roll right off his back and go about his business on the field. After all, the writers have a job to do, too.

Sixth Sense

Jerry Manuel's experimental lineup in Houston did not last long. Tatis went back to the six hole and immediately responded with two home runs. Tatis is playing every day right now, and he's hitting a very productive .316. It is hard to imagine that Fernando was out of baseball just two years ago. In fact, Tatis has been out of the game three of the last four years. Now he has a second baseball life with the Mets—thanks to Omar Minaya, who has taken an interest in him since their paths first crossed, when Omar was scouting for the Texas Rangers in the late 1990s. Tatis been hustling and working as hard as anyone possibly can, and he's been terrific.

And team catalyst Jose Reyes has been terrific as well. The Mets' lead-off man has 80 runs and 37 stolen bases on

Jose Reyes, in 2008, wound up as the second Met in history to collect 200 hits in a season.

the year. In May, June, and July, Jose hit over .300. He hit .336 in July with a .403 on-base percentage. The Mets need Reyes to stay hot, but they need other guys on the team to start getting hot, too. No one can stay hot forever; no one player can carry a team. And with this bullpen, the Mets need all the offense they can muster.

AUGUST 7, 2008

After a loss in the second game of the series, the Mets are again in a dogfight with otherwise struggling San Diego. Adrian Gonzalez singles to left with the bases loaded off Pedro Feliciano in the eighth, but Scott Hairston slides into third when he could have tried to score. On the next play, the Mets turn a brilliant double play on a great stop by Argenis Reyes, the flip to Jose Reyes, and a superb stretch and scoop by first baseman Nick Evans, who barely keeps his foot on the bag to end the threat and keep the Mets in front. With Scott Schoeneweis on in the ninth inning, Jody Gerut—who entered the series with seven homers all year—goes deep for the third time in three games. It is the sixth time and second straight outing in which Johan Santana doesn't get the win because the bullpen allows a lead to get away. But in the bottom of the ninth, David Wright, facing former teammate–turned–bullpen stalwart Heath Bell, hits the first walk-off home run of his career to win the game.

Mets 5, Padres 3. Record 60–54; 2 games behind Philadelphia.

Pulled Wright Out of the Fire

Mets fans have several reasons to be thankful about tonight's win. This was a must-win series for the Mets, playing against a bad Padres ballclub. Mets fans are thankful that the gods of baseball scheduling sent San Diego this way after the disastrous road trip to Miami and Houston. The fans are also thankful for great defense and Wright's clutch game-ending home run in the bottom of the ninth. The Mets had to get back to their winning ways, and even though they struggled in this series, a win is a win, and they welcome it any way they can get it.

The last road trip was the worst the Mets have endured since Jerry Manuel took over. As in early June, the big problem lately has been lack of offense. The Mets' bats have gone silent. The team has scored four or fewer runs in six of their last nine games. Coupled with the loss of Wagner and an already shaky 'pen, every win has been a white-knuckler.

Wright picked up the team today with a two-run home run in the ninth. He brought an 0–15 streak into last night's game before collecting two hits, and he got three more hits today, as did Beltran. One can only hope that this will get them going again, as well as the team as a whole.

With 48 games remaining, David now has 87 RBIs. He could drive in 120 to 130 runs by the end of the season. Beltran has 73 RBIs, and he could drive in 110. To me, neither one is having an outstanding year so far. That could change if each has a strong last month and a half.

Baseball players today compete in an era where offense reigns supreme. Major League expansion in the 1990s, smaller parks, a dearth of quality pitching, smaller strike zones, bigger and stronger players, and balls that observers of the game claim are more juiced than in the past...everything is tilted in the hitters' favor. And who knows the extent and effect of performance-enhancing drug use in the game?

How can I say that a player who drives in more than 100 RBIs is not having an outstanding year? One hundred RBIs simply does not carry the same weight as it did 30 years ago. We've gone through various eras in baseball. The dead-ball era gave way to a proliferation of offense when Babe Ruth ushered in the home-run era. In the 1960s, pitching became dominant again and the mound was lowered. Now we are in another period where offense is dominant and statistical expectations for today's hitters are adjusted accordingly.

Out of Position

The Mets have needed every possible contribution of offense and defense to compensate for the struggles of their over-worked bullpen. The rash of injuries has led Jerry Manuel to play Argenis Reyes, Nick Evans, and Daniel Murphy regularly. Today the team found exactly what it needed in the three rookies.

In this game against the Padres, Murphy and Tatis both played out of position. (They are both third baseman.) Since his call-up, Murphy has been playing left field regularly and doing yeomanlike work there. Tatis also has been predominately playing left field, but today Jerry switched him over to right. And there are differences between playing those two corner outfield positions. Evans was a first baseman in the minors, and he played his first Mets game at that position today with Delgado on a day's rest.

At age 36, Carlos has been playing nearly every day this entire season, and this was a day game after a night game. Today's game was the perfect candidate for resting Delgado, against one of the worst teams in baseball and with nearly two months remaining in the season. The team will rely on Delgado's strength down the wire. Giving him an off-day today was an excellent choice by Manuel.

It was not the best defensive lineup that Jerry has fielded so far this season, but with his team struggling offensively and Delgado out, it was the best possible lineup for the rubber match. He sacrificed defense for some much-needed offense, and he was counting on his pitching ace to play his part.

The Mets got yet another great pitching performance from Johan Santana, who took a 3–1 lead into the eighth inning thanks to Nick Evans and Daniel Murphy, who drove in all three Mets runs. It is the third time in Santana's last four starts that he pitches into the eighth inning. In today's game it is nothing short of heroic.

Everything goes awry when Santana yielded two straight base hits to start the eighth. Jerry called upon Duaner Sanchez, who immediately hit Scott Hairston to load the bases with no outs. Sanchez departed, and Pedro Feliciano took the mound. Feliciano induces a ground ball force-out at home, then served up a base hit to lefty Adrian Gonzalez. Gonzalez singled to Jose Reyes' right.

And then the fun began. The speedy Hairston represented the tying run on second, yet he inexplicably slid into third base on a ball that gets by Jose for a base hit. In this situation, a base runner should be able to read the play as he advances to third. This grounder was in front of him, in plain view. Any good base runner would have been able to determine that

Reyes was not going to make the play. If Hairston was unsure of the outcome of Reyes' dive, he should have looked at his third-base coach, who happened to be waving Hairston home.

This is a textbook example of bad base running. If Hairston scored, as he should have, the game would have been tied at 3–3, with the Pods still threatening with runners on first and second—or worse yet for the Mets, first and third. They would have needed only a sacrifice fly to take the lead.

Manuel brought in Joe Smith to face right-hand hitting Kevin Kouzmanoff, who promptly scorched a bullet up the middle to Argenis Reyes' right. Argenis made an outstanding diving catch to start a 4–6–3 inning-ending double play. Jose Reyes' throw was up the line to Nick Evans' far right. Evans made a spread-eagle stretch, catching the ball in his webbing to end the Padre threat. The Mets got out of the jam because of bad baseball played by a last-place team. I have always said that over the course of a three-game series, a bad club will find a way to demonstrate exactly why it is at the bottom of the heap.

In the top of the ninth, Jody Gerut hit a solo home run off Scott Schoeneweis that tied the game. (Then again, the home run should have put the Padres ahead 4–3, with all-time save-leader Trevor Hoffman ready to close it out in the bottom half.) The blown save marks the sixth time this season that the Mets' bullpen coughed up a late lead for Johan Santana. His won-lost record is only 9–7, but he could easily have 15 wins by now.

I want to underscore again that the Mets are benefiting from contributions from the team's unsung heroes. That is what it takes to win ballgames and pennants. Baseball is a game of 25 players, and winning teams get contributions from them all. Kudos to Jerry Manuel for showing confidence in his young players and putting them out there under the pressure of this tight pennant race. With this series win, the Mets have now taken 13 of 17 rubber matches on the year. Outstanding!

Marlins on Horizon
The second-place Marlins come to Shea for a big three-game weekend series (and every series is big from now on). They arrive on a high after taking two of three from Philadelphia to begin an important road trip and close to within a game and a half of the division leaders. The Mets trail Florida by only a half game when the Marlins arrive at Shea.

The series opener looks as if it will be a pitcher's duel between Ricky Nolasco (11–6) and red-hot Oliver Perez (7–7).

AUGUST 8, 2008
Oliver Perez dominates the Marlins, allowing just two hits in seven innings. David Wright, coming off a game-winning home run in his last at-bat against San Diego, homers with a runner on in the first inning to give Perez a 2–0 lead against Florida's Ricky Nolasco. That is all the backing Perez needs, although nervous Mets fans find themselves wishing for an infinitely larger cushion when Aaron Heilman enters in the eighth inning. Coming off a win the previous day,

Heilman retires all six Marlins for his first save of the year. The Mets have won consecutive games for the first time in two weeks.

Mets 3, Marlins 0. Record 61–54; 1 game behind Philadelphia.

Oliver the Magnificent

Perez is pitching as well as anyone in baseball. He has been on a tear since June 29, after making those all-important adjustments to his delivery. Over eight consecutive starts, Ollie's record is a deceptive 3–2 with a more telling ERA of 1.71, which is nothing short of stellar. Perez could have easily gone 7–1 in those starts if he'd have had the benefit of better run support from his offense.

Coming into his June 29 start against the Yankees, Oliver had been struggling mightily. He had lost his fastball and had minimal command of all of his pitches. Since his subsequent resurgence, Perez's ERA has dropped from 5.29 to 3.90, the equivalent of almost a run and a half per game. It is an astounding turnaround for any pitcher this late in the season.

Oliver simply overpowered Florida today, shutting out the Marlins on two hits with eight strikeouts over seven innings. Twenty years ago, this would have been a day of rest for the bullpen and a complete-game shutout for Ollie. Because it is 2008, however, the struggling Aaron Heilman is brought in to close out the game. Heilman succeeded in fine fashion, going two strong, scoreless innings to register his first save of the year.

Wright and Delgado provided all the offense needed in this game. David hit a two-run home run in the first inning. It is his 22nd home run of the year and his second home run in as many games. Delgado provided insurance with his 24th home run on the year, a solo shot in the fourth.

With this 3–0 win, the Mets have won three out of four, and they leapfrog Florida into second place. In addition, Philadelphia lost tonight, so the Mets are now only a game out of first place.

AUGUST 9 & 10, 2008

Since Billy Wagner has gone down, the Mets have quickly mastered the technique of winning ugly. Brian Stokes, generally a reliever, pitches well as a starter in his Mets debut, except that he allows a two-run homer to his next-to-last batter in the sixth. The Mets regain the lead and hold off a Florida rally with Aaron Heilman throwing the last pitch in the third straight Mets win.

Sunday, though, there is no winning, just ugly. In a battle of strong, young 6'7" right-handers, Florida's Josh Johnson rules the day. The Marlins chased Mike Pelfrey in the fifth. Eddie Kunz, who has the media buzzing that he might be the team's next closer, comes on in the fifth to stanch a Marlins rally and issues a run-scoring wild pitch followed by a walk. The Marlins have won all six starts by Johnson—including a win against the Mets July 30 in Florida—since his return from Tommy John surgery.

Mets 8, Marlins 6. Record 62–54: 1 game behind Philadelphia
Marlins 8, Mets 2. Record 62–55; 2 games behind Philadelphia.

Come From Behind

In the second game of the series, the Mets' pitching faltered, but the offense pounded out 13 hits against Scott Olsen and the Florida bullpen for a resounding 8–6 win. The offensive stars of the game were Carlos Beltran, Carlos Delgado, and

Daniel Murphy, each of whom homered in this game. The struggling Beltran had a 3-for-3 night, with his 16th home run along with three rib-eye steaks. Delgado's titanic two-run shot in the first was his second in two nights, and Daniel Murphy broke the game wide open in the sixth with the first major league home run of his career. These are all promising signs that this Mets offense is breaking out of its 10-day slumber.

Tough Stuff

Josh Johnson is an outstanding pitcher. He's an old-fashioned country hard-baller who works fast and doesn't mess around. He throws hard, and he is not afraid to throw inside. His arsenal consists of a mid-90s fastball, a hard slider and an occasional changeup. I love the way he goes right after hitters. If he stays healthy, Johnson could become one of the top pitchers in the league.

Speaking of promising pitchers, Pelfrey has been dominant since his turnaround, which began in June when he went 6–0 in eight consecutive starts. Mike has been in a slump since his first start after the All-Star break (yes, pitchers go into slumps too). Since that start in Cincinnati, Pelfrey has gone 2–2 with a bulging 5.83 ERA in 29⅓ innings pitched.

I will say this about young Pelfrey: he has guts. He battled in all five of those starts. In spite of his struggles, he never gave in or quit. Perseverance is the quality that separates the men from the boys in this game. It is an intangible that does not show up on spreadsheets or in statistical analyses, but it is a critical element of a player's success.

I am certain that Mike has the potential to become a terrific pitcher in the very near future. He will be a workhorse, someone the Mets can count on to win big games. In the immediate future, the Mets need Pelfrey to break out of this slump and start winning games again—the sooner the better.

AUGUST 11, 2008

After a few days without a major meltdown, the relief corps sabotages a fine start by Pedro Martinez in the makeup game for an April rainout. The Pirates, who beat the Mets in the first-ever game at Shea Stadium in 1964, close out their Shea experience with another buzz kill by scoring three in the seventh and three more in the ninth to overcome a 5–1 deficit. Aaron Heilman, who'd been nearly perfect in his last three outings, takes the loss. Jerry Manuel is ejected for arguing balls and strikes in the ninth. The manager promises change.

Pirates 7, Mets 5. Record 62–56; 2 games behind Philadelphia.

No Relief in Sight

This was a game that got away from the Mets, the kind of game that the team should never lose. Everything seemed to be going their way as they began this make-up. The Pirates were on the tail end of a tough four-city road trip and had played in Philadelphia the previous day. Today should have been their off-day. To make matters worse, there was a long rain delay in Philadelphia, so the Buccos didn't arrive in New York until late. Instead enjoying time off at home, the Pirates were playing an afternoon game in New York on little rest. This easily could have been a game that the Buccos would dial in, particularly after falling behind 5–1 early on.

Unfortunately for the Mets, it was not the case. As the old saying goes, *That is why they play the games.*

Pedro had his best start since coming off the DL at the beginning of the month and gave the Mets six solid innings, departing with a 5–1 lead. Mets fans are praying that Pedro can give the Mets that same level of performance for the remainder of the season.

In the seventh, Joe Smith came in and promptly gave up a lead-off walk, followed by a double by Freddie Sanchez, who was last year's batting champion. Joe Smith out; Pedro Feliciano in. This is starting to seem like a recurring theme.

Feliciano does no better. He issued a walk, a double, and a long sacrifice fly to make it a 5–4 ballgame. Duaner Sanchez relieved Feliciano and prevented further damage, pitching a solid eighth before handing the ball over to new closer Aaron Heilman, going for his third consecutive save. Aaron is coming off a great series against Florida, and I find myself hoping and thinking along with everyone else, *Hey, maybe Heilman can be our guy until Wagner comes back.* Unfortunately, Heilman reverted to his teasing ways and gave up three runs. The Pirates stole a game from the Mets— a game the Mets never should have lost.

After Heilman's bad outing, Jerry said, "All right, he's not going to be in that role anymore." Now he's thinking about using rookie Eddie Kunz as closer. The Mets' bullpen is the target of the fans' wrath, and they deserve it. They have been glaringly bad. A lot of the recent failure has been exacerbated by the loss of Billy Wagner, but this bullpen has been woefully inadequate for most of the season.

In the meantime, someone has to step up and close games for the Mets until Wagner returns, possibly in a week. The Mets are scheduled for a seven-game road trip. Fortunately, this trip takes them to Washington and Pittsburgh, both second-division teams who are out of the pennant race.

AUGUST 12, 2008

Jerry Manuel turns the clubhouse at Nationals Park into the National Zoo, feeding reporters lines about using starters in the bullpen and taking the 'pen to task for blowing too many games, like the previous afternoon's mess against the Pirates. The Mets have four in Pittsburgh after their three-game set in Washington, and the last thing Manuel wants his club to do is miss an opportunity to pick up ground against a pair of teams that have struggled most of the year. Scott Schoeneweis calls a rare relievers-only meeting to clear the air in the leaky 'pen. "When they talk about bringing in other people because you can't get the job done," Joe Smith told *Newsday*, "yeah, that hurts." Smith throws a scoreless eighth, and Pedro Feliciano sets down the side in order for his first save. The last Mets reliever to pick up a save in a Johan Santana win was Billy Wagner on May 27; the bullpen has blown four potential wins for Santana in the interim. *Mets 4, Nationals 3. Record 63–56; 1 game behind Philadelphia.*

Throwing the Gauntlet

Two quotes from manager Jerry Manuel regarding the bullpen set off tremors in the clubhouse and establish the tone for this seven-game road trip. "If you guys can't get the job done, then we'll take drastic measures," was one; "pitching with trepidation to contact" was the other.

I know that Jerry prefers to use a gentle, fatherly, and psychological approach in prodding his players to greater heights, but these statements have nothing in common with the teachings of Dr. Benjamin Spock. This is a 21-gun broadside blasted at the bullpen at close range—and then for emphasis Jerry added that he is willing to use Kunz to close out games and might even try Perez, Pelfrey, or Maine as closers—anyone who can get the job done for the team.

Manuel has seen enough of late-inning losses. He has taken off the kid gloves, and without naming names, he has insulted several pitchers in the bullpen. "Pitching with trepidation to contact" is the ultimate put-down, a way of saying that some of the bullpen pitchers are pitching scared. These are fightin' words.

Jerry has said to me that he is not running a popularity contest and that he does not care whether or not a handful of players like him. He cares more about results—about winning games and pennants—than about being liked. Jerry has given his bullpen a good, old-fashioned spanking, flying in the face of the teachings of the esteemed Dr. Spock. I like it!

In the eighth inning, Damion Easley was beaned with the bases loaded to give the Mets and Johan Santana a 4–3 lead. Once again, Jerry called upon his chastised bullpen to close out the game. From our aerie in the booth, Gary and I watched with great trepidation (to borrow Jerry's word) as Joe Smith began the bottom of the eighth. Joe threw a scoreless eighth and Pedro Feliciano a scoreless ninth, registering his first save of the year and a big Mets victory. It looks like strong words from the skipper have led to positive results.

As I studied the monitor during the last two innings of the game, it was apparent to me that the faces of Smith and Feliciano were markedly different tonight. They were steady with determination and resolve. They had fire in their eyes, which is a fine thing to see. Sometimes a little kick in the pants can go a long way.

On a lighter note, Oliver Perez responded to Jerry's comment and told the press in no uncertain terms that he does not want to work out of the bullpen. I am sure that Jerry or Dan Warthen will take Oliver aside and reassure him that he is in no jeopardy of becoming the Mets' next closer.

There 43 games remaining in the season. The National League standings to this point:

Record/Games Out

NL East	*NL Central*	*NL West*
Phil. 64–55 –	Chi. 71–47 –	Ariz. 61–58 –
N.Y. 63–56 1	Mil. 69–51 3	L.A. 60–59 1
Fla. 63–57 1.5	St.L. 66–56 7	Colo. 53–68 9
Atl. 55–63 8.5	Hou. 60–59 11.5	

Wild Card

Mil. 69–51	–
St.L. 66–56	4
N.Y. 63–56	5.5
Fla. 63–57	6
Hou. 60–59	8.5
L.A. 60–59	8.5

In the NL West, Arizona has come down to earth after a red-hot start in April. Since the acquisition of Manny Ramirez, Joe Torre's Dodgers are closing fast, and they appear to be on the verge of overtaking the Diamondbacks.

In the NL Central, Lou Piniella's Cubs have slipped recently, allowing the Brewers, aided by the newly acquired CC Sabathia to close to three. Even so, I don't think that the Brew Crew can win the Central because of Chicago's complete dominance over Milwaukee this year.

In the NL East, it is still a three-team race, but I don't think that Florida can stay with the Mets and Phillies because of the team's youth and weaker pitching and defense.

My feeling is that the wild-card will not come out of the East because the NL East is the most competitive of the three National League divisions, and those three teams at the top will be scratching and clawing their way to the very end. And I still feel that the Mets will take the division.

The other two NL divisions are much weaker and lacking in depth. Both Milwaukee and St. Louis still have plenty of games against weaker teams such as the Pirates and the Reds, and they could really make hay against those lesser ballclubs. Therefore, I believe that the NL Wild Card will come out of the Central. The losers in the East will have to go home and wait until next year for a chance to play October baseball.

The heat is on. This is the beginning of the stretch run.

Going National

Santana got off to a slow start, giving up two in the first, but then he settled down in workmanlike fashion. He took a 3–2 lead into the seventh but gave up a solo home run to pinch-hitter Ryan Langerhans that tied the game. The Mets got the winning run in the eighth when Damion Easley was beaned with the bases loaded, and the hard luck Santana got his 10th win at last. I am happy for Johan; he has left so many games with the lead, only to have that lead blown by the bullpen.

Beltran had three hits on the night, his third three-hit game in a week after hitting just .248 last month. David Wright is also red hot since his game-winning home run against San Diego last week. Delgado has cooled down a bit, mostly because the opposition is pitching him much more carefully. Fernando Tatis, Damion Easley, and rookie Argenis Reyes have also cooled.

Argenis came up when Luis Castillo got hurt in early July, and he started slow. By the time everyone mastered the pronunciation of his name (ar-**ha**-nis), he was hitting .300, which earned him more playing time. The switch-hitting Argenis is now platooning with Easley at second. Whenever he is called upon to play, he contributes with his glove as well as his bat. The fine-fielding second baseman has excellent range and gives the Mets defensive help on the right side of the infield—which the team needs as a result of Delgado's lack of mobility.

Here's how some of the hitters have done in the first 11 games of August:

Mets	5–6 for month as of August 13
Jose Reyes	.313, 5 runs
David Wright	3 HRs, 10 RBIs, 6 runs
Carlos Beltran	.372, 8 runs, 5 RBIs, .426 OBP
Carlos Delgado	.278, .357 OBP, 2 HRs, 6 RBIs
Daniel Murphy	11-for-24, 5 runs, 6 walks

After two lackluster months, Carlos Beltran heated up in August and stayed hot.

Eye in the Sky in D.C.

This is my first time in the new Nationals Park, because I did not work the Mets' series here in April. My first impression is that the park is beautiful overall, but it has one major drawback from my perspective: the broadcast booth is perched five rows above the last row in the upper tank. We are quite a distance from the playing field. We have to work in the Uecker seats!

At Fenway, the broadcast booth is also up high, but it is right over home plate. I don't much like calling games from Fenway, either. The booth in Pittsburgh is up high, too, but this one takes the cake. It's the worst I've experienced. Being so high up and far back from home plate makes me feel as if I am looking down into deep chasm. It was difficult for me to feel the excitement or intensity, even though it was a thrilling, stretch-run game.

AUGUST 13, 2008

The best tonic for the Mets' bullpen is a rare laugher. John Maine, just off the disabled list, goes five innings. Brian Stokes, in his first relief appearance as a Met, throws the last four innings, qualifying for a save. A save in a 12–0 game bends the spirit of the rule, but the Mets' bullpen will take any save that's being doled out. It's a big enough blowout that the Mets' broadcasters take calls during the telecast, something SNY hoped to try more often during the year. But the 'pen has created too many close calls to open the phone lines mid-game.

Mets 12, Nationals 0. Record 64–56. Tied with Philadelphia for first place.

We'll Take Caller Two

Baseball is about passion and performance. In the booth, we look at the game from a professional perspective, but sometimes it's refreshing to hear from people who watch the game for the sheer joy of it. Our producer, Gregg Picker, had the idea this year for us to start taking phone calls toward the end of games that are blowouts. It is an interesting experiment, engineered to keep the audience from turning the channel in a late-inning rout. I don't mind taking calls in the booth. We obviously won't do it when the score is close, because people at home want to watch a ballgame, not listen to John Q. Public calling in from Mineola.

The fan phone calls are also a nice break for us when it's a lousy game. The calls are screened and they are broadcast on a delay, so there is no way we can get a jerk on the line who would say something silly or offensive. Many of the fans who call in really know what they're talking about and ask legitimate questions about their concerns for the ballclub. It can be very interesting for us, and it helps keep us sharp during some innings that might have otherwise dragged along.

Sometimes people ask what a typical day is like for me on the road or how I prepare for a game. I do have a routine on the road during the baseball season. I usually wake up at 7:00 AM, run for coffee, read the paper, then go to the hotel gym to ride a recumbent bike for 50 minutes. After a shower, I prepare for the game for several hours in my room with my computer and the local and New York newspapers. Then it's naptime at around 1:30 PM, followed by lunch and then off to the park at 4:00 PM. It's a different routine than the one I followed as a player, when I would sleep till noon, but it's still the baseball life. I can't walk around all day sightseeing and then do a night game. The baseball year is just too long. If I want to see the sights in Washington or in an other town, I'll come back during the off-season. Right now I need to be rested and alert for every broadcast. There is a game to announce.

AUGUST 18, 2008

The Mets complete a sweep of the Nationals and then win the first three games in Pittsburgh. David Wright has the Sunday game off and luckily so does the bullpen. Johan Santana throws his second complete game of the year and gets his first shutout as a Met. Even with no work for a day, the bullpen remains a busy place. Luis Ayala is acquired from Washington for a player to be named later (who ends up being Anderson Hernandez).

With the surge, the Mets—who were 7½ games out of first on June 12— find themselves in first place as the Phillies hit the skids on the West Coast, losing five of seven, including a four-game sweep by the Dodgers. The Mets go for a four-game sweep of their own in the wraparound game in Pittsburgh on Monday afternoon, and the Mets take an early 2–0 lead that John Maine preserves through five shaky, shutout innings. Brian Stokes allows a two-run home run to Adam LaRoche in the sixth inning, and Pittsburgh snaps the tie in the eighth. Pirate Paul Maholm goes six innings for the 19th straight start, but the decisions go to the bullpens in what was an otherwise perfect trip for the Mets. *Pirates 5, Mets 2. 68–57; 1½ games ahead of Philadelphia.*

Trip the Light Fantastic

The Mets took advantage of a soft spot in their schedule and were helped by Philly's bad West Coast road trip to take over first place in the NL East. On their last trip to Florida and Houston, the Mets left town one game up and came back three games out; on the next trip—the one just ended—they left New York two games out and now come back 1½ in front. It's been that kind of crazy year for this team.

The Mets won six out of seven on this road trip against teams that they *should* beat. It's what they need to do if they are going to win this thing. They lost the last game of the trip because of the bullpen, and naturally the press is all over them. Duaner Sanchez had a rough outing, and the papers write it up like the sky is falling. The bullpen had an outstanding trip overall, but the media totally disregarded the positive and piled it all on this one negative game. Sometimes life is unfair. When the Mets arrived in Washington last week after blowing a lead the day before at Shea, Jerry asked—actually, he pretty much demanded—that the bullpen step up. He also asked the starters to go deeper and the bullpen to hold the line with Wagner down. And they did.

The Mets are doing the kinds of things that they didn't do last year. The Pirates gave them trouble in 2007—and certainly Washington gave them all they could handle at the end of last year. The Mets have just won six of seven on the road, and that's a hell of a trip no matter what. They fall one win shy of getting the second 7–0 road trip in Mets history, a feat that was achieved by Buddy Harrelson's team in 1991.

I saw a lot of good signs on this road trip, but looking at it with a purely professional eye, the Mets *were* only playing the Nationals and the Pirates. The Mets' bullpen was outstanding overall, but they were also throwing against two teams that just can't hit. The Pirates are without Jason Bay and Xavier Nady, who were both traded last month, and the Nationals have struggled all season. It is up to the Mets to take full advantage of playing weaker ballclubs whenever they are scheduled to face them, and they did.

AUGUST 19, 2008

It's a good news, bad news return to New York for the Mets.

First, the bad news: Billy Wagner, who went on the disabled list August 3 with a muscle injury described as a "strained left forearm," undergoes an MRI that reveals inflammation in the tendon area of his left elbow. He felt stiff following a rehab appearance in Double A Binghamton, perhaps as a result of trying to come back too quickly. With the troubles the bullpen has endured all year, one can understand the sense of urgency.

The good news is that the Mets get another strong performance out of the 'pen after another solid start from Oliver Perez. The Mets still have to rally late, but unlike the previous day, when Pittsburgh put together a big eighth inning against their 'pen, this time the Mets rally for five in the eighth against Atlanta's relief corps. Carlos Delgado launches a two-run double against southpaw Will Ohman, who'd held lefties to a .169 batting average this season, to put the Mets ahead.

Mets 7, Braves 3. Record 69–57; 1½ games ahead of Philadelphia.

Rally Caps

A day after the only hiccup on an otherwise great trip, it's a good sign to see the Mets put together a late charge to beat another team's 'pen. After all, other ballclubs have bullpen problems, too! Atlanta's starting pitching is also mediocre since the Braves lost John Smoltz and Tim Hudson, their number one and two starters.

Jo Jo Reyes didn't have a prayer to win this game for the Braves. The Mets overcame their tendency to score early and then shut down. They scored late in this game by clobbering the Atlanta bullpen. Carlos Delgado had a big opposite-field hit in the eighth inning with the bases loaded. Prior to this game, the Mets had been awful with the bases loaded (3-for-42), so this clutch hit was a welcome change for the team. Easley and Castro follow with hits, and the red-hot Mets made it seven wins in eight days.

The Mets bullpen came through once again, with Luis Ayala looking good in his first game since the Mets acquired the veteran set-up man from Washington. But the euphoria in the clubhouse was dampened when the Mets learned that Billy Wagner will not be available tomorrow as hoped. Billy said he felt something in his elbow after his rehab outing last week in Double A Binghamton. The MRI shows an increased swelling of the elbow. It is an enormous setback for Billy, as well as for the Mets.

The Mets' bullpen spent all of the road trip in Washington and Pittsburgh trying to hold on until Billy could return this week. Now it looks as if Wagner may not come back at all.

We'll see if this bullpen can step up and meet this challenge for the final five weeks of the season.

AUGUST 20, 2008

Umpires approve the use of instant replay for baseball to decide home-run calls during the 2008 season. Among the numerous blown home-run calls by umpires are three that went against the Mets in the first half of the season (April 2 in Florida, May 18 at Yankee Stadium, and July 7 in Philadelphia); all were in games won by the Mets despite the umpires getting it wrong.

Twenty-five general managers voted in favor of exploring the use of instant replay the previous November; the only surprise is getting it in place in the final months of the 2008 season as opposed to trying it out in spring training or early season games.

All 30 stadiums will be wired for replay. Umpires will be allowed to look at a replay to determine only whether a ball is or isn't a home run. The umps will watch from a secure area—usually near a tunnel outside the clubhouse area—and they will have access to TV feeds from both teams so that angles won't be biased for any one club. Replay will be available for use in games starting on August 28.

Mike Pelfrey doesn't offer much reason to look at anything twice as he zips through the Atlanta order and records his first career complete game (the second by a Met in four days). It is in stark contrast to the labor from Atlanta's Jair Jurrjens, who beat the Mets twice earlier in the year.

Mets 6, Braves 3. Record 70–57; 1½ games ahead of Philadelphia.

Contrasting Performances

Pelfrey broke out of his earlier slump and was very clearly in complete command throughout the entire game. Mike pitched ahead in the count and put in a performance on the mound that would do Tom Seaver proud.

Tom has told me more than once, "The most important pitch is strike one." I agree. As a batter, I'd rather hit 1–0 than 0–1. I'd rather hit 2–0 than 0–2. A lot of pitchers in today's game fiddle around too much, fall behind in counts, and as a result, they get themselves an early shower.

Consider Pelfrey's counterpart, Braves starter Jair Jurrjens. Jurrjens is having a terrific year, but in the first inning of tonight's game, he got Jose to ground out; gave up a hit to Argenis; got Wright on a ground-out; and then, with two outs, Jurrjens walked Delgado and Beltran back to back to load the bases. He pitched to both Carloses as if it were late in a tight game instead of the first inning.

I know that Delgado and Beltran can each strike fear into the hearts of hurlers, but pitchers should never pitch afraid. If Delgado or Beltran were to take him deep, the score would have been only 2–0—by no stretch the end of the world with eight innings of baseball left and plenty of time for the Braves' offense to mount a comeback.

So what happened next? Murphy followed with a base hit up the middle for two runs. Tatis singled for another run, and then the Braves made two costly errors. The floodgates opened, and the Braves were out of it early. Walks almost always find a way to score.

From the booth, I constantly see pitchers get cute or pitch scared. It's one of the main differences in the game today from when I played. I cannot begin to estimate the number of times I have seen pitchers going into the ninth with big leads, then throwing 3–2 sliders trying to trick hitters, and often winding up with a walk instead. It's no wonder they get themselves in trouble. That kind of stuff drives me crazy.

Tonight, Jurrjens had only himself to blame. I hope that Jurrjens will learn something from this start. I am sure that Roger McDowell, my former 1986 teammate and current Braves pitching coach, will have a little chat with his young pitcher tomorrow.

Replay

I am against replay in baseball. Gary Cohen likes it but only for judging home-run calls. In some of the new parks, it is tough to determine what is and what is and isn't a home run because of advertising placards on the fence and quirky ball-park configurations. Minute Maid Park in Houston has its home run boundary in the middle of a high wall in left-center. If a ball hits above the line, it bounces back into the playing field. This is a very tough call for umpires as well as for the announcers in the booth. Other stadiums don't have clear lines of distinction at the top of the fence to make it easier to see whether a ball bounced off a fan's hands in the stands or whether it should legitimately be in play. This could be easily rectified with some solid paint to make it as clear as possible when a ball is a home run and when it's in play. It shouldn't be necessary to stop the game and send the umpires off somewhere to watch TV. This measure not only slows down the game, but it also opens up a Pandora's box of demands for using replay to determine other calls. And that would make the already slow game of baseball drag even more. An average of three hours per game, as it stands now, is plenty long enough.

I don't like it when umpires have a town meeting and overrule calls. This happens much more than it used to. If one umpire has a better angle on the play than the ump who originally made the call, fine; it should be overturned. But I've seen instances where a first-base umpire comes all the way across the field to reverse a call down the left-field line when the ump closest to the play got it right. Umpires were much more decisive in my day.

Another difference today is the much smaller strike zone. I've noticed recently that umps are starting to call the inside strike more—and they need to. As I've said before, everything in today's game is in the favor of the hitter. If umpires are going to make the strike zone smaller, then they must give the pitcher the inside corner—they simply *have* to. Ask any pitcher, if he had the choice of getting the high strike or the inside corner, I guarantee you that he will opt for the inside strike. If a pitcher can't pitch inside, then he's in big trouble—no matter which era or ballpark he is pitching in.

AUGUST 21, 2008

After winning the first two games against the Braves, the Mets send out Pedro Martinez to try to complete the first sweep of the Braves at Shea since 2003. Pedro is not overly sharp with his pitches, but he is economical. He pitches into the eighth inning and leaves after allowing a leadoff hit and passing the 100-pitch mark. Luis Ayala, in his second game since joining the Mets, puts out a fire in the eighth and throws a scoreless ninth. Carlos Delgado completes a five-hit night as well as the sweep when left fielder Omar Infante butchers his line drive and David Wright dives across the plate with the winning run for the Mets' ninth win in 10 games and their 18th victory in their last 23 games at Shea.

Mets announcers Keith Hernandez and Ron Darling have the best view in the house. They spend the last few innings broadcasting from directly behind home plate while Gary Cohen works from the booth.

Mets 5, Braves 4. Record 71–57; 1 game ahead of Philadelphia.

Sweep on the Down-Low

In the course of this season, Ronnie and I have each broadcast games from the lower-level field box seats, but we did these broadcasts solo. This time we sat down there together. Our seats were in the first row, right behind home plate. These are some great seats. I would much rather sit down here than in the booth. It's certainly a far cry from calling the game on top of the Washington Monument in D.C.!

Jerry Manuel has kept his bullpen on a short leash. He does not have a lot of confidence in this bullpen, even though they have been pitching well overall during the winning streak. He has made the executive decision to take his starters as deep as he can into games. He proved his intentions when he let Pedro pitch into the eighth inning against the Braves, in spite of his age and all of his injuries. I was shocked by that, but the starters have responded, offering up two complete games this week. The Mets had only two complete games all of last *year*, and both of those were rain-shortened wins that didn't go past six innings.

This is without doubt the worst Braves team of the Bobby Cox era. In the first game of the series, Atlanta's bullpen

The Mets mob Carlos Delgado after his liner glances off the glove of Atlanta left fielder Omar Infante in the bottom of the ninth. It gave him a 5-for-5 night and the Mets a 5–4 win to sweep the Braves at Shea.

coughed up the lead in the eighth. The following night, the starter walked the bases full in the first, the defense made two critical errors, and the game was essentially out of the team's reach after the first inning. Tonight, the Braves threw a ball away in the seventh inning to allow the tying run to score, and they botched a line drive that brought in the winning run in the bottom of the ninth. This team in no way resembles the Braves I've been accustomed to seeing here all these years. They dialed it in with the Mets this week; it was as if they could hardly wait to leave.

The Mets scored early again to go up 3–1, fell behind by one, tied it in the seventh on an error, and them won it in the ninth to finish the sweep. Left fielder Omar Infante butchered a play that allowed David Wright to score the winning run. If Infante had caught the line drive off the bat of Carlos Delgado, as he should have, David Wright would have been doubled up at second base to end the inning. Instead, David got caught in no-man's-land, not knowing what to do, but ended up heading home to score after the misplay in left field. The Mets are sizzling, and whenever a team is hot, it usually catches the breaks.

AUGUST 24, 2008

The suddenly surging Astros team beats the Mets for the second straight day, hitting two home runs off Pedro Feliciano in the tenth inning. Although the climax of the game is a downer, the Sunday matinee started on a upnote. The Shea Countdown, the numbers displayed in center field counting the games remaining at the 44-year-old home of the Mets, goes to 17. Who better to do the honors than Keith Hernandez, without a doubt the best of the 33 Mets to have worn No. 17?

Astros 6, Mets 4. Record 72–59; ½ game ahead of Philadelphia.

No. 17, Come on Down

It was nice to pull down my number today. I wasn't about to cry or get sentimental over it, but it was fun.

People ask me all the time why I chose No. 17 when I joined the Mets. I wore No. 37 in St. Louis for 8½ years, and won my first World Series with 37 on my back. Throughout my entire life in baseball, going all the way back to Little League, I always wore a jersey with No. 7 on it because I was a Mickey Mantle fan growing up. I was born on his birthday, too: October 20th. *That* would make a kid in the 1950s a Mickey Mantle fan! October 20th is Juan Marichal's birthday, too. It is a pretty good day for baseball players to be born. When Mantle retired, I stopped rooting for the Yankees. Growing up in the San Francisco Bay Area, I was a National League guy, not an American League guy. When Mantle was winding down his career, the future Oakland A's were still in Kansas City; San Francisco was a one-team town in those days.

As a kid, I was both a Cardinals and a Yankees fan, but I was a Cardinal fan first. In 1964, when the Yanks and the Cards faced each other in the World Series, I rooted for St. Louis—and the Cards won! It was a great World Series. My school played the radio broadcast of Game 4 at Yankee Stadium for us, and I remember jumping for joy when Ken Boyer hit that grand slam off Al Downing, which was the turning point in the series. I was 11 years old; I never dreamed that Ken Boyer would be my manager one day.

I was never in love with No. 37 when I played in St. Louis, but how I came to wear it is an interesting story. As a call-up in 1974, I was given No. 18 by longtime Cardinal clubhouse man Butch Yatkeman. (Butch started working for St. Louis back in 1924.) In those days, a rookie took the number he was assigned whether he liked it or not, and I certainly was not going to tell the crusty Yatkeman that I wanted a different number because I had always worn a 7.

The next year I was allowed to pick my own number, but veteran All-Star Reggie Smith wore No. 7, so that was out of the question. The Cardinals had retired 17 in Dizzy Dean's honor, 27 was worn by veteran outfielder Mike Anderson, and 47 belonged to Lynn McGlothen, a veteran starting pitcher. I certainly did not want No. 57, which was my first number when I was an invitee in spring training in 1974. That number is better suited for a middle linebacker in the NFL. So there wasn't much choice if I wanted a number with a 7 in it—my best option as a Cardinal was No. 37, and I took it.

When I was traded to the Mets, I knew that No. 37 had been retired for Casey Stengel, and I was happy to take No. 17 instead. I have always liked 17 better than 37, anyway. I often joke about all of the Mets who have been assigned No. 17 since I left the team in 1989. It's up to 15 players now, but who's counting? One thing that makes me very happy is that some of my former Mets teammates wore that number later in their careers to honor me. David Cone switched from 44 to 17 for his last two years as a Met, and my '86 Mets team-mates Ron Darling, Roger McDowell, and Bob Ojeda all wore No. 17 on other teams after leaving the Mets. That tribute means a lot to me.

AUGUST 25, 2008

The Mets beat the Astros to split the four-game series. Ryan Church, after appearing in just seven games since June 6 due to lingering effects from his second concussion of the year, starts three games in the Houston series and hits 5-for-12. Carlos Delgado, following his fourth multi-homer game of the season, comes out for a curtain call—something he didn't do back in April, at a time when Mets fans were doing a lot more booing than requesting encores. "I didn't think it was the right time [then]," Delgado says in the Daily News. "Six RBIs, a couple of homers. I think it's the right time."

Mike Pelfrey throws his second consecutive complete game, the first Met to do so since Rick Reed in 2001. The same day as Pelfrey's triumph, John Maine goes on the disabled list for the second time in a month with a bone spur on his right elbow. When asked whether he thought about removing Pelfrey, whose turn in the rotation the manager had considered skipping to keep him strong, Jerry Manuel does a complete turnaround. "You're trying to win a championship, period," Manuel said in the *Newark Star-Ledger*. "And in the course of winning a championship, there'll be some damage to some folks. That's the cost. That's the price you pay. Are you willing to pay it? Depends how much you want a championship."

The bullpen, which has a rough day Sunday, gets a chance for a breather before the Phillies series that pits two evenly matched teams who are nearly even in the standings in a taut two-game mid-week set in Philadelphia. *Mets 9, Astros 1. Record 73–59; ½ game ahead of Philadelphia.*

Mike Pelfrey emerged as a dependable major league starter in 2008. In late August and with the bullpen a shambles, he threw successive complete-game victories.

Going the Distance. Again.

Mike Pelfrey is a horse. To me, Pelfrey is developing into the future ace of this staff. He has a chance to be a Bob Gibson, a Steve Carlton—the guy you can look to when you need the big game. Mike still has to *do* it. This is his first full season, and he'll be pitching in September for the first time, right in the heat of the race when the team is really counting on him. But I think he's on the verge of very big things.

John Maine, on the other hand, is out for the second time in a month with a shoulder spur. Maine had already established himself as a quality major league starter. This year John has had health problems and control issues, but he has still won 10 games and was someone the Mets could count on. I don't know if we'll see him in a game again this year, which would be a major loss. Along with Billy Wagner, John Maine is not easy to replace in the final month of the season. Their absence bodes poorly for the Mets.

Destiny Awaits Down the Turnpike

The two-game series coming up in Philadelphia is a critical one. This is what it's all about. I liked it that Jerry Manuel was quoted in the newspapers as saying, "We've got to face it. We've got to go out there and do it." This team still has that monkey on its back from the way the 2007 season ended, and the only way to get it off is to win this division.

The Phillies have to hit in this series if they're going to beat the Mets. They have been struggling offensively as a team for quite some time. Aside from Cole Hamels, their starting pitching is suspect, but the Phillies' bullpen has been outstanding all year. Brad Lidge has been perfect: 31-for-31 in saves. They call him "Lights Out Lidge," and in his case it's not just hype.

With Wagner on the DL, Mets lefthander Pedro Feliciano will have big responsibilities in this series. Feliciano will be called upon to get two big left-handed hitting Phillies, out in Chase Utley and 2006 NL MVP Ryan Howard. I like Feliciano against these two.

The light part of the schedule is officially over for the Mets. They begin their most important road trip of the year with a half-game lead over the Phillies. They are 5½ up on the Marlins. On this trip, the Mets will play two in Philadelphia, three in Florida, and three in Milwaukee. This could be a season-defining road trip for the Mets.

The Phillies won't catch a break with their upcoming schedule either. After the Mets leave, they go on the road to play four in the Windy City against the first-place Cubs. In addition to playing in-division in September, the Phillies will also have to play four against NL Wild Card–leading Milwaukee at home.

The Mets also play in-division after they get back from Milwaukee, except for four games at Shea against the Cubs during the last week of the season. The Mets hope that they can have the division wrapped up before they have to face those tough Cubbies. I think they will get the job done.

After this two-game series, the Mets and Phillies will have only one more head-to-head confrontation in the regular season: a three-game weekend set at Shea September 5–7. They won't face each other in the remaining three weeks of the season, which is too bad. It would be great baseball if these two rivals could play one another during the last week of September.

If the Phillies are going to win the NL East, they will need their All-Star shortstop, Jimmy Rollins, to pick it up. Rollins is not having the year he had in 2007, when he won the NL MVP with a .296 batting average, 139 runs, 30 home runs, 94 RBIs, and 41 stolen bases. His offensive numbers across the board are down this year, but he got three hits to finish the Phillies' four-game sweep of the Dodgers.

The Mets were hoping to get some help from the red-hot Los Angeles Dodgers, who played four in Philadelphia over the weekend. The Phillies were swept in four earlier in the month in L.A., but they returned the favor by sweeping four from the Dodgers in this set, and they picked up two games on the Mets in the process. Instead of doing the Mets a favor, the Dodgers allowed the gap to close to a half game between the Phillies and the Mets. The Phillies are starting to hit.

Pedro Martinez gets the call in the first game of the critical series. Facing the Phillies' lineup will be Pedro's first real test since coming off the DL at the beginning of the month. If anyone can do it, Pedro can. He's not throwing hard, but he doesn't have to throw hard to win. Fans are keeping their fingers crossed.

AUGUST 26, 2008

The Mets arrive in Philadelphia a half game in front, with something to prove after falling flat there at the end of August 2007. It looks to all of the world as if this is a statement game as the Mets knock out Jamie Moyer in the third, take a 7–0 lead in the fourth, and seem to be in cruise control with Pedro Martinez on the mound. But the Phillies, who'd broken up the shutout in the fourth, smack a pair of two-run home runs off Pedro in the fifth before Brian Stokes follows with two scoreless innings. The Phils pull to within 7–6 in the eighth. After Luis Ayala retires the first two in the ninth, a broken-bat hit by Jayson Werth keeps the Phillies alive. Eric Bruntlett doubles to right, and the tying run crosses the plate as Brian Schneider can't handle a tough hop on the relay throw. Aaron Heilman tosses three scoreless innings, but Scott Schoeneweis, the last pitcher left in the bullpen, relieves in the thirteenth and allows a walk-off hit by Chris Coste, who did not even start the game yet finishes with four hits. The Phillies regain first place, and the Mets and their fans are once again in shock.
Phillies 8, Mets 7. Record 73–60; ½ game behind Philadelphia.

Philly Showdown: The Excruciating

I'm troubled by Pedro—though today is the hardest he's thrown all year. I think that he's going to have problems against good-hitting teams. Pedro just doesn't have enough stamina to maintain his command through the fifth. He was hurt by the home runs from Rollins and Howard. Both of them are pitches that Pedro wishes he could have back, big mistakes.

Even so, there were big two positives I saw in Pedro's performance today. He threw a good change-up in this outing, and more important, he had good velocity on his fastball, throwing consistently in the mid- to high 80s and even hitting 90 a few times when he needed to. Despite those two positives, and the fact he had the benefit of a seven-run lead going into the fourth, the Phillies still managed to clobber Pedro. In his heyday, Pedro used to throw in the mid-90s. My concern is that the ability to throw in the high 80s will not be good enough for Pedro any more.

The Phillies started their comeback in the fifth when reliever Clay Condrey, a career .083 hitter, led off with a double. That's right, Charlie Manuel did not pinch hit for his reliever with his boys down six runs and plenty of game remaining in which they could mount a comeback. I know that the Phillies' bullpen has been overworked lately, but for Charlie not to pinch hit for Condrey in a game of this importance is staggering to me. It is as if he were conceding the game and trying to save his bullpen for another day.

Both teams wound up using their entire bullpens in this thirteen-inning game, though Charlie Manuel was able to stretch three of his relievers over multiple innings while Jerry Manuel used four relievers to get just one out apiece.

The Phillies can rave about their bullpen, but it's getting a little worn down, especially Chad Durbin. Durbin is a hard sinkerballer who was picked up in the off-season from Detroit and has been the workhorse in that Phillies 'pen. After Philadelphia lost veteran Tom Gordon in early July, Durbin has taken on most of the heavy lifting in the second half of the season. It seems to me that he has been getting his pitches up more frequently of late, a sure sign of fatigue. Even so, Charlie Manuel still has the big trump card up his sleeve: his All-Star closer, "Lights Out" Lidge, who provides a definite edge for the Phils.

The Mets' bullpen is a different story altogether. Luis Ayala made his Mets debut a week ago, and he is now the team's closer. A pitcher the last-place Nationals thought couldn't be effective is suddenly closing for the first-place ballclub in the NL East. Wagner is hurt, Kunz isn't ready, Sanchez and Heilman aren't the same pitchers they used to be, Smith can't get out lefties, Feliciano can't get our righties, Stokes is an unknown quantity, and Schoeneweis can't be trusted. This is what Jerry Manuel has to contend with right now with his 'pen. So Ayala, the new veteran guy, gets the field promotion.

It's hard to criticize Ayala's performance in this game. He retired the first two batters in the ninth, leaving the Mets one out away from winning the opener. But Jayson Werth got a broken-bat bloop single to center, and Eric Bruntlett ripped a pinch-hit double down the right-field line. With Werth attempting to score the tying run, Easley's relay throw short-hopped Brian Schneider at the plate. Schneider was not able to handle the throw, and the ball-game was tied. Werth would clearly have been out and the game would have been over if Damion had made a better throw. Instead, the game went on into extras, and there was constant drama until the Phillies finally won it in the thirteenth against Schoeneweis.

Heilman deserves praise for throwing three scoreless innings against the Phillies. Aaron was in trouble each inning, but he pitched out of it every time. I've noticed that

Heilman seems to pitch better on the road, away from disgruntled Mets fans.

The knee-jerk reaction to tonight is to blame the bullpen once again for this loss, which leaves the game saddled with its 22nd blown save—an awfully big number for a team that is a postseason contender. But allowing three runs in almost eight innings of relief certainly isn't terrible. It pales next to the Philly bullpen's effort in this game (10 IP, one run), which leads me to put the spotlight on the Mets' offense.

The Mets' offense deserves a fair share of the blame for this loss as well. The team scored seven early runs and didn't score again after the fourth. That's nine long innings of shutout ball. The lineup's bats going silent early in games is getting as tiresome to the fans as hearing about the bullpen's shortcomings.

AUGUST 27, 2008

This time the Phillies take the early lead, and they do it against Mets ace Johan Santana. Ryan Howard's two-run home run in the bottom of the first trumps the RBI single by Carlos Delgado in the top of the inning. Jayson Werth homers to lead off the second, but Santana allows only two more hits and goes six innings before leaving for a pinch-hitter. Delgado winds up the hero of this game, though. His homer off Kyle Kendrick in the sixth draws the Mets within one run, and his two-out, opposite-field home run in the eighth off Rudy Seanez, the previous night's winning pitcher, ties the game. Carlos Beltran's infield hit knocks out Seanez and brings in closer Brad Lidge.

When Beltran steals second, Lidge walks Ryan Church to face Daniel Murphy. The rookie's double gives the Mets the lead, and Brian Schneider's opposite-field hit plates two more runs. The Mets follow the previous night's bullpen implosion with three scoreless innings from four relievers—Brian Stokes, Pedro Feliciano, Joe Smith, and Luis Ayala—to secure the win, a split in the series, and first place.

Mets 6, Phillies 3. Record 74–60; ½ game ahead of Philadelphia.

Philly Showdown: The Invigorating

Tonight's game was a complete reversal of the previous night's game. This time, the Phillies score first and the Mets shut *them* down—except for a solo home run by Werth—for the last eight innings. The Mets win, get a split of the two-game series, and move back into first place.

This is a huge swing game. The Mets came into Philly a half game up, and they leave with exactly the same lead, instead of being 1½ back and having all the talk shows and newspaper articles rant about how they can't beat Philly, how they're the same old Mets. Well, this makes five series now they've played with Philly, and this is the first time the Phillies have even managed a split. After last night (the offense falling asleep after the fourth, the big blown lead, losing in thirteen), the Mets picked themselves up and won in comeback fashion in a must-win game.

Santana gave up three runs in the first two innings. If it were a tie game or a one-run game (or an American League game with the godforsaken DH), Santana probably would have stayed in the game and shut them down the rest of the way. Instead, Jerry pinch hit for him after six innings.

This could end up being the pivotal game of the division race right here. In the last three series between these teams, the Phillies have come back to win in the ninth inning of the series opener, and the Mets have responded each time by not allowing the Phillies to win again. The Mets suffered a body blow on Tuesday and then delivered the counter-punch tonight, something they were unable to accomplish last year.

It all comes down to the bullpens, and the Mets' bullpen got the job done tonight. Stokes is throwing really well. He has impressed me. I haven't seen enough of him yet, but he throws hard, and I've watched him beginning to get his breaking ball over in the last two outings. He's definitely throwing a lot better, which is good to see.

On the other side, the Phillies find themselves with a bullpen that is crying out for a lefty to face Delgado in the eighth. Delgado came up with two outs and a one-run lead—and he's been on fire. Phillies lefty J.C. Romero had thrown three days in a row, and Charlie didn't bring him in. Charlie said he was unavailable for today's game because he pitched in the last three. Oh, really? Romero can't come in to get one big out against the team's closest divisional rival?

This is astounding to me. It was the eighth inning, and if the Phillies got out of the jam, Lidge would be in to close it out in the ninth. Because of this, the Phillies end up losing the game and splitting a series they should have swept.

Maybe Charlie was thinking ahead to that four-game series looming before the team in Chicago the next after-noon. The Mets have an off-day after this series before they play the Marlins in Miami. Charlie does not have the same luxury. The Phillies have to board a plane after this game, fly to Chicago, and then play an afternoon game after arriving late the night before. That is some tough scheduling.

After Pelfrey's second straight complete game, someone asked Jerry whether he should have taken Mike out to preserve his arm. In essence, Jerry said that extraordinary times call for extraordinary measures, and some people may get hurt. Jerry Manuel is pushing back hard against the rising tide of pencil pushers and pitch counters who decide who can or can't pitch.

In my humble opinion, there are too many people making executive baseball decisions based on computer analyses. Statistics and analysis can be helpful to a manager, but there is one unquantifiable thing that computers will never be able to read: a player's heart. Over the course of my playing days, I saw a host of great arms, with great stuff, but the pitchers themselves lacked that one intangible component. Heart, guts, *cojones*—call it what you like, but every good ballplayer needs to have it. There are a lot of talented guys who didn't make it in the big leagues because they didn't have that quality.

Getting back to that eighth inning, the veteran Rudy Seanez stayed in the game to get a big out with Delgado. (Seanez has been around the game so long, he and I were teammates when he was coming up in Cleveland.) Protecting a one-run lead, he needed only one out—but more important, he needed to keep Delgado in the park. He didn't. In fact, the worst of all scenarios happened, and Delgado hit a game-tying opposite-field home run.

Beltran followed with a squib infield hit and then promptly stole second base. Charlie Manuel called on Brad Lidge with the tying run in scoring position in the middle of an inning, an unfamiliar spot for the closer. Lidge imploded by walking Church. Murphy then hit an RBI double to break the tie. Brian Schneider followed their lead, providing the insurance with a two-run single. As fast as lightning, the Mets took the lead, and the score became 6–3.

Stoppers today are not conditioned like the savers of old, such as Rollie Fingers, Goose Gossage, or Bruce Sutter. Today's stoppers come in only in a save situation, and then for only one inning. If a closer blows a save, he does not go out to the mound again in the next inning.

I understand the philosophy behind this. When guys like Fingers and Gossage came in with runners on base and a game on the line, there was really no margin for error. They had to come in from the very first pitch with everything they had. In Goose's case, that everything would have been the ability to throw the ball 100 miles per hour.

If a closer is brought in to start the inning, it is less stressful on the pitcher, psychologically as well as physically. If a closer comes in to start the ninth with a two- to three-run lead, he should be able to get the job done. I agree with today's approach to closers since it helps preserve their arms, but there are times when a team *needs* an important out in the eighth from its best reliever.

This doesn't happen anymore in baseball, and it didn't happen in this particular game. I do not wish to denigrate the hard work and accomplishments of today's closers, but stoppers of this era simply aren't mentally conditioned to handle the kind of situation that Brad Lidge faced today. It has been argued that the average save today doesn't not carry the same weight as it did in the past. One exception to this argument would have to be Mariano Rivera of the New York Yankees, who has been nothing short of outstanding throughout his long career as a closer, particularly in post-season play.

But I have digressed. *This* game is all about Carlos Delgado.

Most Valuable Delgado

Delgado should be considered as a candidate for MVP. If the Mets win the division and Delgado keeps playing like this through September, and he could be the Mets' first NL MVP. At this point in the season, no clear front-runner has emerged in the National League. In Delgado's last 57 games, he has 58 RBIs and 19 homers; he has had the National League lead in both of those categories for more than two months. He has accomplished this after his terrible start. Heading into the last Friday in June, Carlos was hitting only .229 with 11 homers and only 35 RBIs. This is a truly amazing turnaround.

There are several worthy MVP candidates this year: Ryan Braun, Albert Pujols, Ryan Howard, and Chase Utley among them. The Cubs are having a great season as a team, but there is no one player having an MVP year on that club.

With his two-month surge, Delgado has officially thrown his hat in the ring. He hit a truly clutch home run against the Phillies, one in a very long line of clutch hits he has delivered

Carlos Delgado launches one of the 27 home runs he hit after June 27. He wound up with 38
homers for the year.

since early July. The Mets have to win the division for Carlos to have a chance at the award, but without doubt Carlos is the Mets' MVP. This would have been a very different season without him. I have said earlier that Jerry has created a new mentality in this ballclub. It started on day one of his tenure with Jose Reyes' first at-bat in Anaheim. Jerry is communicative and honest, and he doesn't care about hurting feelings in order to inspire the highest level of performance from his players. Jerry intends to win this division, and he's going to do it his way.

Lost in the shuffle in the two-game split in Philadelphia is Ramon Castro's lingering leg injury, which forces him onto the disabled list. Infielder Argenis Reyes, whose slump has taken him from a .302 average at the start of month to .250 after the Philly series, has lost his job at second base. Damion Easley has been playing regularly again—he had four hits in the extra-inning loss to the Phillies—and Luis Castillo is back again after missing 30 games with hip and leg ailments. Pitcher Nelson Figueroa returns after starting the season in New York and spending almost all summer in New Orleans. (He will take the injured John Maine's spot on the staff, but another pitcher will be recalled to take Maine's start—speculation is that it will be Jon Niese.) Catcher Robinson Cancel, also on the Zephyr yo-yo between the majors and minors, returns to the big club.

AUGUST 29, 2008

The Mets follow their big comeback in Philadelphia by looking flat in their first 8⅔ innings at Florida. A Jose Reyes error, just his second since July 20, sets up a second Florida run. That looks as if it might hold up as the Mets can't cash in on opportunities in the seventh and eighth. Kevin Gregg has two outs and none on in the ninth when Luis Castillo singles, David Wright singles, and Carlos Delgado is hit by a pitch. Carlos Beltran then steps in and crushes the first pitch for a grand slam. Beltran accounts for all five runs in the game for New York, and the Mets need every one.

Luis Ayala allows four hits in the bottom of the ninth, including Jorge Cantu's double, which makes it a one-run game with pinch runner Alfredo Amezaga holding at third as Daniel Murphy gets the ball in quickly and keeps his footing despite the wet, chewed-up turf. (The University of Miami played its football home opener there the previous night.) Wes Helms grounds out for the final out, and the Mets take a two-game lead on the Phillies, who drop the first two games in their series with the Cubs.

Mets 5, Marlins 4. Record 75–60; 2 games ahead of Philadelphia.

Beltran's Big Night

Beltran got a cripple pitch down the middle. I think he surprised everyone, myself included, by swinging at the first pitch. Over the course of his four years as a Met, I have seen Carlos take a first-pitch strike countless times in that situation. In fact, just before the first pitch was delivered, I said in the talkback to my producer, Gregg Picker, in the truck, "If he takes a first-pitch strike, I'm going to explode." And he didn't. Carlos got a fat pitch, a hanging split-finger, and he hit it a country mile. It was a tremendously clutch shot deep into the right-field seats.

Maybe this is the beginning of a great finish to the season for Carlos, something the New York Mets will need if they are going to win this thing. Beltran hits behind Delgado in the batting order, and I guarantee you one thing: with NL pitchers pitching carefully to Delgado, Beltran is going to have a lot of opportunities to drive in runs down the final stretch. Right-handed pitchers in particular are going to walk Delgado, because the switch-hitting Beltran has not been swinging a great bat from the left side for quite some time. He has admitted this publicly in the papers, saying that he has felt better from the right side all year long. That homer off Kevin Gregg in tonight's first inning was from the left side, so perhaps that will get him going from that side of the plate.

We still have to see what this team does at home in September; there is only one more road trip after this one. This team has been less comfortable playing in front of the home folks; they tend to play tight at Shea.

Florida started this three-game series six games back. The Marlins are hanging on by a thread. After this series, there remains a month to play, and Florida cannot afford to lose any more ground to Philadelphia and the New Yorkers. They really need to take two out of three from the Mets, or, better yet, get a sweep. If they lose two of three or get swept by the Mets, it will be all over for Florida.

This first-game loss is a devastating one for the Fish. In the ninth, they were one out away from not only winning but closing the deficit to five games. Now they are seven back—a two-game swing with time running out. Kevin Gregg took two losses on Florida's last road trip, and tonight's is the ugliest loss yet for them.

Mets reliever Luis Ayala wasn't pretty in this game, either. He got hit all over the park again. His groin is bothering him, and it seems obvious to anyone paying attention that it is affecting his performance. Once again Mets fans have another nail-biter, this one featuring a game-saving play by the rookie in left field. Murphy made a very nice play in left, cutting off a double down the right-field line by Jorge Cantu to prevent the speedster Alfredo Amezaga from scoring the tying run from first. With tying and go-ahead runs in scoring position, Ayala induced Wes Helms to ground out to end the game at last.

The Mets are getting it done in grand fashion. These are the kind of wins that uplift ballclubs down the stretch. Since the Pittsburgh series when the schedule toughened up, the Mets have gone 7-3. They still have five tough games remaining on this road trip, two in Florida and three in Milwaukee, before the three-game weekend series against Philadelphia at Shea. We also learned that the Mets will miss Josh Johnson in this series as well as CC Sabathia in Milwaukee. How fortunate for the New York Metropolitans, who need to play .500 on this trip at the bare minimum. Anything above that is gravy.

The Phillies have two more tough games in Chicago after losing the first two in Chi-town. They then move on to Washington for three. At this stage of the season, with the pennant race so close, Philly must not let the Nationals ambush them if they are to maintain their lead; taking two of three from the Nats would be acceptable for them, at the very least. The Fightin' Phils need to stay with or pick up ground on the Mets before their big showdown at Shea.

During that bloodbath of a two-game series against the Mets, an already overtaxed Philadelphia bullpen was pushed even closer to the limit and then moved on to Chicago without luxury of an off-day like the Mets had. In the first game at Wrigley, the Phillies took a 4–1 lead into the eighth behind another great performance by Cole Hamels. Hamels was lifted after the seventh, and then the exhausted Philly 'pen coughed up the lead. That's a game in which the manager should have gone to Hamels and said, "Close it out, son, or at least give me one more inning" and at the very least gotten the ball to Lidge. All you longtime Mets fans, can you imagine if Davey Johnson had pulled Dwight Gooden out in the seventh in a game of this magnitude? You would have hung Davey up on the highest oak tree in Flushing!

Philly lost the second game in Chicago this afternoon, and the Mets have a two-game lead for the NL East crown. With two games still to play this weekend against those Cubbies, Philadelphia could be in trouble in the Windy City.

AUGUST 31, 2008

After a disheartening loss on Saturday night (Aaron Heilman walked four batters, two intentionally, and forced in the winning run in the bottom of the ninth), the rubber match of the three-game set in Miami has Pedro Martinez pitching on Sunday. Florida scores twice off Pedro in the first, but the Mets get

solo home runs from Carlos Beltran, Nick Evans (his first major league home run), and David Wright. Even after the Mets score three times in the seventh, they still use five relievers to finish off the Marlins. Jose Reyes makes a diving catch to end the game for Brian Stokes with two runners aboard.
Mets 6, Marlins 2. Record 76–61; 1 game ahead of Philadelphia.

Sunday Spin

Pedro pitched well against a team with a strong lineup, and Brian Stokes also threw well in this game. Jerry is now using the bullpen often, particularly in situations where they match up well against their opponents. It has become commonplace to see Jerry use three relievers in a inning, sending each one to get specific outs.

Stokes has been an unsung Mets hero. He has provided the team with journeyman-like middle relief. A former starter, Brian is a true middle-reliever, someone who can come in and go two, three, or four innings. He throws hard but his fastball is straight as a string. He doesn't have great command of his breaking stuff, and his changeup is a work in progress. Still, he has had what it takes to get the job done for the Mets.

Using Stokes only once through the lineup is perfect. That's what Whitey Herzog did with Jim Kaat on our 1982 World Champion St. Louis Cardinals team. Kaat was in his forties then and in the waning days of a Hall of Fame–caliber career. Jim didn't throw hard anymore, but he was a sinker/slider, control pitcher. This is the rationale behind using someone like Kitty or like Brian: if a pitcher with marginal stuff goes once through the lineup only once, hitters don't have the chance to zero in on him by facing him a second time. That strategy worked well for us in 1982, and it is working well with Stokes for the 2008 New York Mets.

The Mets won yet another rubber match in Florida on Sunday. Taking two of three from the Marlins enables the Mets to cling to a one-game lead over Philly as they begin the final month of the season. This series has cost the Marlins dearly. They have fallen seven back with the sun setting rapidly on their horizon. And those Atlanta Braves are a distant fourth place, 17 games behind and on the verge of another season without postseason play.

August has been another good month for the Mets, who had another 18-win month (18–11) after starting August with three straight losses at Houston.

Twenty-five games now remain to be played, a friendly 15 at home and only 10 on the road. The toughest stuff lies ahead. Looming is the ugly month of September. Mets fans already know more than they care to about what Septembers can bring.

Chapter 8

SEPTEMBER

SEPTEMBER 1, 2008

The Brewers, leading the NL wild-card race, have played solid ball for the first five months of the season, but they ended August with controversy in Pittsburgh. Prized acquisition CC Sabathia is unsuccessful bare-handing a ball hit back to the mound in the fifth inning at PNC Park Sunday. The official scorer rules it a hit, and Sabathia winds up with a one-hitter. As the Mets hit Milwaukee, the Brewers soon find that they have bigger worries than an official scorer's decision.

Pitcher Ben Sheets thoroughly dominates the Mets on Labor Day, but he comes out of the game after the fifth inning with tightness in his left groin. Sheets is still in line for the win as the seventh inning begins. Milwaukee holds a 2–0 lead, and Johan Santana is pulled for a pinch-hitter. A bases-loaded wild pitch by Mitch Stetter puts the Mets on the scoreboard, but he gets out of the jam. Stetter is one of 10 Brewers called up with the expanded rosters—a call-up to arms that the Mets will match with their own 10 brought up from New

Orleans. The Met of the day is Carlos Delgado, who hits a two-run home run off Eric Gagne in the eighth, despite the glare and encroaching shadows at home plate. Ryan Church drives in a key insurance run for the second straight day, and the Mets' bullpen holds off the Brewers to maintain first place.
Mets 4, Brewers 2. Record 77–61; 2 games ahead of Philadelphia.

Extras

The bench overflows with reinforcements. Baseball rules allow major league clubs to expand their rosters after the minor league season ends, allowing each team to have up to 40 players available for play during the last month of the season. It's nice to add a third or fourth catcher, but the true advantage lies in being able to add a multitude of pitchers for September.

In Milwaukee, Gary and I have an on-air discussion about whether September call-ups are fair—and if not, why not? Gary recalls the strong opinion of Bobby Valentine. The former Mets manager was dead-set against it and is on the record stating that because a manager goes the first five months of a season with only a 25-man roster, he should not have the luxury down the stretch of adding additional arms.

Granted, a manager on a contending team is not likely to use young call-ups in tight September games, but he would very well use them in blowouts. Whether his team is winning or losing, he could bring in one or more call-ups to finish a game. A game could be a blowout by the fifth or sixth inning, in which case a manager could use young kids to gobble up the remaining three to four innings instead of the relievers he has leaned on heavily all season. Having a team in contention in the middle of August may lead a manager to use his bullpen less judiciously, knowing that relief (in every sense) is on the way for September.

One could argue that every team has an equal opportunity to make additions to its roster, so the system is therefore an equitable one. If one examines it more closely, however, this does not prove to be the case. Perhaps one contending team's weakness has been starting pitching, and therefore that team's bullpen has been more overworked than the other contender's 'pen. Perhaps one manager has managed his pitching staff better than another. The use of September call-ups negates much of what the latter manager has accomplished and levels the playing field for the former. I agree 100 percent with my good friend Bobby Valentine's stance on this subject.

Regardless of his opinion or mine, September call-ups are here to stay, and the Mets' 2008 call-ups have arrived in the clubhouse. A total of six new arms have been added to the pitching staff. Among the new additions are two veteran pitchers, each of whom is older than Pedro Martinez: Al Reyes, a right-hander, and Ricardo Rincon, a lefty. The Mets also re-call Carlos Muñiz and Brandon Knight, both of whom were with the team earlier in the season. To many, the most interesting call-ups to observe will be the Mets' top two pitching prospects, Jonathan Niese and Bobby Parnell.

I mentioned earlier that Jerry has been using his bullpen differently of late. He has been mixing and matching in his overworked and much-maligned 'pen. A glaring flaw in this Mets bullpen has forced Jerry to take this tack. That serious shortcoming has led to all of the pitching changes Jerry has made late in games, such as using three pitchers in one inning to get three separate hitters out.

Scott Schoeneweis and Pedro Feliciano are the lefties in the Mets' bullpen. Both of them get left-handers out fairly well, but they definitely have trouble against right-handed hitters. The right side of the 'pen consists of Nelson Figueroa, Brian Stokes, Aaron Heilman, Duaner Sanchez, Joe Smith, and Luis Ayala. Because Figueroa and Stokes are middle relievers, I will leave thme out for the purpose of this discussion. I am concerned only with the relievers Jerry calls upon from the sixth or seventh inning on.

Joe Smith and Aaron Heilman have been tough on right-handed hitters, but they struggle woefully against lefties. Because of his devastating change-up, Duaner Sanchez gets lefties out, but he has issues against right-handers; Luis Ayala can't get lefties out, and he is tougher on righties. Therefore the Mets are lacking a "crossover pitcher," which is modern baseball parlance for someone who can get both lefties and righties out. Ideally, a team would prefer to have several crossover pitchers in the bullpen; the 2008 Mets have none.

Manuel has found a way to optimize his bullpen in spite of its inadequacies, but the burning question in Met fans' minds is how long the bullpen will be able to withstand this constant usage. It doesn't matter whether a reliever takes the mound every day. Daily warm-ups in the 'pen take their toll on a pitcher's arm as well. If Manuel has to continue employing this strategy day after day to win games, will the bullpen pitchers even able to wipe their proverbial rear ends by the last two weeks of the season?

SEPTEMBER 2, 2008

One of the September call-ups, Jonathan Niese, makes his major league debut in Milwaukee. He allows a leadoff home run to Rickie Weeks, but he settles down and has a 5–1 lead when the Brewers erupt with five straight hits and chase him from the game in the fourth. Nelson Figueroa comes in and allows the game-tying hit, but J.J. Hardy tries to score on the hit, takes too wide a turn around third, makes a bad slide into the plate, and is tagged out by Robinson Cancel. Later, Weeks, enjoying a four-hit night, makes a poor slide and is thrown out by Endy Chavez trying to take second on a hit down the left-field line. An error by Milwaukee on a sacrifice bunt brings Daniel Murphy all the way to third on the play and sets up a go-ahead sacrifice fly by Chavez in the tenth inning. The bullpen holds the Brewers scoreless for the final six innings.
Mets 6, Brewers 5. Record 78–61; 2 games ahead of Philadelphia.

Defense Worthy of Praise

The team continues to play good baseball. They hit and they use their speed, putting pressure on their opponents' defense. The Mets made only one error during this entire trip. With Church back in right field, the defense has improved greatly. Credit also belongs to Nick Evans and Daniel Murphy, both of whom are doing a great job in left field, not their natural position.

The 2008 Brewers typify what Milwaukee teams have always been: an old-fashioned American League team with good hitting, team speed, and lots of power but too many guys who strike out a lot and bad defense—and they don't run the bases very well either. In addition, the Brewers suffer from mediocre pitching. Even though Milwaukee has been incredibly hot lately, I am not impressed.

In the second game, Milwaukee had a chance to take the lead in the fourth after knocking out rookie Jonathan Niese, making his major league debut. With the bases loaded and one out, Corey Hart hit a single to center that brought in Rickie Weeks with the tying run. J.J. Hardy tried to score on the play from second but took a wide turn rounding third base. Beltran's great throw to Cancel was right on the money, Hardy was out for poorly executing a hook slide, and the Brewers lost a chance to take the lead 6–5.

At that point in the game, eight Brewers had come to bat in the fifth, and only one failed to reach base. They did score four to tie, but Hardy's bad base running was the saving grace for the battered Nelson Figueroa, relieving for Niese. Weeks repeated that same hook slide in the eighth and killed any chance of a Milwaukee rally when the strong-armed Endy Chavez threw him out at second as he tried to stretch a single into a double with one out.

The Mets' outfield defense has improved with Church back on the field. Chavez was inserted late in this game, and along with Beltran and Church—all three of them have strong and accurate arms—there is not a better defensive outfield in baseball. Defense helped win this game.

The Brewers did not score again, as the Met bullpen shut them down in the next six innings. The Mets did not score until the top of the tenth, when the winning run came in on Endy Chavez's sacrifice fly. This game could have very easily been a 6–5 Brewer win, but instead the score was reversed in New York's favor. The Mets will take it.

In a game where Jerry used 20 players, the Mets improved their road record to 37–36, climbing over the .500 mark for the first time since early April.

SEPTEMBER 3, 2008

The Mets score six times in the first—including a Ryan Church grand slam—and have the lone lopsided win of their excellent 6–2 trip against three teams. Oliver Perez has a few tense moments, but Nick Evans singles in two runs in the eighth to insure the sweep and a three-game cushion with Philadelphia coming to Shea for the final time.

Mets 9, Brewers 2. Record 79–61; 3 games ahead of Philadelphia.

Road Warriors

The first game in Philadelphia at the start of this trip was an exceedingly crushing defeat and a difficult way to start an eight-game road trip against competitive teams. The way the Mets bounced back late the next day with Delgado's heroics was terrific, and then they won the following game in Miami in much the same fashion, that time with Beltran playing the hero.

After losing the middle game of the series, the Mets rebounded yet again—Pedro threw well, and the Mets took another rubber match. In the three-game sweep of the

Brewers, the first win was a come-from-behind victory, the second was an extra-inning win, and the series finale was resounding defeat.

The bullpen pitchers were also heroes on this tremendous trip. Not one Mets starter went more than 6⅔ innings, so Jerry had to call upon his bullpen early and often. In that first game in Philly the Mets used seven relievers. Granted, the game went thirteen innings, but the Mets used every guy in the 'pen. The next night, in the 6–3 win, the Mets used four. In the opener in Florida with Ollie pitching well, they used three. The next night, with Pelfrey starting, they used four. And then five were called upon the next day in Pedro's start. In the opener in Milwaukee, four. The next night in ten innings, the Mets used six relievers, then three in the last game.

Here is a look at the outstanding work done by the 'pen on this trip:

Reliever	Games on Trip	Innings Pitched
Smith	7 of 8	3⅔
Stokes	6 of 8	7⅔
Feliciano	6 of 8	2⅓
Ayala	5 of 8	5
Sanchez	4 of 8	4
Heilman	3 of 8	3⅔
Figueroa	2 of 8	3

Jerry went to the well often on this trip, but most of the time the bucket came up full. Take Brian Stokes, for example, who made his Mets debut August 9 as a starter.

Since his move to the 'pen, Stokes has been brought in 10 times, with half of those appearances requiring him to pitch multiple innings. Brian pitched in five straight games on the road trip. He's become the workhorse of this 'pen, except that they're all being worked hard. Stokes is just working the hardest.

As for the others in the bullpen, Ayala had four saves in five appearances, with one blown save. He did a terrific job and showed a lot of guts by working with an injured groin. Smith somehow missed pitching in the Saturday-night loss in Miami, but otherwise he had his card punched for every game on the trip.

The bullpen pitched really well on the road trip. The late home runs provided by Delgado and Beltran get all the press, and rightly so, but the unsung heroes in the bullpen toed the line beautifully. If the 'pen had been shelled on the road trip, then those home runs wouldn't have meant a thing. There would have been no comeback, the Mets wouldn't have had a great trip, and they wouldn't have a three-game lead over the NL East.

Ever the psychologist, Jerry said in the paper that as a result of the recent success of the mix-and-match strategy, the guys in bullpen are now "starting to feel good about themselves." What a lift it would be if the Mets can get Wagner back for the final push!

So the Mets completed a tremendous 6–2 road trip and came charging home on a tremendous high. This is the stuff that pennant-winning teams are made of. This team is energized, confident and ready to face the Phillies, who are coming in for a weekend series. The Phillies, on the other hand, come into town on a low after losing two of three in Washington. They dropped two games in the standings and fell three games behind the Mets.

The Mets catch another break with the scheduling. Because of a couple of fortuitously scheduled off-days, the Mets won't have to use a fifth starter until they play at Washington in mid-September. With Maine on the DL, this is a huge break for the Mets.

Boldly Going

Put me on the record: the Mets are going to the World Series. I've been right so far, and I didn't quit on this team when they were floundering earlier in the year. I've said they're going to win this division going away. The last week of the season won't matter, just you watch. And if I'm wrong, I'm wrong. I won't go back and cover my tracks in print.

I have seen every contender except the Dodgers, and the Mets match up well against all of them. I don't know if the Mets can *win* the World Series, but they can play with anyone in the American League this year, too. It's amazing how well this team has played under Jerry. He's got a lot of people believing.

SEPTEMBER 5, 2008

The Phillies come into Shea Stadium for the last time. The Mets have played the Phillies more often than anyone else in the history of Shea—they are the only team that has consistently been in their division—but with the Mets leading the defending NL East champs by three games, few series between the two have held more at stake. So when arguably the greatest Phillies player ever sends a message, it gets noticed.

A sheet of paper taped next to the lineup card in the Philadelphia clubhouse from Mike Schmidt alludes to the Mets fumbling a seven-game lead in September 2007. "The Mets know you're better than they are," Schmidt wrote. "They remember last year."
Phillies 3, Mets 0. Record 79–62; 2 games ahead of Philadelphia.

Blanked by Brett and Brad

With only 21 games remaining, the Phillies came to New York needing to win a minimum of two out of three. If Philadelphia drops two of three, they will fall back four; if they get swept, they will be six games behind, a nearly insurmountable deficit with 19 left to play.

The Phillies have been sputtering of late. After splitting the two-game series at Citizens Bank Park with the Mets, they traveled to Chicago for a tough four-game set, losing the first two and then showing something by winning the remaining two. Then they went to Washington, where they proceeded to drop two of three to a team that will probably lose 100 games by the time the season is done.

The Phillies could use a sweep in this series at Shea, but I don't think they're going to get it. The Mets' four starting pitchers make it difficult for any team to sweep them, particularly as a visitor. I've said it before and I'll say it again, pitching is the name of the game.

In game one, it was the Phillies who get the dominant performance from their starter, Brett Myers. Mike Pelfrey pitched a good game for the Mets, but Myers threw as fine a game as any I've seen pitched this year. He was dominant. The matchup reminded me of the golden era of baseball: two superb pitchers in complete command, resulting in a minimum of offense and a very crisp game. You don't see this often enough today.

It was hard to believe that this was the same Myers who walked four straight batters in the first inning here in July. Today he gave up only three hits in eight innings, walked two and fanned 10: a 180-degree turnaround for someone who was sent down to the minors in July.

Brad Lidge was actually hittable in the ninth, but he got out of it. He hasn't blown a save all year. The Mets had a glimmer of hope of breaking Lidge's streak before he shut the door. This Phillies win closes the lead to two games.

Schmidt Speak

The New York press tried to make a big deal out of Mike Schmidt's written exhortation to his former team. He sent a note saying that the Mets know that the Phillies are better than they are because of the way last year ended. The note was posted in the Phillies' clubhouse before game one of this series.

I see nothing wrong with an ex-Phillies Hall of Famer trying to inspire this current bunch with a rallying cry. I don't think Mike Schmidt's words have any great effect on the team, either. Nonetheless, the media ran with the story. Every effort was made by the press to encourage the rivalry between New York and Philadelphia in this close division race.

SEPTEMBER 7, 2008

Amid a crush of stories hinting at a possible repeat collapse by the Mets in 2008, the elements intervene. Tropical Storm Hanna washes out Saturday afternoon's game. A split doubleheader is slated for the next day. An afternoon game is added because a game was already scheduled for ESPN on Sunday night.

The Phillies hammer Pedro Martinez in the opener while the Mets manage just two hits in seven innings off Jamie Moyer, the same 45-year-old southpaw that they pounded for six runs and nine hits in three innings to start the last road trip. The interval between games on Sunday brings yet more bad news. Closer Billy Wagner, pitching in a simulated game at Shea in front of Mets brass, walks off in pain after only a few throws. Wagner had hoped to return to the club Tuesday, but it now appears doubtful that he will be able to pitch again in 2008. A torn medial collateral ligament and flexor pronator muscle is the diagnosis. The injury requires major surgery and one year of rehabilitation before he can pitch again.

The Mets take the field in the night portion of the twin bill with a slim one-game division lead. Johan Santana is clipped for a run in the first inning, but Carlos Delgado singles in two runs to give the Mets the lead. Delgado later hits two mammoth home runs—coming out for a curtain call for the second one—and is even lauded with chants of "MVP" after he strikes out in the seventh. Johan Santana, pitching on his own bobblehead doll night, is superb, beating Phillies ace Cole Hamels. Though this is the first series the Mets have lost to the Phillies all season—and the first time they've dropped a series at all since they were swept in Houston at the beginning of August—emerging from this head-to-head showdown with the lead is clearly a positive step for the Mets. Their record since Wagner went down is 22–10.

Phillies 6, Mets 2. Mets 6, Phillies 3. Record 80–63; 2 games ahead of Philadelphia.

Weather Lessens the Blow

Because of injuries, the Mets have been plugging infielders into corner outfield spots for most of the year. In the first game of the doubleheader, the resulting defensive deficiencies were on full display. Tatis, who has mostly played left this year, misplayed a ball in right; Reyes and Evans failed to communicate on a short fly in left. These out-of-position outfielders (Tatis and Evans, as well as Murphy, Easley, and even Anderson) have all played admirably; it is unfortunate that today's outfield miscues occurred in such an important game.

That first doubleheader game was probably the worst game the Mets have played since that 1–5 trip to Florida and Houston in early August. I don't think it would have mattered either way if those plays were successfully executed, however, because veteran pitcher Jamie Moyer followed the lead of his fellow starter Brett Myers and completely dominated the Mets with seven shutout innings. Third baseman Greg Dobbs supplied all the runs the Phillies needed with a three-run blast off Pedro Martinez in the fourth. It seemed as if the Mets were never really in it.

In view of the opening loss in the Sunday split doubleheader, Tropical Storm Hanna (formerly Hurricane Hanna) might have proved a godsend to the Mets by washing out Saturday's game. If there had been no rainout and the Phillies had beaten the Mets on Saturday, the Metropolitans would have gone home and slept on that second consecutive loss, only to wake up on Sunday morning to glut of negative media coverage. I can imagine the back-page headlines: "Collapse

Relapse," "The Choke Is On...Again." Instead, with today's split doubleheader, the Mets are spared that ignominy, and in addition they benefit from an unscheduled day off to lick their wounds and regroup after losing the opening game.

I have always maintained that doubleheaders are hard to sweep, especially on the road. Hanna's deluge may turn out to be the best thing that could have happened to the Mets, because the odds were against Philly taking both games on Sunday. I am reminded of the wonderful Elia Kazan film about middleweight champ Rocky Graziano, *Somebody Up There Must Like Me*. Today it seems as if somebody up there must be a Met fan!

Holy Moses!

Basically, today's game was *The Carlos Delgado Show*. Under a national spotlight (both ESPN and SNY broadcasted the game), Delgado had the sort of night that most players only dream of. Tied in the first inning, Carlos singled in two to give the Mets a lead they would never relinquish. He followed with two solo home runs off Cole Hamels in the third and fifth, which gave the Mets all the runs they needed to prevent a three-game sweep by the Phillies. His second home run, a bomb, represented his 33rd of the season and his 100th RBI. This marks the ninth time in Delgado's illustrious career that he has hit 30 or more home runs and driven in 100 or more runs in a season.

This night could make a big difference in the MVP voting. I have heard the argument that a player who hit only .228 during the first three months of the season should not be eligible for an MVP award. It is a valid point, but Carlos' July, August, and this first week of September have been nothing short of Ruthian. He has overcome his earlier struggles and has gone on to carry this ballclub, coming through with most of the Mets' clutch hits.

As I have said before, to have any chance at the coveted award, Carlos needs to continue being "the man" for the Mets down the stretch, and the Mets need to win the division. If those two things happen, then I don't foresee a problem with Delgado being MVP-eligible.

Delgado should also be under consideration for the NL Comeback Player of the Year. He did not have a particularly good year in 2007, but it wasn't a terrible one, either. He hit .258, with 24 home runs and 87 RBIs in 2007; however it may not be sufficiently bad for him to be eligible for Comeback Player in 2008.

The only player to have ever won both awards in the same season was Terry Pendleton, with the Atlanta Braves in 1991. Whether or not Delgado wins any award at all this season, he has certainly been this team's Moses, leading the tribe triumphantly out of Egypt.

Today had the potential to be a devastating one for the Mets. If Philadelphia had swept the Mets at Shea, it would have resulted in a tie for first place in the NL East, and the momentum would clearly have gone to Philadelphia's side. The news of Wagner's season-ending diagnosis coupled with the Phillies' two wins could have been a tsunami too large to overcome. But along with Johan Santana, Delgado took care of the situation handily.

Santana is a battler. Signing him has paid off dividends. He's 13–7 on the season, but the bullpen has cost him six wins; his last loss was in June. Having a *bona fide* ace provides an emotional lift for a team as well, since one good outing from an ace can snap a losing streak. That's what Johan did today. It was only a two-game losing streak, but the Mets were facing the possibility of a sweep by their arch rivals. They definitely wanted Johan standing on the mound and in the way of a Phillies win, and Johan delivered the goods once more for his team.

Now They'll See the Phillies Only on TV
It is a shame that these two teams won't face each other again this season. Each team can affect only its own destiny from this point forward. If the Mets continue to win, Philly can't catch them. All Philadelphia can do is keep on winning, applying pressure to the Mets, and hope for help from other teams. Who has the advantage? I would take a two-game lead with 19 left to play any day of the week. Advantage: Mets!

SEPTEMBER 10, 2008
With Billy Wagner officially gone, the bullpen approach can longer be "hold the line until the closer returns." It is now up to them and only them, the 10 pitchers who have relieved in September up to this point (plus a few others who have yet to get the chance). Since Wagner's injury to start August, the bullpen mustered a surprising 3.56 ERA, including almost 26 innings over eight games in which only one unearned run was scored off the 'pen. That ERA was sixth-best in the

Billy Wagner struggles through his press conference after learning he would miss the rest of 2008 and most, if not all, of 2009 due to surgery. Mets fans were saddened by the team's bullpen alternatives.

majors in that span, according to the Elias Sports Bureau; the Mets starters' mark of 3.31 was fifth. That changes against Washington, although the results are the same. The Mets sweep the two-game set, but they have to score 23 times to win twice, allowing 18 runs. The seven earned runs in the series opener off Oliver Perez are the most allowed since August 31, 2006, in Denver. Yet the Mets rally for a 10–8 win over the Nats.

Mike Pelfrey, staked to a 7–1 lead in the second game, barely makes it through five innings and gets in a confrontation after throwing inside to hot-headed Elijah Dukes, who later antagonizes the crowd. Aaron Heilman and Brian

Stokes each allow home runs to Cristian Guzman with men on base for the Nationals. New York and Washington score the same total (23) as the NFL teams from the same cities did in the Giants' 16–7 win over the Redskins in the season opener the previous week.

Mets 13, Nationals 10. Record 82–63; 3½ games ahead of Philadelphia.

Sluggo

The Mets outslugged the Nationals in an ugly series. Oliver Perez and Mike Pelfrey each had poor outings, rare for them, but the offense picked them up with a 23-run burst over the two-game sweep.

Perez couldn't get out of the fourth inning in the first game. He gave up seven runs, all earned, matching his April 30 season high. He retired only 10 of the 20 men he faced and gave up four consecutive hits in the fourth. Jerry Manuel had no choice but to give Perez the hook. Oliver's last 13 starts have been stellar, six innings or more in each of them. But even the best pitchers are only human; one could probably claim that Ollie was long overdue for a bad outing.

Offensively, the Mets combined for 14 hits, four of them home runs. Beltran and Church had big nights, hitting their 23rd and 12th homers respectively, but once again the main attraction was Carlos Delgado. The man is on fire! Delgado hit two more titanium home runs (numbers 34 and 35 on the year) to lead the Mets to victory. That's right—he hit four home runs, two each in two consecutive games.

This is the seventh time this year that Delgado has hit multiple home runs in a game. Let's take a look at the stark difference between Delgado's numbers from his first 81 games and his last 67 games:

Carlos Delgado	HRs	RBIs
March 31–June 26 (81 games)	11	35
June 27–Sept. 10 (67 games)	24*	69#

* most in MLB

\# most in NL

These numbers don't lie.

Washington might well have the worst pitching staff in the NL, and they did everything possible to show it tonight. Washington's pitchers gave up 13 hits and an incredible eight walks in the second game. A team that walks so many men in the course of a game will not end up winning a lot of games. On the other hand, this is the same Nationals team that beat Philly soundly in two out of three last week. Go figure.

Bullpen Angst

Everyone is talking about Delgado's chances at MVP, but bigger questions exist for the Metropolitans, particularly about the team's pitching. Can the Mets get to the playoffs with this bullpen? And if they do get there and end up facing teams in October that can hit, will the Mets' bullpen be sufficient for the challenges of the postseason?

I have a feeling that Jerry Manuel bet on his offense in this series. After all, the Nationals unquestionably have the worst pitching staff in the National League. Manuel used

Nelson Figueroa and call-up Brandon Knight early after Perez got knocked out in the opener, hoping that they could hold the line. Nelson and Brandon did their bit, and Met bats came to life to win the game. Jerry knew that he can't afford similar outings from his starters for the remainder of September; starting pitchers need to go seven innings, minimum, or else the bullpen will collapse from overwork.

The inability of the some of the starters to go deep into games has forced Jerry to rely more heavily on his bullpen than he would like. If not for September call-ups, the Mets might not be able to maintain their lead of the NL East down the home stretch. Manuel is counting on those extra arms to help ease the burden of the team's nightly reliance on the bullpen.

There are no off-days remaining over the course of the final 17 regular-season games, and there is also no John Maine. Without their fifth starter, the Mets will have to find one or more pitchers to start three of the remaining games. With Pedro struggling, Manuel is relying on both Pelfrey and Perez to put these two aberrational starts behind them and pitch as well as they ever have in each of their remaining outings.

Record Men

Today Jose Reyes officially became the Mets' all-time stolen-base leader, surpassing Mookie Wilson's record of 281. By age 25, Jose has already amassed an incredible 282 stolen bases. Reyes has remarkable talent; if he continues at this rate, Ricky Henderson's career stolen-base record will be in jeopardy in another decade.

Gary Cohen and I had a discussion on the air about how the Mets have never had one player who played the majority of his career for the team, the way Stan Musial did for the St. Louis Cardinals. To date, the only contender for this role has been Ed Kranepool, the Mets' leader for career games played. Ed holds the record for most of the Mets' career offensive categories, but he was never an everyday player; he finished the final third of his lengthy career as a pinch-hitter. As a result, a lot of all-time Mets team records for offensive numbers are relatively low and attainable.

Now the Mets have two young, star-caliber players who came up in the organization and are likely to anchor the team for years to come. Before their careers are over, Jose Reyes and David Wright will be the all-time Mets leaders in most categories. Their names will be inscribed all over the top of the team record books, and they should accomplish this while they are still fairly young. Without doubt, David and Jose are the Mets' greatest tandem in the franchise's 46-year history.

SEPTEMBER 13, 2008

The number 17 hasn't been mentioned this often at Shea Stadium since Keith Hernandez played here. There are 17 games left in the 2008 season—a grim reminder of the exact number of games remaining in 2007 when the Mets blew a seven-game lead. This correlation is not lost on the press.

The last 17 games will also be played without a break. The Mets have bene-fitted from having four scheduled off-days during a two-week span, plus two more games that were rained out. A rainout on Friday night against the Braves actually gives the Mets three days off in a five-day span. It is rescheduled for a single-admission doubleheader Saturday with a late afternoon start because it was already scheduled to be the Fox national game. Now, the season will end with 17 games in 16 days.

Johan Santana throws shutout ball for seven innings. He takes the mound for the eighth inning with a 2–0 lead, but the first two Braves each stroke singles. Santana is replaced by Scott Schoeneweis, who allows another single. Brian Stokes surrenders a two-run single and sacrifice fly. The Braves go on to beat the Mets, who had won 20 of 27 overall and had been 5–1 against Atlanta at Shea in 2008. The Mets take the nightcap behind call-up Jon Niese's eight shutout innings for his first major league win. It is the sixth doubleheader the Mets have played this season, the most twin bills for the club since 1998.

Braves 3, Mets 2. Mets 5, Braves 0. Record 83–64; 2½ games ahead of Philadelphia.

At 17

Because of Friday's rainout, the Mets played a twi-night make-up doubleheader the following day. A split double-header was not possible because Fox Sports is broadcasting the originally scheduled Saturday Mets-Braves contest as its *Game of the Week* with the first pitch to air at 4:00 PM. Nationally televised games take precedent over rescheduled games, so this game would have begun at 4:00, come hell or high water.

The Mets probably would have preferred to schedule a split doubleheader on Sunday, but negotiated labor rules stipulate that no team can schedule a makeup doubleheader on get-away day without a majority vote in favor from the players on both teams. So the Mets played an old-fashioned

Johan Santana leaves after a brilliant performance against the Braves only to have the bullpen pour gasoline on a potential win for the seventh time.

two-for-the-price-of-one doubleheader, their sixth of the year.

The Mets sent ace Johan Santana to the mound. Johan threw seven strong innings of shutout ball but was pulled in the eighth after giving up two straight base hits to lead off the inning. Santana has been unbeaten since June 28, and he left to a thunderous ovation from Mets fans. Scott Schoeneweis came in to face left-handed hitting Casey Kotchman, who promptly delivered a base hit to load the bases with no outs. Exit Schoeneweis, enter Stokes—a familiar pattern for the

Mets. Jeff Francoeur singled up the middle on the first pitch, a good fastball on the inside corner, to tie the game at 2–2. With that, the Mets' bullpen blew a lead for Johan Santana for the seventh time this season.

But the inning was not over. With runners on first and second, Josh Anderson executed a sacrifice bunt to move both runners into scoring position. Bobby Cox pinch hit the switch-hitting Greg Norton, and Jerry Manuel employed the proper strategy of walking Norton intentionally to load the bases and brought the infield in, hoping for an inning-ending double play. Up stepped Omar Infante, who hit a sacrifice fly, and in the blink of an eye, the Braves took the lead, 3–2. How much more tough luck must Santana endure?

Blown Saves for Santana

Date	Opponent	Lead	Culprit	Result
Apr. 29	vs. Pit.	4–2	Wagner	W
May 4	@ Ari.	2–1	Smith	W
June 12	vs. Ari.	4–0	Wagner	L
July 22	vs. Phi.	5–2	Feliciano	L
Aug. 2	@ Hou.	4–1	Wagner	L
Aug. 7	vs. S.D.	3–1	Schoeneweis	W
Sept. 13	vs. Atl.	2–0	Stokes	L

There was plenty of blame to go around in today's loss. The Mets had no outs with the bases loaded in the fourth, facing former Met ace Mike Hampton, and scored only two in the inning. They again loaded the bases with no outs in the sixth, and this time they came away empty handed.

Atlanta came into this game with a Major League record of 22 one-run road games in a row this year and a total of 29 dating back to August 2007. Unfortunately for the Mets and their fans, the Braves' streak ended as they hung on to deal the Mets a heartbreaking defeat.

After the painful loss, Jerry Manuel handed the ball to rookie Jonathan Niese in game two. The team was counting on young Niese to prevent a sweep. Jonathan responded to the challenge with a brilliant eight-inning shutout performance. The Mets' offense clicked. Jose Reyes, Carlos Beltran, and David Wright hit home runs, Wright, a two-run shot in the first; Jose Reyes, Beltran, and Tatis contributed three hits apiece; and the Mets cruised to an all-important split of the doubleheader. Niese was in complete control of this game, showing poise beyond his years in a tough spot.

SEPTEMBER 14, 2008

If the first game Saturday is bad, Sunday is worse. Oliver Perez looks good for seven innings, leaving with a 4–2 lead. Joe Smith makes it hold up by quelling a rally to end the eighth inning. In the ninth, Luis Ayala allows hits to the first two batters and then surrenders a three-run, pinch-hit home run by Greg Norton. The five-run ninth gives the Mets their 27th blown save of the year, the 11th squandered in the ninth inning. In the last four games, the bullpen has allowed six home runs over a nine-inning span for an ERA of 11.00. And they somehow won two of those games.

Meanwhile, the Phillies complete a four-game sweep by taking a makeup doubleheader from the staggering Brewers to cut the NL East deficit to the same number it had been a week earlier.

Braves 7, Mets 4. Record 83–65; 1 game ahead of Philadelphia.

Bloody Sunday

This Sunday brought yet another rubber match, one the Mets needed to win. Oliver Perez bounced back from his previous disappointing start by throwing seven brilliant innings before exiting the game, handing the bullpen a 4–2 lead. David Wright provided 75 percent of the offense, going 4-for-5 with two home runs (his 30th and 31st) and three RBIs.

Jerry Manuel called on Scott Schoeneweis in the eighth, and he gave up two hits in one-third of an inning. Joe Smith came in to bail out the Mets and recorded the remaining two outs without allowing either of the two inherited runners to score.

New Mets closer Luis Ayala got the call in the ninth from Jerry Manuel. Because of Billy Wagner's uncertain physical status, the Mets had traded for Luis on August 17th as insurance to bolster the back end of the New York 'pen. Ayala has spent most of his career as a set-up man; he has limited experience as a closer. In fact, over the course of Ayala's five years in the major leagues, he has been in only 24 save situations, of which he has saved only nine. In spite of this mediocre track record, not to mention his current groin strain, Luis enters this important game already having notched seven saves in eight opportunities for the Mets.

Luis faces three batters and doesn't get anybody out. The *coup de grace* comes as a pinch-hit, lead-surrendering three-run home run to Greg Norton. Luis is a gutty pitcher, but it couldn't have been a worse time for a bad outing. Once again, in a blink of an eye, the Mets' bullpen relinquished another late-game lead.

I did not like the way Luis Ayala pitched the previous game in the nightcap of Saturday's doubleheader. His pitches were ominously up, not a good sign in a sinkerball pitcher. Yesterday's struggles clearly carried over into today's game for Luis.

Feliciano relieved Ayala and promptly gave up two more Brave insurance runs on two hits and two walks. Then Stokes came in with the bases loaded and managed to stave off the Atlanta rally. But the damage had already been done during the five-run ninth inning that staggered the Mets like a right cross from Mike Tyson.

It is horribly difficult for a team to bounce back from losses like these, which, in the Mets' case, mirror last year's bullpen failures. As Yogi would say, "It's déjà vu all over again." The Mets' everyday players must be looking over their shoulders wondering what will happen next.

It must be hard for Jerry Manuel to trust anyone in this bullpen right now, but he has no choice, because today's starters seem unable to finish games. Mets fans are wondering whether the relievers are worn down from overuse, not that good, or both. It is true that the 'pen has been overworked, but to be perfectly honest, this bunch leaves a lot to be desired. I'm guessing that it's all of the above for the Met relievers.

No Love Lost

One thing is certain: the Mets are not liked around the NL East. I have asked opposing players in the division to explain the reason for the animosity toward the Mets, and, almost to a man, they take umbrage with the extravagant dancing on the field and in front of the dugout after Met home runs.

It is true that my 1986 Mets teammates and I could be arrogant with our curtain calls after home runs, but today's dancing and bumping in front of the dugout takes home run celebrations to an entirely different level. Opposing teams view this behavior as hot-dogging, and it rubs them the wrong way. I am not saying the entire team behaves this way, but it takes the actions of only a handful of players on a team to upset the opposition. Anyone who behaves that way on the playing field had better be prepared to face a determined opponent, and, more important, had better be prepared to back it up.

After the game, Chipper Jones put everything in perspective with his quote when asked by the press, "What do you take out of your last game at Shea Stadium?"

His answer? "Pride."

It is easy to read between the lines.

I Hear You Knocking...

With this Mets loss and the Phillies' four-game sweep of the faltering Milwaukee Brewers at Citizens Bank Park, the Mets now cling to a one-game division lead over the Phillies. In the wild-card race, the Fightin' Phils have tied the Brewers for the lead, with the surging Houston Astros surprising everyone by being only two games back. The Cardinals are 4½ back in third place, and the Marlins are 5½ behind in fourth. Both these teams are fading fast, however. The wild-card race is still far too close to call.

SEPTEMBER 15, 2008

The Mets lose again, this time to the Nationals. They do, however, hold a half-game lead on the Phillies in the division (one game in the loss column) and a half-game on the Brewers in the wild-card. Both teams had off-days today. Milwaukee entered the month with a 5½-game lead in the wild-card before dropping 11 of 14, starting with a three-game sweep by the Mets and ending with a four-game trouncing by the Phillies, who are now tied with the Brewers for the wild-card lead. The surging Astros can't recover from Hurricane Ike, losing two rescheduled rained-out games against the Cubs in Milwaukee of all places. The Brewers take a flyer and fire manager Ned Yost. The NL Wild Card race is a mess. *Nationals 7, Mets 2. Record 83–66; ½ game ahead of Philadelphia.*

Feeling the Heat

The Mets finish with a disappointing 4–4 homestand, one that could easily have been 6–2. If the Mets had gone 6–2 on that homestand, they would now be embarking on this seven-game road trip with a three-game lead over the Phillies and only 14 left to play. Instead, they opened a four-game set in Washington in front by only one game, up two in the loss column.

Pedro had another disappointing start for the Mets. He left the game in the sixth, behind 4–1, as John Lannan out-pitched Martinez through seven. With the game still within reach, Duaner Sanchez gave up a three-run blast to Elijah Dukes to point the Mets toward another difficult defeat.

In the eighth, down 7–2, the Mets loaded the bases for David Wright with one out. Nationals manager Manny Acta decided to leave in lefty Mike Hinckley to face David Wright. This was obviously the big out of the game, and I was stunned that Acta left Hinckley in to face Wright. Wright is hitting .376 against lefties this season, and he has been scorching the ball of late.

With a 2–0 count, David hit into an inning-ending double play. I think that Wright seemed slightly overanxious and too quick on this pitch, hitting the ball toward the end of the bat. Even though Hinckley got the out, Acta was living dangerously by keeping the left-hander in to face Wright with the Mets one clutch hit away from getting back in the game.

As a result of today's loss to the last-place Nationals combined with an off-day for the Phillies and the Brewers, the Mets now hang on to a half-game lead over Philadelphia in the division, a half-game lead over Milwaukee and Philadelphia in the wild-card, and only three over Houston.

Incredibly, to me, the Mets are now talking about simply *making* the playoffs any way they can. They should never let it enter their minds. They're still in first place in the NL East. They're in control!

The fact that the team is thinking this way gives credence to the notion that they are feeling the heat. The wild-card is second-best. Their sole focus should be on winning their division in the remaining 13 games.

The only way to get free of the burden of last year's collapse is to win the division in 2008. There would still be redemption if the Mets were to win the division and lose in the playoffs. If they back into the postseason with the wild-card, the only true redemption at that point would be to win the World Series. I simply refuse to entertain the thought of this team *not* playing in October.

The Mets can't let Philly take the lead in the division. I have the uneasy feeling that if they relinquish the lead this late, they might never get it back.

The Mets have faced every challenge in 2008 when things haven't gone their way. They fought through controversy, played for two managers, survived without a true closer, and showed incredible heart in the second half of this season. They are in front of the Phillies; the Phillies have to catch *them*. If the Mets keep on winning, the Phillies can't do that.

SEPTEMBER 16, 2008

The Mets hold a team meeting before Tuesday night's game and fall out of first place after it. Odalis Perez, knocked out by the Mets after three innings at Shea in his last start, pitches into the eighth and hands Mike Pelfrey his second 1–0 loss against the Nationals in 2008. Even worse, Fernando Tatis separates his shoulder diving for a ball during the inning that Washington scores the game's only run. He's out for the year. Damion Easley is already on the bench with a strained right quadriceps.

Nationals 1, Mets 0. Record 83–67, ½ game behind Philadelphia.
Wild Card: ½ game ahead of Milwaukee, 3 games ahead of Houston.

Good News, Bad News

The Mets played the first game in Washington with low energy. After they lost, Jerry Manuel called a team meeting before today's game. I believe Jerry's reason was not to chide the team about last night's loss but rather to voice his concern about the team's lackluster, lifeless performance that led to it.

Pedro Martinez delivers a pitch against the Nationals September 15 in the Mets' third straight loss.

There is valid reason for concern. The Mets just suffered two deflating losses against Atlanta—the kind of losses that can make a rebound difficult. Although I can't know for sure, it is my feeling that Jerry delivered a good old-fashioned pep talk to his troops prior to today's game. I have liked everything Jerry has done since taking over this ballclub, and this meeting is no exception. Difficult times like this call for words of encouragement from the manager. Unfortunately, the Mets responded to Jerry's pep talk by getting shut out 1–0 by Odalis Perez.

Aside from the loss, there is good news and bad news for the Mets in tonight's game. The good news is that Mike Pelfrey followed Oliver Perez's lead and threw a good game, going seven strong innings and allowing only one run before he was lifted for a pinch-hitter in the eighth.

Tonight's bad news is that hot-hitting Fernando Tatis separated his shoulder diving for a line drive in the fifth inning, an injury that could sideline him for the remainder of the season. Tatis got hurt in that fifth inning trying to catch a sinking line drive off the bat of Odalis Perez. Fernando charged aggressively, diving unsuccessfully for the ball and allowing Perez to coast into second with a stand-up double.

After a delay while Tatis was examined by medical personnel, Pelfrey started out by walking Willie Harris and then gave up an RBI double to recent Met-killer Cristian Guzman as Perez scored the winning run. The Mets had only two opportunities to score in this game, in the sixth and eighth innings. In the sixth, with two runners on, Wright hit a bullet to left, which was momentarily misjudged by Willie Harris. Harris quickly adjusted and made a remarkable diving catch to end the threat. In the eighth, with one out, two Met pinch-hit singles fell by the wayside as Reyes and Church failed to deliver.

Fernando Tatis' separated shoulder is yet another in the long line of injuries the Mets have suffered this year. Tatis has had a tremendous comeback year until tonight's game. He has played a significant part in the Mets' offensive resurgence since late May, when he was first inserted into the starting lineup. The team will miss his contributions. His injury tonight will put the onus on two young rookies, Daniel Murphy and Nick Evans, whose playing time should now increase in the final two weeks of the year.

The Mets have lost four of their last five, including three consecutive losses. This Met losing streak has enabled the Phillies to take the lead in the NL East. I expressed concern earlier about the implications if the Mets were to lose their lead in the East. Contrary to my previous prediction that the Mets would win the division handily, it now looks as if this race is going to go down to the wire.

SEPTEMBER 17, 2008

The Mets regroup as the offense unloads, but the bullpen loads it up for the Nats. The Mets use eight pitchers before finally subduing Washington in the third game of the four-game series. Carlos Beltran homers twice and makes a running catch in the deepest part of Nationals Park, robbing Ryan Zimmerman with two men on in the eighth. A David Wright error in the ninth, however, helps the Nationals plate two unearned runs before Luis Ayala finally ends it. It is the third time in a week that the Mets have beaten last-place Washington despite allowing seven runs or more.

Mets 9, Nationals 7. Record 84–67; ½ game behind Philadelphia.
Wild Card: ½ game ahead of Milwaukee.

The Carlos Beltran Show

Carlos Beltran took the field in tonight's game with a look in his eyes that I recognize but one that I do not recall seeing on his face before. Tonight he was a man on a mission, and that mission was to stop the losing streak and get this club back on the winning track.

He played one of the best games a major leaguer could hope to play, certainly the greatest game I have ever seen *him* play as a New York Met. He had a great night at the plate, going 2-for-3, scoring twice, hitting two home runs (his 25th and 26th) and driving in three. Beltran did everything tonight, winning the game almost singlehandedly. But this is not the full measure of Beltran's contributions to this game: he also exuded a level of determination, leadership, and willfulness to win that I have not previously observed in this future Hall of Famer.

Reyes also had a big night, getting on base three times and scoring twice. He hit his 15th home run and stole his 50th and 51st bases. As usual, Jose catalyzes team.

The vacant fifth spot in the pitching rotation came up once again in this game. Veteran Brandon Knight landed in the seat tonight in Jerry's ongoing game of musical chairs. After a shaky start, Knight settled down nicely. He left the game after five innings with the Mets ahead 7–2, hoping to get his first Major League win at age 32, but the bullpen made him sweat it out. The apparent blowout against the last-place Nationals turns into another nail-biter. Jerry Manuel used seven relievers before Luis Ayala turned away a ninth-inning Nats rally, ending the losing streak and allowing the Mets to keep pace with the red-hot Philadelphia Phillies.

SEPTEMBER 18, 2008

The Mets eke out another win against the lowly Nationals, but it's anything but easy as they approach the season's end. With only 10 games remaining, every outing is crucial.

Mets 7, Nats 2. Record 85–67; ½ game behind Philadelphia.
Wild Card: 1½ games ahead of Milwaukee.

Lucky 14

This game was all Johan Santana and Brian Schneider. Schneider's two home runs led the offensive charge to dominate the Nationals early in the game. Johan was in complete command on the mound, and strong run support from his teammates allowed him an easy outing. Santana cruised to his 14th victory.

Most important, with 10 games remaining, the Mets stayed a half-game behind the Phillies, who are riding a seven-game winning streak. With this win, the Mets also took a 1½ game lead over the fading Brewers in the wild-card race.

There is valid cause for concern regarding the Mets' offense. Church, Delgado, and Wright did not swing the bat well during the four games at Nationals Park. Jerry Manuel's experiment with playing the slumping Argenis Reyes (currently 0-for-24) at second base has come to an end, as Jerry announced that Luis Castillo will play second for the remainder of the season.

More troubling is the lack of productivity from Wright, Delgado, and Church. Here are their stats for the four-game series in Washington:

	Hits-At Bats	Strikeouts	LOB
Wright	1-18	7	10
Church	3-15	5	7
Delgado	3-16	5	4

The Mets desperately need these three key players to hit as well as they ever have if the team is to make it to the postseason.

Fortunately for the Mets, Carlos Beltran, Jose Reyes, Brian Schneider, Brandon Knight, and Johan Santana pick up the slack over the final two games. The Metropolitans showed me something by bouncing back and gaining the split in Washington.

The Onus on Wright

David came into this Washington series red hot. He was 12-for-19 with four home runs in his last five games. For whatever reason, overnight David looked as if he has never swung a bat before in his life. One of the great mysteries of the game is when, how, and why a player can go into a slump. A player can be on a hot streak, and then suddenly he can fall into a deep, prolonged funk. Then two weeks later, equally unexpectedly, that same player will get a hit, and just as quickly as he went into his slump he is out of it. I know first-hand the frustrations of a slump from my own playing days, and I have no explanation for the hows and whys of slumping. I know only that slumps can happen to the best of us.

This series was the first time I have ever seen David take his bad at-bats out onto the field with him. He seemed especially affected by the error he made on Wednesday that almost cost the Mets the game in the ninth inning. His demeanor and his body language clearly showed that his sub-par performance is bothering him.

David's offensive woes were compounded by committing two errors (and he could have been charged with three) in the series, highly uncharacteristic for him. One of the lessons I learned from my father is that when a player is in a slump, that is the time he must bear down the hardest. Even if a player isn't helping his team offensively, he can always help win a game with his glove.

David Wright is one of the key players on this Mets team who cannot allow rough patches to dishearten him. The best players always have to be exemplary in their attitude and approach to the game, both on and off the field, through good times and bad—and David Wright is one of the best. When a player is a star, this responsibility comes with the territory.

Mets fans tend to forget that Wright is only 25 years old. Because of his talent, his character and his demeanor, everyone assumes he's a 10-year vet. David is still very young, and he's still learning. I hope he will learn from this as well.

SEPTEMBER 19, 2008

Ryan Church commits his first error of the year, allowing the Braves to tie the game in the seventh. Though Nelson Figueroa gets charged with the club's 28th blown save, a trio of relievers follow to get the Mets out of the inning with the score still even. Daniel Murphy's pinch-hit double gives the Mets the lead, and some shoddy defense by Atlanta provides New York some insurance. The club's third-straight win puts the Mets back into first place, thanks to Philadelphia's loss in Florida. It is the first win in seven tries by the Mets at Turner Field in 2008. *Mets 9, Braves 5. Record 86–67; ½ game ahead of Philadelphia.* *Wild Card: 2½ games ahead of Milwaukee.*

Dial "M" for Murphy

The Mets have faced lefties in eight of their last nine games, during which time the team began to cool. Jerry has been platooning Murphy and Nick Evans since Tatis' injury. Daniel Murphy, who had formerly platooned with Tatis in left, sat for all nine of those starts. He was in the starting lineup for the last two games in Washington, collecting two hits in each of those wins. Murphy went 4-for-9 in those two games and is hitting .467 for the month of September.

I feel that Daniel has the potential to be a good number three hitter in the near future if he continues making progress. There is no guarantee that Murphy is going to be a star. He's

Daniel Murphy connects for a two-run double to break a tie in Atlanta and spark what would be New York's only win at Turner Field in 2008. In a season full of unpleasant developments from expected sources, Murphy, in just his second year of professional baseball, was a pleasant surprise for the Mets.

had a great six weeks, but six weeks don't make *bona fide* .300 hitter, which is what a three-hitter has to be. There have been a million guys who have had good rookie seasons only to fall flat the next year. From everything I've seen of young Daniel so far, however, I don't think he will fall into that category.

I've had a few conversations with Murphy, and he has good ideas about what he wants to do at the plate. His talent is far ahead of his experience, which thus far has been limited to Double A until his call-up in Houston. I don't know where the Mets are going to play him. There is talk of Daniel going to instructional league in Arizona to play second base. I don't necessarily think second base is the ideal position for him. His future may be in the outfield or at first base.

In Atlanta, against lefty Jo Jo Reyes, Evans got the start and hit his second home run of the season to give the Mets a 5–3 lead in the fourth. But in the four-run Met eighth, Manuel pinch hit Murphy for Evans with the right-hander Julian Tavarez on the mound.

I am surprised that Bobby Cox didn't bring in lefty Will Ohman to face Daniel Murphy, who stepped to the plate with two runners on. It is even more of a surprise that Bobby didn't have Ohman start the inning, because Delgado and Church were due up. Cox and his Atlanta Braves would like nothing better than to play the spoiler against their longtime rivals, and Bobby has certainly managed this game as if his Braves were in the thick of the pennant race. This entire inning screamed for the left-hander Ohman, who hadn't pitched in the last two days and should have been raring to go.

Murphy came through in the clutch with a big opposite field, two-run double that put the Mets ahead to stay. Cox kept Tavarez in the game until Reyes, Castillo, and Wright all got hits after Murphy. By then it was a 9–5 ballgame, and for all intents and purposes, the game was over.

It was a sloppy game all around, as both teams combined for four errors. The Mets made three: another error from Wright, one from Reyes, and Church's first of the season. But it was the Braves' error that proved most costly. With two outs and the score 7–5 Mets, Murphy got caught in a run-down between second and third. Second baseman Kelly Johnson arrived late, failing to back up Infante at shortstop in time, and botched the throw from Martin Prado at third. Instead of Murphy tagged out to end the inning, Daniel was not only safe, but also advanced to third on the misplay. The Mets followed with three consecutive hits and two big insurance runs.

Pitching In

Oliver Perez didn't have his good stuff in this game. He was in constant trouble, but he battled and managed to minimize the damage. His final line was six innings pitched, six hits, four runs (three earned), three walks, and six Ks. This is hardly spectacular, but Perez did hand a one-run lead to his teammates in the bullpen.

The bullpen coughed up its 28th blown save, but this was actually the result of shoddy Met defense—back-to-back errors—that enabled the Braves to tie the game at five apiece. In what should have been an easy seventh, Jerry Manuel had to use four pitchers to get out of the inning with a tie. After the Met four-run outburst in the eighth, Stokes came in and threw two fine innings.

Stokes hit a rough patch in late August because of over-work. Jerry realized this and has used Brian sparingly in September. The workhorse of the 'pen has thrown only 9⅔ this month, which, considering this bullpen, is hardly working up a sweat.

The Mets' bullpen is not very good, and it is particularly lacking whenever bullpen pitchers throw to batters who hit from the opposite side of the plate. To illustrate my point:

Opposites Detract

Relievers (through Sept. 18)	vs. LH	vs. RH
Schoeneweis	.172	.330
Feliciano	.202	.351 (5 HR)
Figueroa	.377 (2 HR)	.188
Sanchez	.206 (3 HR)	.260 (3 HR)
Ayala	.357	.200
Stokes	.348	.200
Heilman	.314 (8 HR)	.224 (2 HR)
Smith	.340	.189 (4 HR)

The chart above clearly illustrates the Met bullpen's need for a crossover pitcher. That need has forced Jerry to make mid-inning pitching changes in game after game, which in turn has resulted in the surfeit of three-plus hour games the Metropolitans have played in the last six weeks.

This lack of a crossover pitcher forced Jerry once again to use three pitchers to get three outs in tonight's game after

Figueroa got in trouble in the seventh. The left-hander Rincon got a lefty out, only to be lifted in favor Heilman to get a righty out, only to be pulled in favor of Feliciano to get another lefty out. In this particular game the strategy is successful, but the result is interminable. The only people smiling are our Met sponsors, as we had to go to commercial break four times in this inning.

SEPTEMBER 21, 2008

For the second time on the road trip, Pedro Martinez allows a two-out hit in the sixth inning that makes the Mets' uphill climb too steep to overcome. Pedro also provides the only offense, driving in both runs off Jorge Campillo with his first extra-base hit of the year. The 4–2 Saturday night loss knocks the Mets out of first, though their wild-card lead on the Brewers remains at 2½ games and three in the loss column.

On Sunday, they have a chance to stay on Philadelphia's heels and solidify their hold on the wild-card. Mike Pelfrey pitches out of trouble through six shaky innings, leaving with a lead that the Mets have nursed since scoring twice in each of the first two innings to knock out September call-up James Parr. The Mets suffer what will be their last blown save of 2008, but it is as costly as any of the 29 coughed up by the bullpen.

The Braves score four times off four relievers in the eighth, yet the one that winds up stinging the most is Martin Prado's two-run double off Aaron Heilman after the Mets elect to walk the injured Chipper Jones with two outs. Those runs prove to be the winning margin after Carlos Delgado's two-run home run off of Mike Gonzalez, the only runs the Mets score against the Braves closer during his three saves in eight days against New York. (His only outing in between those appearances, aggravatingly, was a blown save against the Phillies.) To further rub it in, former failed Met Jorge Julio—with an ERA of 0.87 since joining the Braves—gets the win against his former team for the second straight Sunday. The Mets end the year 1–8 at Turner Field.

Braves 7, Mets 6. Record 86–69; 1½ games behind Philadelphia.
Wild Card: 1½ games ahead of Milwaukee.

Another Bloody Sunday

It seemed as if Mike Pelfrey woke up on the wrong side of the bed this morning. Mike was uncharacteristically uptight from the very first inning of this game. Though the Met offense scored two in the first and second innings, Pelfrey returned the favor to the Braves by giving up one run in those same two frames. The score remained unchanged until the Brave seventh, when Pelfrey issued a leadoff walk. In yet another game where Jerry Manuel used his bullpen extensively, Brian Stokes and Ricardo Rincon were called upon to finish the inning. They completed the job, but not without giving up a run.

In that fateful Braves four-run eighth inning, Jerry used four pitchers, all of whom fared poorly. The loss went to Schoeneweis, but the big blows come from a bases-loaded triple by Jeff Francoeur off Joe Smith that gave Atlanta the lead, and Martin Prado's opposite-field 2-RBI double off Aaron Heilman. Delgado had four hits on the day, including a two-run shot in the ninth (his 37th home run of the year), but the Mets still fell short.

These two losses in Atlanta were gut-wrenching. Compounded with the two games at the beginning of this road trip in Washington where the Mets inexplicably played flat and lost to the Nationals, it all added up to a 3–4 trip. Although the New Yorkers started this trip with a one-game lead over the Philadelphians, they now return home a week later and 1½ game behind. The Mets are clinging to a 1½ game lead in the wild-card the Brewers with seven left to play. The Phillies and Brewers have six apiece to play, as they each get an off-day in this last week of the season.

The tables are now turned, and Philly is in the driver's seat. If they continue to win, the Mets can't catch them. Now, for the first time, I am thinking wild-card for the Mets.

Here Come the Cubs
The NL Central Champion Chicago Cubs come to town with nothing to play for, having clinched their division as well as home field advantage throughout the playoffs. Mets fans have been claiming that this will be advantageous for the Mets in their four-game set with the Cubs. I don't buy this for a minute. Lou Piniella knows that his Cubbies may well have to face this Mets team in the playoffs, and believe me, they will want to set the tone from the outset in this series at Shea.

THE FINAL HOMESTAND
SEPTEMBER 23, 2008
The last homestand at Shea Stadium begins ominously. Jon Niese has a lead early on Monday night, but it disappears as quickly as a Jason Marquis grand slam. The Cubs pitcher's homer with the sacks full ends Niese's night and the Mets fall 9–5. The last Met to surrender a grand slam to a pitcher takes the

mound Tuesday, but this is September—not June—and Johan Santana's toughest opponent seems to be home-plate umpire Phil Cuzzi. Santana allows single runs in the second and third, but he makes up for it by starting a rally in the fifth when his shattered bat hits the ball a second time and redirects it for an infield hit. David Wright singles in Nick Evans and Santana to tie the game. Jose Reyes' 200th hit is a bases-clearing triple and gives the Mets some breathing room. Santana's four-run lead becomes drama at the hands of the Mets bullpen, but Luis Ayala gets the save to stop New York's three-game skid.
Mets 6, Cubs 2. Record 87–70; 1½ games behind Philadelphia.
Wild Card: 1 game ahead of Milwaukee.

Santana Adds Life

After last night's loss to Chicago in the first game of the series and a Philly win, the Mets came into tonight's game 2½ games behind Philadelphia with six to play. Milwaukee benefits from the Cubs' victory, which whittles the Mets' wild-card lead to only one game.

It goes without saying that the Mets can't afford many more losses. Under the circumstances, there is no one better to send to the mound than ace Johan Santana, who hasn't lost a single game in the second half of the season. And Santana delivered eight dominant innings for the Mets, giving up one run in the second and third innings. After the third, the Cubs never threatened again.

David Wright tied the game at 2–2 with a clutch bases-loaded single in the fifth. Jose Reyes provided the Mets with everything else they needed in the next frame with a bases-loaded, three-run triple. It is Jose's 19th triple on the year, and it also marks his 200th hit of 2008.

Santana threw 125 pitches in those brilliant eight innings, and he also contributed with his bat, scoring twice and hustling on the base paths. His performance tonight is a *tour de force* from a superb athlete. Santana did everything and more that could possibly be expected from an ace. He had that look in his eye that clearly said, "The three game losing streak stops here." It was an inspirational performance.

What If...?

At times like these, I look back on the 1980s Met teams I played for, and I wonder how we would have fared with today's divisional alignment and playoff format. With the current three-division setup, we would have won our division in every year of my Mets tenure except for 1989. The Cubs and Cardinals were the two teams that sent us packing in 1984, 1985, and 1987, and 1989, none of which would have been in our division. That's a lot of October baseball that our guys missed out on. Ah, the things that might have been for the '80s-era Mets and our loyal fans... Oh well; that's just a big hang-with-em for all of us.

SEPTEMBER 24, 2008

A blown save is the only element missing for this game to join the myriad choices for the most agonizing Mets loss to date in 2008. A bases-loaded walk followed by a Carlos Delgado grand slam off Carlos Zambrano gives the Mets a four-run lead in the third. Oliver Perez can't get out of the fifth as the Cubs tie the game. After Chicago takes the lead, the Mets have a runner on third and none out in the seventh, eighth, and ninth. The result? One run, coming on a bases-loaded walk drawn by Ramon Martinez in his third career Mets plate appearance. After Daniel Murphy's leadoff triple in the ninth goes for naught—David Wright fans after being ahead 3–0 with the infield and outfield in—the Cubs score three times with two outs in the tenth inning. The wild-card race is tied. The division is now almost an afterthought.

Cubs 9, Mets 6. Record 87–71; 1½ games behind Philadelphia.
Wild Card: tied.

Stranded at the Drive-In

For several reasons, this game could end up being the proverbial straw that broke the camel's back. Things looked promising initially, as the Mets dominated Cubs ace Carlos Zambrano and took a 5–1 lead thanks to a five-run third featuring a grand slam off of the mighty bat of Carlos Delgado.

Oliver Perez was cruising along through four when the Jekyll-Hyde routine reappeared, to the dismay of Met fans everywhere. Perez fell apart completely in the fifth, departing after two runs scored and leaving two on base for Duaner Sanchez.

Sanchez failed to meet the challenge, and both inherited runners scored on two base hits before Chicago was through with the inning. Before the dust settled, the game was tied 5–5. Perez's line is 4⅓ IP, six hits, five runs (all earned), 5 BB, 6 K, 1 HR. This outing was particularly disappointing given the critical juncture in the season. The Mets needed dominance in every game from their starting pitching, but Perez's five walks tell a very different tale. Oliver was all over the place in a totally inexplicable disintegration after his fine performance in the first four innings.

To make matters worse, I looked up at the scoreboard and saw that Atlanta had added six runs in the fifth at Philadelphia to blow that game open 9–3. It is scoreboard-watching time.

All was not lost at Shea, however; the Mets were tied in this game with plenty of game left to play. The Mets could have closed to ½ game back with a win tonight, if Philly ended up losing to the Braves (and it looked as if they would). The Phillies would have had an off-day the next day, so if the Mets could win tomorrow's game after winning tonight's, the NL East could be tied going into the final weekend. But as the old saying goes, *One day at a time*. This is just as true in baseball as it is any other aspect of life. First the Mets needed to regroup and win this one tonight before they could start worrying about tomorrow.

Chicago took a one-run lead into the top of the seventh when the extraordinary occured. The Mets ended up with runners on third with no outs in each of the last three innings of the ballgame. They managed to score only one run in these three golden opportunities, and that one run was gift-wrapped: a bases-loaded walk issued to Ramon Martinez to tie the game at 6–6 in the eighth.

More exasperation followed in the bottom of the ninth. Daniel Murphy hit a lead-off triple off the hard-throwing Bobby Howry. With the infield and outfield playing in, the heart of the Mets order was due up: Wright, Delgado, and Beltran. Game over, right? *Not so fast*, in the immortal words of *Laugh-In* host Dick Martin.

Wright got ahead in the count 3–0, fouled off a few a pitches, then struck out on a high-and-away fastball that was out of the strike zone. Ouch! Lou Piniella intentionally walked Delgado and Beltran to load the bases. Up came Church, who grounded to second for the force at home; then Ramon Castro struck out on three pitches; and just like that, the inning was over. You could have heard a pin drop. The stadium was completely silent!

Mets fans have just witnessed their team fail to score a run twice in three innings with a runner on third and no outs. They were justifiably astonished and in shock. In fact, as each of these excruciating innings transpired, the crowd grew quieter and quieter. Our brilliant director Bill Webb whispered to Gary, Ronnie, and me to mention the silent stadium, and we obliged with a description for the fans at home as Webby focused various cameras on the crestfallen faces in the crowd.

The Cubs immediately scorde three in the tenth off Luis Ayala, and the Mets lost this most devastating game. All of Reyes' and Delgado's signature top-step dancing after Carlos' grand slam in the third was for naught. If a team can't drive in runners from third with nobody out on two separate occasions—well, that team deserves to go home, plain and simple.

The Mets lost a golden opportunity to close on the Phils, but more important, the Mets have blown a 2½-game lead over Milwaukee in the wild-card race. They are now tied with the Brewers with four left to play. All bets are off. If the Mets don't get into postseason, they will look back on this particular game and think of what might have been. Remember Archie Bell and the Drells? Tonight, the Mets did the "Tighten Up."

SEPTEMBER 25, 2008

Pedro Martinez, who is 5–6 on the year and the loser of his last three decisions, allows three runs early and exits to cheers in the seventh in his last start at Shea. Ricardo Rincon comes in with two men on, and call-up Micah Hoffpauir launches his second home run of the game. With Chicago's two All-Star relievers staying dry on a cold, drizzly night, the desperate Mets go to work against Chicago's second-line relievers. Ramon Martinez and Robinson Cancel—third-stringers starting because of injuries—each deliver two-out RBI singles in the eighth. Cancel's hit scores Ryan Church, who fakes out catcher Koyie Hill and sprawls across home plate with the tying run. First baseman Hoffpauir, having a 5-for-5 night, has Carlos Beltran's liner deflect off his glove to bring in the winning run in the bottom of the ninth. The Mets pick up a half-game on the Phillies, who are idle, but the Brewers put together their own walk-off win against Pittsburgh to keep the wild-card race even.

Mets 7, Cubs 6. Record 88–71; 1 game behind Philadelphia.
Wild Card: tied.

Facing Facts

Pedro Martinez took the mound tonight in what may be his last regular season start as a Met. I have the greatest respect for Pedro, who is a consummate pro. Certainly my admiration stems from his Hall of Fame career, but I feel it now more than ever, witnessing the way Pedro has handled the waning moments of his career with enormous dignity and class. It is not easy for a player to run out there on the field unable to do the very things that he always took for granted or perform at the level to which he was accustomed. Players handle this adversity differently as they age or face injuries; Pedro Martinez has unfailingly demonstrated courage, determination, and grace, along with his trademark good humor and intelligence throughout this entire difficult season.

He hasn't thrown well down the stretch. Every recent start for him has been similar: he has rocky early innings, settles down to a good middle, and then he runs out of gas by the sixth or seventh.

Tonight's start did not vary from this pattern as the Cubs got to Pedro early, scoring two in the first and another in the third. He then settled down and threw three scoreless innings before the roof caved in during the seventh when Jerry Manuel attempted to squeeze another inning from his veteran pitcher.

With the score tied 3–3, Pedro hit a wall. Manuel lifted Martinez with rookie Micah Hoffpauir at bat. The first two Cubs hitters had already reached base, and Hoffpauir, a left-handed hitter, had already enjoyed a great day off Pedro, going 3-for-3 with a home run and a double. Ricardo Rincon relieved Pedro and promptly gave up a three-run home run to Hoffpauir. Quick as lightning, the bullpen had done it again.

With this lead, Piniella didn't bring in the front line late relievers who have been among the very best in the National League. Instead, Lou called on Chad Gaudin, who gave up one run in the seventh. In the eighth, he brought in lefty Neal Cotts instead of his flame-throwing set-up man, Carlos Marmol, who got a night's rest. Cotts couldn't get anybody out, and he was followed by Bobby Howry, who didn't do much better, giving up two hits and allowing two inherited base runners to score game-tying runs for New York.

To the Mets' credit, they did not go gently into that good night after Hoffpauir's three-run shot. They did not quit; they fought back. The Mets were led by two virtual unknowns during this comeback: Robinson Cancel and Ramon Martinez. Cancel got his ninth start of the season because of Brian Schneider's rib-cage injury, and Ramon Martinez got his first start of the year because Jerry Manuel had lost all faith in both Argenis Reyes and Luis Castillo at second base.

Met fans have also lost all patience with Castillo, who has been having a bad year because of the various injuries he has sustained this season and last. Luis has become the target of frustration and wrath from Met fans, and he is greeted with a chorus of boos every time his steps onto the field. I feel for Castillo; he is a gentleman and a real gamer, and he deserves better treatment from the fans. This can't be much fun for him.

In the two-run eighth, both Cancel and Martinez provided RBI hits to tie the game. Ramon drove in Ryan Church, who made an incredible slide at home to avoid the tag from the Cubs catcher. It was a very close and exciting play, and Met fans went wild. In the ninth, the Mets completed the comeback on yet another clutch hit from Carlos Beltran, an RBI single off the glove of first baseman Hoffpauir. Reyes scored, and the Mets earned a dramatic win.

The Cubs didn't play their regulars or use their frontline relievers late in this series, but the Mets will take the win any way they can get it. Combined with the Phillies' loss to Atlanta followed by an off-day, this win suddenly puts the Mets one game out of first in the East with three to play. It is an amazing night for the Mets and their fans.

Meanwhile, in the wild-card race, Milwaukee wins just as dramatically at home tonight against the lowly Pittsburgh Pirates on a ninth-inning grand slam from MVP candidate Ryan Braun. The Brewers have won four straight, snapping a 4–15 skid (during which they lost 11 of 13). The Astros have not recovered from Hurricane Ike, and they have faded quickly out of contention. The wild-card is now a two-horse race between the Mets and Brewers. But you can throw Philadelphia in the mix, if the Mets go on to win the division.

There are so many variables in a possible ending for the 2008 season. The Mets could finish in a tie with Philly; the Mets *and/or* Philly could finish in a tie with Milwaukee. An extra game may be required to decide the NL East, with the loser playing *another* extra game to decide the wild-card. Fasten your seat belts, baseball fans: it's going to be a wild final weekend!

THE FINAL WEEKEND
SEPTEMBER 26, 2008

The threat of rain creates scenarios for single- and double-admission double-headers, postponing games until Monday, complicated by the plans of dozens of former Mets coming into town for Sunday's closing ceremonies at Shea. Yet the rain passes through, and the Mets—needing to win to maintain a share of the wild-card lead—play as if they're holding an umbrella in their free hand.

The Marlins score twice in the first inning and twice more when Mike Pelfrey exits after six innings. Pelfrey hits the 200-inning mark and is hit hard by the Marlins…again. He is 0–4 with a 7.11 ERA on the season against Florida and drops his third-straight decision.

Marlins 6, Mets 1. Record 88–72; 2 games behind Philadelphia.
Wild Card: 1 game behind Milwaukee.

Florida Rains on the Parade

The forecast was grim: rain all day, with intermittent showers to come later that night. The last thing Mets management wanted was a rainout, which would force the Mets and Marlins to play a make-up doubleheader on Saturday. I have already told you my feeling that doubleheaders are nearly impossible to sweep. The Mets cannot afford to lose a single game over the weekend, so if the game can possibly be played tonight, it will be.

In spite of ominous clouds above, the game started on time. The crowd of barely 30,000 did not fill the stands at Shea for the opening game of this pivotal series. I was shocked by the number of empty seats in the house and also by the lack of energy in the stadium. The fans were all but silent as the game began. In this gloomy atmosphere, Mike Pelfrey took the mound against his nemesis, the Florida Marlins.

From the very first batter, it was more than apparent that the Marlins were pumped up and ready to play the spoiler again for the 2008 Mets. All-Star shortstop Hanley Ramirez led off with a base hit and immediately stole second. Marlin catcher John Baker singled to left, scoring Ramirez. Jorge Cantu ripped a double down the left-field line for a double, advancing Baker to third. In a New York minute, Pelfrey and the Mets were in big trouble.

Much to Pelfrey's credit, he did not crumble. He impressed the crowd by settling down to prevent the Marlins from blowing the game wide open. Mike gave up only one more run in the first, then escaped that precarious inning with a score of 2–0.

I've watched Mike Pelfrey enjoy the kind of season that he can look on back years from now and say, "It all turned around for me in 2008." And so it has. Pelfrey has made giant strides forward this year, physically as well as mentally.

After he capped a spectacular August with the first two complete games of his career, Mike went 0–3 with a 4.06 ERA in September. An ERA of 4.06 is hardly terrible in today's game, and it certainly is better than his April or May ERAs by a longshot. Pelfrey has pitched in some tough-luck games, getting shut out twice in a three-start span. He didn't get any run support in tonight's game, either.

The seventh inning proved decisive for the Marlins. With the score 3–1, the Fish added two more insurance runs, courtesy of another Met bullpen implosion. Rookie Bobby Parnell started the inning and gave up a walk and a wild pitch, followed by an RBI single to Hanley Ramirez. Exit Parnell, enter Feliciano.

Pedro Feliciano was brought in to get the lefty John Baker out. He didn't manage to do this. The worst imaginable scenario came to life as he hit Baker with a pitch, putting runners on first and second. Exit Feliciano; enter Heilman.

Aaron got Cantu to pop out, then walked Mike Jacobs to load the bases. Dan Uggla softly lined out to third, and the Mets were one out away from stemming the tide. But Heilman followed Feliciano's lead and walked Josh Willingham to bring in the second Marlin run of the inning. Just like that, Florida had a comfortable 5–1 lead.

Starter Chris Volstad was in complete command for the Marlins, silencing the Met bats through six innings. Florida's bullpen was the Met 'pen's polar opposite, throwing the final three innings without allowing a run.

All in all, the Mets were outplayed and outhustled by the Florida Marlins tonight. They didn't play this game with any apparent sense of urgency. The Marlins, on the other hand, are in the midst of a meaningless September. They are a team playing out the string on the road; it is the last weekend of the year, and they have nothing to play for, yet they came out tonight with more spring in their step than the Mets, a team fighting for its life in order to make the playoffs. It was nothing short of amazing that the Mets came out flat. It was a dreary, rainy night, and there aren't many fans in the ballpark, but the Metropolitans had so much to play for tonight. They are fighting for their postseason life. There should be no need for motivation beyond that.

The potent Mets offense never threatened in this game, collecting only seven base hits, six of them singles. The lone run came on a fielder's choice ground-out by Brian Schneider in the sixth. The New Yorkers never gave tonight's somnambulant Mets crowd a reason to wake up. This game was a total disconnect in many ways.

With Philadelphia's win today, the Mets are now two games out for the division title with two games left to play. The Mets not only need to win those remaining two games, but they also need the Cubs to end Milwaukee's five-game winning streak if they are to be in contention for the wild-card.

Under the circumstances, Santana will get the ball on three days' rest tomorrow. There's no other option now, because Maine is out and Jerry can't take a chance with the other fifth starters (Niese and Knight) in a game of this much importance.

So the Mets are one game behind with two to play. If they are tied in the wild-card standings with the Brewers after the 162nd game, there will have to be a one-game playoff at Shea Stadium on Monday.

SEPTEMBER 27, 2008

The Mets need to win to keep from being eliminated from postseason contention. With no alternative, the Mets take Johan Santana up on his offer to pitch on three days' rest instead of having Jon Niese make his fourth career major league start. Oliver Perez and Santana both volunteered to pitch on short rest, if needed. It's needed. Santana exceeds all expectations and makes even the meager Mets offense look like a mountain. How rare is a complete-game shutout on three days' rest? It has happened only five times since 2000, and Santana has never before started a regular-season game on three days' rest.

Though the Phillies win and clinch the NL East—their first outright back-to-back division titles in 30 years—Ted Lilly's six no-hit innings in

Milwaukee propel the Cubs to victory and put the Mets back into a tie for the wild-card.
Mets 2, Marlins 0. Record 89–72; 2 games behind Philadelphia.
Wild Card: tied.

Smooth

I will be succinct regarding today's Met victory. This time it was *The Johan Santana Show*. He put on a performance worthy of great pitchers of the past and present—Dwight Gooden, Bob Gibson, Sandy Koufax, Tom Seaver, and Greg Maddux, to name a few.

Looking dominant in spite of having only three days' rest, Santana threw a three-hit shutout in a game that lasts two hours and 17 minutes. In fact, Johan hasn't lost a single game in the second half of the season. Santana is 9–0 in 17 starts since July 4. He is the league leader in ERA (2.53) and innings (234⅓), and he is second in strikeouts (206). If the bullpen had only managed to hold four of the seven leads they blew for him, Johan would have had 20 wins and probably another Cy Young Award, his first in the National League. It is obvious why he already has two of those awards from the American League. Santana has lived up to all of the Mets' hopes and expectations and then some: he is truly a magnificent pitcher.

When Santana took the mound in the first, he was the personification of spirit, fortitude, and grit. In an organization steeped in pitching tradition, Johan put on a performance that will long be remembered by Met fans. With nothing less than everything on the line, Johan proved why the Mets signed him to that very expensive contract. He is worth every penny.

With Philadelphia's win today, the Mets are mathematically eliminated and the Phillies are once again the champions of the NL East. The Mets do get help from Chicago, however, as the Cubs defeat the Brewers 7–3. The wild-card race is a dead heat with one game left to play. The Mets have one last gasp left, one final chance at postseason life.

The Mets send Oliver Perez to the hill where he will be opposed by left-hander Scott Olsen. The Mets have killed Olsen all season long, so Mets fans have reason to be hopeful. The Brewers will start their ace, CC Sabathia, against the Cubbies in an attempt to ice the wild-card title. Playoff chances are no longer in the Mets' hands; they are solely at the mercy of Sabathia, who has gone 10–2, with a 1.78 ERA, in 16 starts since joining Milwaukee in July.

FINAL GAME
SEPTEMBER 28, 2008

Amid the hype and hoopla of the last game at Shea Stadium's 44-year history, there is a game to be played, and it is the most important game of the year and a defining moment for the franchise. One year after the same opponent knocked the Mets out of contention on the last day of the season, the scenario is identical.

The game starts an hour late because of a downpour, so the first pitch comes at almost the same time as the start in Milwaukee a time zone away. After the Marlins take a 2–0 lead, Carlos Beltran blasts a home run with a man on to tie the game in the sixth. Scott Schoeneweis surrenders a home run to pinch-hitter Wes Helms in the eighth, and Florida regains the lead. Dan Uggla follows with another

blast off Luis Ayala. It is the last home run ever hit at Shea Stadium. Ryan Church's long fly in the ninth off ex-Mets farmhand Matt Lindstrom falls short. At 5:05 PM, the Mets' season and Shea's tenure as a baseball stadium conclude.
Marlins 4, Mets 2. Record 89–73; 3 games behind Philadelphia.
Wild Card: 1 game behind Milwaukee.

The End

This final game was a pitcher's duel through the first five innings, with Perez and Olsen each throwing wonderfully. Oliver cruised right along, retiring the first 15 of 18 batters (and nine of the last 10) that he faced. Unfortunately, Scott Olsen matched Perez inning for inning. Fans were on the edges of their seats.

I heard a loud roar from the crowd, and I realized that this could mean only one thing: the Cubs have scored. And indeed they had, taking a 1-0 lead in the second inning of a game that started an hour later than the Mets-Marlins game.

Perez took the mound in the sixth, and much to their chagrin, Met fans witnessed yet another inexplicable middle-inning meltdown from Oliver. After he gave up a go-ahead run on three straight hits, Jerry Manuel correctly issued an intentional pass to Dan Uggla to load the bases and set up a potential double play. This was the only viable strategy.

Exit Perez, enter Joe Smith. Manuel brought in the sub-mariner in the hope of getting a ground ball from Josh Willingham. The tension in the ballpark was palpable; the season hung in the balance. Joe Smith proceeded to follow Aaron Heilman's lead in the first game of the series; he walked Josh Willingham for the second run. Met fans were muttering every expletive they could think of! Much to Joe's credit, he settled down and put out the fire, but the damage was done. The Mets were losing 2–0.

In the bottom half of the inning, Robinson Cancel drew a lead-off walk. Two batters later, Carlos Beltran breathed life back into the Mets by hitting a clutch two-run homer to tie the game. The stadium went wild! Beltran has been tremendous this September, and today he did it yet again.

For the second year running, Closing Day meant a heart-wrenching end to Mets hopes.

The game remained tied until the Marlins' eighth. With Scott Schoeneweis on the mound, Fredi Gonzalez pinch hit right-handed hitting Wes Helms in place of the lefty Mike Jacobs. Helms rewarded his manager with a solo shot over the left-center field fence to give the Marlins a one-run lead.

Exit Schoeneweis, enter Ayala. Uggla greeted Ayala with a solo bomb to left, and the Mets were suddenly down 4–2. As the inning ended, I heard a collective groan from the Mets faithful, who were watching the game with one eye on the scoreboard: the Brewers had just taken the lead in their game. Coincidentally, they had scored two runs in the eighth, just as the Marlins had at Shea.

The Mets went down without a whimper, and suddenly reality set in for their fans everywhere: the Mets have done it again. Another promising September has melted away, and the team will not take the field again until 2009.

Director Bill Webb panned his cameras through the stands at Shea, focusing on individual shots of a bevy of distraught Mets fans. It was a montage of despair—some fans were crying, others were speechless, with gaping mouths and hands on top of their heads.

The 2008 season ended in another heartbreak, but this one stings more for me, even more so than last year. I can only imagine how the Mets players must feel.

Fans can justifiably shower all of their scorn upon the bullpen, but the offense has to shoulder its share of the blame as well. In this three-game series, the Mets' offense managed to score only five runs on a meager 17 hits. Of those 17 hits, only four were extra-base hits. The Mets' powerful lineup was completely shut down in this series, as they were in that painful loss against the Cubs when Met bats scored only once in three-straight late innings with a runner on third and no outs. To me, that loss was the turning point that ended the season for the 2008 New York Mets.

It's Over View

At the end of a long baseball season, it is always interesting for someone who follows a particular team to review the past eight months, from spring training through the last regular-season game, and mull things over like a general manager. Looking back over the Mets' fascinating, agonizing, and ultimately disappointing 2008 season is an exercise in exploring the *whos*, *whens,* and *why*s that led such a promising and talented group of players to fall short of winning a division title and going on to play October baseball.

As it does every year, the Mets' 2008 saga began in spring training. The team looked promising in many respects. As far as pitching was concerned, the Mets had an upper-echelon starting rotation in Johan Santana, Pedro Martinez, Oliver Perez, John Maine, and Orlando "El Duque" Hernandez. Mike Pelfrey had an outside chance of making the club as the fifth starter, but it was more likely that he would start the season in Triple A.

Offensively, the team was strong as well, anchored by Carlos Beltran, David Wright, Jose Reyes, and Carlos Delgado. New Mets Ryan Church and Brian Schneider looked like excellent additions to an already strong squad.

Age and injury were the big question marks going into the new season. Would Pedro Martinez, Moises Alou, Luis Castillo, El Duque, and the bullpen be able to weather the season? Was Pedro Martinez fully recovered from his 2007 surgery? Would the aging and injury-prone Alou stay healthy? Luis Castillo underwent off-season surgery to clean up the creaky knees that hobbled him in late 2007 and was signed to an astonishing new four-year contract; would he be ready and able to play? And then there was El Duque, also now a seasoned veteran, who came into camp with a bad bunion on one of his big toes. He had to alter his windup as a result, forgoing his signature high leg-kick, to pitch without pain. Would he still be able to dominate?

Bullpen problems were the main cause of the 2007 collapse, and these issues were not addressed by Omar Minaya in the off-season. He still had faith in this group of relievers. Aaron Heilman, Scott Schoeneweis, Pedro Feliciano, Jorge Sosa, Duaner Sanchez, Joe Smith, and Billy Wagner all returned to the Mets' 'pen in 2008. The only new addition, Matt Wise, proved an early disappointment and did not pitch again after May 26.

As the season started, so did the injuries. Moises Alou, El Duque, and Duaner Sanchez fell off the roster. This made room on the ballclub for Mike Pelfrey, who took Hernandez's place in the rotation as the fifth starter. Offensively, the Mets lost Alou in spring to a hernia that required surgery, and Castillo's knees prevented him from performing like the player he used to be.

The most significant injury incurred in spring training was the Grade 2 concussion sustained by Ryan Church when he collided with Marlon Anderson while fielding a shallow fly ball to right. Of the myriad Mets injuries, this one would hurt the team the most. Church was the Mets' best overall performer in the first seven weeks of 2008, and it looked as if he was on the verge of a breakthrough season. Then he suffered *another* concussion in Atlanta. He floated on and off the DL for the remainder of the season and never again played to early season levels.

Adding to the problems of the already-depleted starting rotation, Pedro Martinez pulled a hamstring in his first start, the second game of the season; the injury was so severe that he would not take the mound again until June. Minaya tried to fill the vacancy by calling veteran Nelson Figueroa up from Triple A, but as the season wore on, there was a revolving door of starting and relief pitchers as Omar tried to find the right formula not only to replace Pedro, but also to bolster a deficient bullpen.

After John Maine went down in late August, the fifth starter problem was irremediable. For a time the schedule favored the Mets with an inordinate amount of late-season off-days, allowing the Mets the luxury of going 2½ weeks with only four starters, but it came to an end in mid-September with telling consequences.

Every ballclub has injuries, and juggling the roster is always part of a general manager's job. The Mets' injuries are not a global excuse for the team's failure to win the division in 2008. But the fact that Mets *did* lose an inordinate amount of their key players over the course of this season certainly had negative effects on their performance.

I think that all general managers need to rethink their philosophy regarding aging veterans. Two years ago, Omar Minaya said that he was not concerned with age as a factor for the composition of a team. He has always fielded an older, veteran club in his tenure with New York Mets. I think he will have to have a change of direction, given the recent exposure of rampant illegal use of performance-enhancing drugs in the major leagues. If the drug testers can stay one step ahead of the criminal laboratories and diminish, if not eradicate, steroid use, then we will no longer see men over the age of 40 performing as they did at age 30. I am by no means saying or implying that any Mets players were using steroids or other performance-enhancing substances; I do not think that they were. As the 2008 season unfolded, Mets fans were reminded time and again that young players, while less seasoned, bring much-needed vitality to a team during the course of a season, whereas older players, however experienced, are more apt to break down over the course of a 162-game schedule.

The first half of the year was anything but sterling. The club floundered under manager Willie Randolph, a few players exhibiting a marked lack of desire and hustle. The club played with a huge cloud over its collective head in the seemingly endless weeks before Willie was fired on June 17.

It was acknowledged by the media that a handful of Mets didn't seem to like Willie; some even virulently disliked him. When Jerry Manuel took charge, it was obvious that the players liked and respected him and instantly took to him as manager. In fewer than 10 days after Manuel took the helm, the team completely altered they way they played. This was not reflected in the won-lost record as much as in their increased hustle. Suddenly the Mets were playing inspiring ball again. Jerry Manuel deserves kudos for the turnaround.

Another bright side of the season was the opportunity given to more than a few worthy Mets farmhands. These young players had an unprecedented chance to play this year because of the many injuries sustained by the veterans on the team. The Mets certainly profited from the youthful infusion. Mike Pelfrey blossomed as a pitcher, and Nick Evans and Daniel Murphy made great contributions to the club on the field and with their bats in the second half of the season. All three have bright futures ahead of them.

Playing in New York is much more difficult than anywhere else, regardless of a player's experience level or talent. New Mets ace Johan Santana was incredible in his first season pitching in the National League, particularly in the latter half. Santana should have won 20 to 23 games; he will be even better next year.

Pelfrey should improve next year as well. He had his first taste of a pennant race in 2008, and he will benefit from that experience. Mike is young; he'll get only stronger. I think he is on course to become a true rock of this Mets starting rotation, alongside Santana.

John Maine had off-season surgery to remove a bone spur from his throwing shoulder. I think he will bounce back and be the big sleeper on this staff next year. He is also young— and we must not forget that he won 15 games for the Mets in 2007.

Oliver Perez is probably one of the most gifted pitchers on the staff. He has overpowering stuff, and he should become a dominant pitcher before he is through. He also has many years ahead of him. Oliver's biggest disappointments came in his last three starts down the stretch. His inability to stay focused throughout an entire game is the only factor preventing him from becoming a true star pitcher. If he can learn to maintain his focus for 2½ hours in every start, he can easily be a 20-game winner. He is a free agent this off-season, and I think that the Mets *must* sign him. There is too much upside to Ollie to lose him to another team.

If the Mets do sign Oliver in the off-season, the team will have Santana, Pelfrey, Perez, and Maine as the starting four. This outstanding, and, most important, *young* rotation will be the envy of other ballclubs. Of course, Omar will search for a fifth starter in the off-season, but with these four pitchers as the bedrock, Mets fans and Minaya have to feel confident about next season.

It is in the bullpen where the Mets must make wholesale changes this winter. This same group should not be back for another year. As a unit, they blew an amazing 29 saves last year. Phillies closer Brad Lidge was picture perfect; the Mets lost Wagner in late August. Therein lies the difference between winning and losing the NL East. With Wagner out for the 2009 season (and possibly at the end of his career), Omar's first order of business will be to acquire a closer.

He will also have to search for a new group of relievers, especially in the back end of the 'pen. Met fans hope that he will not have to give up too much offense to get it, particularly the young Fernando Martinez. Nonetheless, strengthening the Met bullpen has to be top priority in view of the heartbreak of the last two seasons.

The offense must also shoulder its share of the burden of blame for last year's collapse. As in 2007, the team's powerful lineup scored early and then shut down in far too many games. It happened time and again, allowing opponents ample opportunities to come back and win. The self-destructive pattern of early scoring followed by silent bats should never have become habitual down the stretch. In fact, with the exception of two games against the Cubs, the Met offense went into complete hibernation during the last seven-game homestand of the year.

Once again, Jose Reyes struggled in September after hitting exceptionally well through August. David Wright's strong numbers are deceiving; he did not drive in many clutch runs during this final month. Carlos Delgado had a good month—until the final homestand. Ryan Church was completely lost at the plate the final month because of his two concussions. Castillo played his way out of a job in September, when Jerry Manuel inserted Ramon Martinez at second base for the final four games of the season.

The one Met who produced in September was Carlos Beltran, who hit .344 with six home runs and 19 RBIs. He played in 161 games in 2008, which is remarkable considering that he had surgery on both knees in the off-season. He drove in 112 runs on the year, scored 116, hit 27 home runs, and 40 doubles, and had 25 stolen bases and an on-base percentage of .376. He is the only Mets player to drive in 112 or more runs in each of the past three seasons. He reached base safely in 114 of his 159 starts in 2008 and won his third Gold Glove. He is an excellent center fielder with a strong and accurate arm.

Much has been written and said in the New York media about Carlos being soft, of not wanting to play hurt. I have been guilty of it, too. Whatever has been written or said in the past, it is an irrefutable fact that this year, Carlos Beltran started in 159 games and appeared in 161 games, less than a year after double knee surgery. No one should ever make that criticism of him again after this season.

Beltran's numbers are staggering. He is a natural athlete, one of the finest I have ever seen play. But to me, this was the year that Beltran added his greatest improvement and achievement to his other considerable talents: leadership. It doesn't always take a rah-rah guy to be a team leader. Carlos' reserved and dignified demeanor is the antithesis of gung-ho leadership. He comes to the park every day and quietly puts in a solid day's work, day in, day out, all season long. He prefers to remain in the background rather than vie for attention. This year, however, it was imperative for someone on this team to step up and take charge, and Carlos Beltran did it.

After all the corner outfield injuries, the Mets were forced to fill those vacancies with three men who were infielders by trade: Tatis, Evans, and Murphy. All three needed guidance and assurance, and Beltran never failed to provide it. I cannot tell you how many times over the course of the second half I saw Carlos positioning young Evans and Murphy during a game.

Beltran shouldered this tremendous added responsibility, and he never complained or made a fuss. He had to cover much more ground in the outfield because of the inexperienced teammates on either side of him, and he seemed to do it effortlessly. His demeanor and performance were a study in team play and good sportsmanship.

I also remember the great game that Beltran played in Washington in September, after the Mets lost the first two games of that four-game series. He came out to play the third game with a determination that I have never seen from him before. This is the stuff that greatness is made of, and I think that Carlos has crossed the threshold at last. He has become a truly great player.

With Delgado's resurgence in the second half of the year, one can say with confidence that this team is anchored by five future Hall of Famers, four of them everyday players: Johan Santana, Jose Reyes, David Wright, Carlos Delgado, and Carlos Beltran. Mets fans will have the great fortune to be able to watch these terrific players all season long at the ballpark or on SNY.

To my mind, the Mets have been the best team in the National League since 2006. If Minaya can strengthen the bullpen without having to give up any of the five players mentioned above, the Mets will be the best team in the National League.

In spite of the way the 2008 season ended, so many positives remain with this ballclub. They stayed competitive until the very end of the season, even though they were plagued with injuries and riddled with pitching woes. They were a gritty bunch who faced all challenges and played with determination in the face of adversity. There was plenty in 2008 to agonize fans but even more to make fans proud. The only thing left for the Mets to do in 2009 is *win*!

The Wilpons had hoped that the Mets would win in their last season at Shea Stadium and carry a world championship into the new Citi Field. Unfortunately, it didn't happen. But there is nothing to prevent Mets fans from believing that the 2009 Mets will inaugurate their new ballpark with a world championship.

The Mets have their own network, and they have their new stadium. The Wilpons are determined to keep them competitive. They want to win; the team wants to win. The fans are *screaming* for a win. Jerry Manuel has taken the team to the next level, and with his first full season as manager in 2009, I think the team *can* win with Jerry, joining the very small club of winning Mets teams: 1969 and 1986. (I do not include 1973, 1988, 1999, 2000, and 2006 in this club because, as Fred Wilpon told the Mets in spring training at the beginning of the 2008 season, only a world championship will do.) Can the 2009 Mets get over the hump and win a world championship? Stay tuned to SNY, and we'll all find out together.

As for me, I think this team is ready.

Banners and signs followed the Mets from the Polo Grounds to Shea...and now move on from Shea to Citi Field. *AP Photo/Kathy Willens*

Chapter 9

SHEAING GOOD-BYE:
THE LAST TIME

With Ryan Church's fly ball to right settling into Cameron Maybin's glove, Shea Stadium's life as a baseball stadium came to a close with 1,856 wins, 1,709 losses, and five ties. Oh, but for one more win! Maybe two.

There were a few minutes to contemplate the tragic end to the season prior to the stadium's closing ceremonies. Love it or hate it, Shea has been identified with the Mets since it opened on April 17, 1964, with the World's Fair occurring simultaneously. Shea saw the first National League perfect game in 84 years on its first Father's Day, just two weeks after a marathon, 23-inning game. Shea saw its last no-hitter (not by a Met, regrettably), the clinching of the first NL East title, the winning of the first NLCS, and the first expansion team crowned world champion—all within a four-week span in 1969. The fans tore the place apart again after clinching the pennant in 1973, the culmination of a wild six weeks that saw the Mets rise from last to first with a carom, a fight, and shouts of "Ya Gotta Believe!" Shea was also the site for the longest night game in National League history in 1974, a blackout in 1977, a "fog out" in 1979, its smallest crowd in 1980, and the first 3 million attendance season in New York history in 1987. There were 1986, 1988, and 2006 NL East titles, plus a walk-off home run to claim the 1999 Division Series, a one-hit gem to clinch the 2000 NLDS, and another shutout eight nights later to secure the first Mets pennant in 14 years. There were many non-baseball events—the Jets earning a trip to the Super Bowl, Pope John Paul II, and performers from the Beatles to the Who to Bruce Springsteen—but never to be forgotten among the Mets fans who bought nearly 100 million tickets throughout the years was the victory at Shea that clinched the Mets' last World Series title in 1986. The team is still remembered with great pride and fondness by the fans and the men who won it.

Of the 56,059 who came to Shea for the last day, relatively few left after the game—amazing given the overwhelming temptation to flee after the season-ending, heart-rending, doomed repeat of 2007. Ceremony specifics were kept from most of the participants, who were as surprised as those watching from the stands and on TV at what happened as the ceremony unfolded. As late afternoon progressed, Keith Hernandez left the booth, slipped on an '86 jersey, and headed down to the diamond for the final time.

Cathartic Closure

I thought the ceremony was nostalgic consolation, a tonic of sorts for Mets fans—although Gary, Ronnie, and I all agreed that it should have been held *before* the game, the way the Yankees did it. But after such a disappointing end to the season, the closing ceremony was therapeutic for the fans. After all, Mets fans have been through more disappointing endings than they'd care to admit.

Ron Darling still makes the right pitch in the Mets' broadcast booth.

Keith Hernandez and broadcast partner Gary Cohen.
(Photo courtesy of Keith Hernandez)

The closing ceremony itself was well done; I wish only that they had invited more former players. I would have loved to have seen every living 1962 Met, along with every surviving member of the 1964 team that first took the field at Shea. It would have been nice to include the survivors of all the pennant-winning Mets teams (1969, 1973, 1986, and 2000) as well. Even so, the ceremony was nearly perfect.

Former Mets were on hand to represent every era. The great Mets who are no longer living were represented by those who survived them: the Agee family, Joan Hodges, the McGraws, Joy Murphy, and more. Some were asked to attend and were unable to come (Mookie Wilson, Davey

Darryl Strawberry and Dwight Gooden stand a head taller than Yogi Berra at the closing ceremony at Shea Stadium, but Yogi, who managed the Mets to the 1973 pennant, is a giant among New York ballplayers. *(Photo courtesy of Keith Hernandez)*

Jerry Koosman, who won the deciding game of the first Mets world championship, stands on the field at Shea for the last time. *(Photo courtesy of Keith Hernandez)*

Dwight Gooden, Jerry Koosman, Al Leiter, John Franco, Jesse Orosco, and Cleon Jones enjoy their last time at Shea. *(Photo courtesy of Keith Hernandez)*

Johnson, Ray Knight, Nolan Ryan, Jerry Grote, and a few others). Their names were called, and they were honored by the crowd along with everyone on the field. If Mookie had been there, the chanting would have been deafening; he is one of the all-time Mets favorites.

The crowd gave Ralph Kiner a standing ovation. Ralph was busy winning National League home-run titles years before I was born, and he called the first game the Mets played back at the Polo Grounds. He has been a voice of the Mets without interruption since 1962. Ralph Kiner is a great man to work with—and a great man, period.

As they were announced, the former Mets took the field wearing the uniforms they wore when they played. Here's a list of the honorees as they were introduced at the stadium:

Jack Fisher	Tim Teufel	Edgardo Alfonzo
Ron Hunt	Todd Zeile	John Franco
Al Jackson	Ron Swoboda	Rusty Staub
Frank Thomas	Lee Mazzilli	Lenny Dykstra
Jim McAndrew	Wally Backman	Gary Carter
Ed Charles	Ron Darling	Jerry Koosman
Art Shamsky	Sid Fernandez	Yogi Berra
Wayne Garrett	Howard Johnson	Me (the only No.
George Theodore	Bobby Ojeda	17 on the field
Dave Kingman	Robin Ventura	not named Felix)
Felix Millan	Al Leiter	Darryl Strawberry
Craig Swan	Ed Kranepool	Dwight Gooden
Doug Flynn	Cleon Jones	Willie Mays
John Stearns	Buddy Harrelson	Mike Piazza
George Foster	Jesse Orosco	Tom Seaver

From the broadcasting booth, I had to take the press elevator down to get to field level for the ceremony. I was underneath the stands and making my way around to the field entrance when most of the honorees were introduced, so I didn't get to hear as much of the cheering as I would have liked.

After the ceremony was over, a lot of people commented on the way I leaned against the bullpen gate in left field when they announced me. Someone said I was posing like Fonzie from *Happy Days*. For anyone who wondered, I have a bad back. When I stand up for an extended period of time, my legs go numb. I was afraid that if I let that happen while I waited to go on the field, I might stumble and fall. I didn't want to walk out on that field for the very last time and make a fool of myself.

I had my camera, and I took shots of everyone on that historic day. I wanted to capture everything I could, because I don't ever want to forget these last moments at Shea Stadium. Even though Shea wasn't the greatest park in the history of baseball—and it certainly wasn't a great *hitter's* park)—it has been my home for the better part of the last 25 years.

It made me happy to hear the enthusiastic reception that the crowd gave to many former Mets, especially Dave Kingman. He was a Met during the lean years, just like John Stearns and Craig Swan. It took those teams a week to draw 55,000, so it was nice that the crowd cheered for them like victorious warriors on the final day at Shea.

Willie Mays was there, which was wonderful, though it was a shock to see him straining to get around. I always think of him running through the outfield and zooming around the bases. Seeing him on the final day reminded me of seeing Stan Musial at the Cardinals' 2005 closing ceremony at Busch Stadium; it made me realize once again that even our heroes get old.

Speaking of heroes, it's always nice to see Yogi. I'm glad he was there. He's always good for a story. Everyone knows about Yogi's great lines, and he came up with a classic just a few days earlier, at the Yankee Stadium closing ceremonies. He and Whitey Ford were standing out on the field together as the Yankees paid homage to the greats who had passed away. He said to Whitey, "Boy, I hope I'm not alive when they do that for me."

I did not know in advance that each former Met would step on home plate as part of the ceremony. It was a nice gesture. When my turn came, I walked over and touched home plate, and then without thinking about it, I stepped into the batter's box and got into my batting stance one last time. It felt like the right thing to do.

It was the perfect ending when Seaver and Piazza threw one final pitch and left together through the center-field gate with the rest of us assembled on the field. I only wish that the 1962 and 1986 Mets had been represented at the very end. There could have been a third person out there with Seaver and Piazza to stand for our 1986 World Champion team. Our manager, Davey Johnson, would have been a good choice to represent us, but he wasn't there for the ceremony. It also would have been a perfect time to bring back all the surviving members of the 1962 Mets. If they had come out at the very end, after Seaver and Piazza left the field, I think the fans would have gone berserk. Grown men and women would have been in tears.

All in all, even so, it was a wonderful ceremony. Everybody left feeling sentimental about Shea and all the years of Mets baseball played there. That wasn't an easy feat, after the way the game ended. I think the ceremony turned a rainy day into a partly cloudy day for Mets fans and players alike.

I know that everyone on the field was touched by the out-pouring of affection and appreciation from the fans at Shea. We all played a lot of games on that field, in front of big crowds, in pressure situations, with all those curtain calls and all the cheers, so after all these years, we know how to be in control, to contain ourselves in front of a crowd. I'm sure a lot of former players went in thinking, "Shea's closing. It's not the end of the world." But everybody on the field with me seemed swept up by memories of their experiences there. I would bet that a lot of the former players were as surprised as I was by how emotional we all felt.

No current players came out for the ceremony (though later I read that Daniel Murphy had gathered up some dirt from the batter's box during the ceremony). Some of the honored Mets were miffed that the 2008 team didn't come out to watch the closing ceremonies, but I wasn't. I wouldn't wish the outcome of this season on my worst enemy. After the way today's game ended, along with their playoff hopes, I completely understand why they weren't out there.

I did the SNY postgame on the field in front of the first-base dugout, and it hit me like a sledgehammer that the fans were still there. I am used to being on the field for BP, when no one is in these stands. It was the first time in a long time that I had been on the field in front of a packed house. Standing in front of the dugout that day brought back a flood of old memories of being on that field, playing in front of a sold-out crowd. It was very poignant moment.

The fans are what I will always remember best from my playing days at Shea. Their passion fed our passion. Our

The rising structure of Citi Field loomed over Shea's shoulder throughout the final year of the 44-year-old stadium. *(Photo by Dan Carubia)*

team wanted to win for ourselves, certainly; but we also wanted to win for our fans. I was on the field at Shea in Game 7 in 1986, and Met fans have never forgotten that. To this day, they treat all of us like long-lost brothers.

The way that Mets fans continue to embrace our 1986 team is something that none of my teammates or I will ever take for granted. And that closing ceremony showed me that the same feeling extends to players from *every* Mets team. A ballpark is only a ballpark, after all; it's the people that made Shea special. I hope that the Mets will continue to be so blessed at their new home, Citi Field.

A Citi Awaits

The next time I am in Flushing, I'll be walking into Citi Field. It will feel strange driving to a new place and a new ballpark, strange to have to learn my way around a new stadium, and stranger still that Shea will no longer even exist. I'm looking forward to the change, though. It's a break from the past, and we'll all get used to it.

Ah, the past…to be sure, along with the glory of 1969 and 1986 and the high hopes of 1973, 1988, 1999, 2000, and 2006, there were some very rough years for Mets fans. Everyone loves the 1962 Mets, even though they went 40–120 on the season. The '62 Mets were an expansion team, so there were no expectations. They may have been losers, but they were loveable losers.

No time in Mets history was worse than the years after the team traded Tom Seaver in 1977. Everything went downhill from there. The mid-1970s until 1983 were the dark ages of Mets history, followed by Davey Johnson's golden era (1984–90), when the Mets were in contention every year and took home the team's second world championship in 1986. Then darkness descended upon the franchise again, but it lasted only six years.

A new Mets manager arrived in 1996, and for the next seven seasons, Bobby Valentine brought the team back into the light. Mike Piazza led the Mets to their third World Series appearance. They lost to the Yankees in a subway series New Yorkers will never forget.

After playing lackluster baseball in the early 2000s, the Mets responded when Willie Randolph took the helm in 2005. Beltran, Reyes, and Wright became the nucleus of the current team. Along with their teammates, these players have ushered in a new era of competitive Mets baseball. Although no Mets fan will soon forget the way the 2007 and 2008 seasons ended, the Jerry Manuel era seems full of promise.

Part of my job in the booth is to talk about what happened when Ronnie and I were playing, to compare those days with what's happening in the game today. And Gary will never let us forget anything that's happened to the Mets over their 47-year history. But the majority of our job is to focus on the present, and from now on that present will take place in Citi Field.

I hope that the new stadium will help the team turn the page on the failure and disappointment that, along with the triumphs, played such a part of Met history for more than 40 years. Citi Field should be the symbol of a new Mets era, one of strength, dominance, and success. It holds all the

The final day. It really is time to say goodbye. *(Photo by Dan Carubia)*

possibilities of a bright future. I like the fact that everything will be new at Citi Field, that the 2009 season will be a fresh start in every sense. I will never forget Shea and everything that happened there over the years, the good as well as the bad. But now we have said goodbye to our old home and will say hello to our new one. As long as the Mets are playing there, Citi Field will still be home.